ILLINOIS'S WAR

THE CIVIL WAR IN THE GREAT INTERIOR

Series Editors
Martin J. Hershock and Christine Dee

Ohio's War: The Civil War in Documents, edited by Christine Dee
Missouri's War: The Civil War in Documents, edited by Silvana R. Siddali
Indiana's War: The Civil War in Documents, edited by Richard F. Nation
and Stephen E. Towne
Kansas's War: The Civil War in Documents, edited by Pearl T. Ponce
Illinois's War: The Civil War in Documents, edited by Mark Hubbard

FORTHCOMING:

Michigan's War: The Civil War in Documents, edited by John W. Quist
Wisconsin's War: The Civil War in Documents, edited by Chandra Manning

ILLINOIS'S WAR

The Civil War in Documents

~

EDITED BY MARK HUBBARD

Ohio University Press

Athens

Ohio University Press, Athens, Ohio 45701
www.ohioswallow.com
© 2013 by Ohio University Press

To obtain permission to quote, reprint, or otherwise reproduce or distribute
material from Ohio University Press publications, please contact our rights and
permissions department at (740) 593-1154 or (740) 593-4536 (fax).

Cover image: Mr. Lincoln. Residence and horse. In Springfield, Illinois,
as they appeared on his return at the close of the campaign with
Senator Douglas, by Louis Kurz. *Courtesy Library of Congress.*

Printed in the United States of America
Ohio University Press books are printed on acid-free paper ⊗ ™

20 19 18 17 16 15 14 13   5 4 3 2 1

Cover art: Mr. Lincoln. Residence and horse. In Springfield, Illinois, as they
appeared on his return at the close of the campaign with Senator Douglas.
Lithograph by Louis Kurz. Courtesy Library of Congress LC-DIG-pga-10932.

Library of Congress Cataloging-in-Publication Data
Illinois's war : the Civil War in documents / edited by Mark Hubbard.
    p. cm. — (The Civil War in the great interior)
Includes bibliographical references and index.
ISBN 978-0-8214-2010-2 (pb : alk. paper) — ISBN 978-0-8214-4430-6 (electronic)
1. Illinois—History—Civil War, 1861–1865—Sources. 2. United States—History—
Civil War, 1861–1865—Sources. I. Voss-Hubbard, Mark.
E505.I46 2013
973.7—dc23
                                    2012032542

For Kim

Contents

One

Illinois and the Politics of Slavery 8

Two

The Emergence of Lincoln and the Secession Crisis 34

Three

Improvising War 56

Four

Illinois and Emancipation 80

Five

Divided Houses 101

Six

The Soldiers' War　124

Seven

Hearts and Minds in the Days of Total War　153

Eight

In the Shadows of War　175

Illustrations

Series Editors' Preface

The Civil War in the Great Interior series focuses on the Middle West, as the complex region has come to be known, during the most critical era of American history. In his Annual Message to Congress in December of 1862, Abraham Lincoln identified "the great interior region" as the area between the Alleghenies and the Rocky Mountains, south of Canada and north of the "culture of cotton." Lincoln included in this region the states of Ohio, Indiana, Michigan, Wisconsin, Illinois, Missouri, Kansas, Iowa, Minnesota, and Kentucky; the area that would become West Virginia; and parts of Tennessee and the Dakota, Nebraska, and Colorado territories. This area, Lincoln maintained, was critical to the "great body of the republic" not only because it bound together the North, South, and West but also because its people would not assent to the division of the Union.

This series examines what was, to Lincoln and other Americans in the mid-nineteenth century, the most powerful, influential, and critical area of the country. It considers how the people of the Middle West experienced the Civil War and the role they played in preserving and redefining the nation. These collections of historical sources—many of which have never been published—explore significant issues raised by the sectional conflict, the Civil War, and Reconstruction. The series underscores what was unique to particular states and their residents while recognizing the values and experiences that individuals in the Middle West shared with other Northerners and, in some cases, with Southerners.

Within these volumes are the voices of a diverse cross-section of nineteenth-century Americans. These include African Americans, European immigrants, Native Americans, and women. Editors have gathered evidence from farms and factories, rural and urban areas, and communities throughout each state to examine the relationships of individuals, their communities, the political culture, and events on the battlefields. The volumes present readers with layers of evidence that can be combined in a multitude of patterns to yield new conclusions and raise questions about prevailing interpretations of the past.

The editor of each volume provides a narrative framework through brief chapter introductions and background information for each document, as well as a timeline. As these volumes cannot address all aspects of the Civil War experience for each state, they include selected bibliographies to guide readers in further research. Documents were chosen for what they reveal about the past, but each also speaks to the subjective nature of history and the decisions that historians face when weighing the merits and limits of each piece of evidence they uncover. The diverse documents included in these volumes also expose readers to the craft of history and to the variety of source materials historians utilize as they explore the past.

Much of the material in these works will raise questions, spark debates, and generate discussion. Whether read with an eye toward the history of the Union war effort, a particular state or region, or the Civil War's implications for race, class, and gender in America, the volumes in The Civil War in the Great Interior help us consider—and reconsider—the evidence from the past.

Martin J. Hershock
Christine Dee

Preface

"We live in revolutionary times," observed the Chicago writer and newspaper reporter Horace White, ten days after the secession of South Carolina.[1] One hundred and fifty years have passed and White's words continue to resonate. An enormous corpus of writing confirms the central place that the Civil War holds in the story of America, even as that story is continually debated and reinterpreted. The countless roundtables and meetings devoted to Civil War–related topics; the millions who visit Civil War battlefields, monuments, and museums each year; the popularity of Civil War artifacts and memorabilia; and the many commemorations that Americans attend bear witness to the public's enduring connection to the Civil War. Instinctively we recognize the war was a transformative moment in our past, and we seek to give meaning to it in our present.

This modest volume treats the meaning of the sectional conflict for a diverse people residing in what was, at the time, the most consequential state in the Union. It tells the dramatic story of Illinois's role in the sectional crisis, as well as the multiple ways in which the revolutionary times that White spoke of recast the destiny of the state and its citizens. The documents that constitute the bulk of *Illinois's War* illuminate the actions and experiences of Illinoisans as they struggled to come to terms with slavery and western expansion, with explosive economic growth, with terrible bloodshed and wartime sacrifice, and with postwar efforts to reconstruct the South and give substantive meaning to black freedom. The documents reveal the deep-seated divisions—ethnic, regional, economic, and political—that shaped the bitter and sometimes violent conflicts among Illinoisans over the war's origins, prosecution, and legacies. *Illinois's War* reveals the struggle of the state's free black population as it battled against racial oppression before, during, and after the war, and it presents the perspectives and experiences of Illinois women as they carved new political and economic roles for themselves. It traces the profound economic transformation that Illinois underwent in the mid-nineteenth century through the voices of travelers, civic boosters, urban workers, and rural farmers. It uses correspondence between soldiers and their loved ones back home to show how Illinoisans interpreted the costliest war in American history. Throughout, *Illinois's War* treats these and other aspects of the state's history through the complex and sometimes contradictory views of its diverse people, from the well known to the obscure.

Illinois's War, like all histories, is the product of choices. My chief concern was to present the story of the state's social, economic, and political development in relationship to the sectional crisis, while giving attention to as broad an array of voices as feasible. Inevitably, there are important people, events, and themes that are absent or underdeveloped in a volume of this kind. Readers interested in delving deeper into Illinois's history during this era will find relevant works listed in the selected bibliography, which also includes some influential national studies. Early in the writing process I chose to organize the chapters more or less chronologically. I did this in part for stylistic purposes, but also to convey a sense of the contingency of Illinois's war as experienced by those who lived through it. Nineteenth-century Illinoisans perceived their world as a relatively open field of contingent choices and volitional possibilities (even if, as historians, we see the deeper political, economic, and ideological structures that impinged upon the options available to them). In hindsight, of course, we know how Illinois's war played out. But Illinoisans at the time did not, and their decisions and actions at any given moment reflected a belief in the essential mutability of events. In the midst of those "revolutionary times" it *was* possible to believe that Lincoln might lose in 1860 or in 1864, for example, or that emancipation might hurt, not help, the Union cause, or that Grant and Sherman might fail in their various campaigns. Throughout the period, it was possible to imagine altogether different outcomes in the story of Illinois's war.[2]

I hope students, educated readers, and professional scholars alike find the documents in this volume exciting and informative. Each chapter opens with an introduction that establishes key themes and background for the documents that follow. A headnote introduces each document, providing further context. Outside of a handful of cases where spelling or typographical errors were silently corrected for clarity, the documents themselves are allowed to speak on their own terms in the language and spelling of the day. Typesetting, including the use of italics, boldface, and small caps, appears as it does in the original documents. Ellipses indicate where material was omitted for purposes of length. Brackets indicate where information was included for clarification, such as a definition of a term not readily recognized in today's English usage, or to make transitions in the documents smoother. In no case was the intent or meaning of the author altered.

Acknowledgments

It seems a long time ago when Christine Dee and Marty Hershock initially approached me about doing "the Illinois book" for Ohio University Press's Civil War in the Great Interior series. No problem, I thought. How much work could an edited collection be? I soon realized that I had taken on a more substantial project than I first imagined. I've learned a great deal researching, documenting, and writing the story of Illinois's war, and for that and more, I owe Christine and Marty a lot. They not only showed great patience and faith in me, they also offered advice at various stages in the writing process that made this a much better book.

The same can be said of the several scholars who read early drafts of *Illinois's War*, or portions thereof. I thank Susan-Mary Grant, Theodore Karamanski, Mark Neely, Jr., and two anonymous readers, whose critical assessments saved me from several errors and pointed me to both important sources and to larger themes in Illinois's past.

The folks at Ohio University Press have also made this a better book. I thank Gillian Berchowitz, editorial director, for showing patience when I needed it, and for prodding me to move forward, also when I needed it; Nancy Basmajian, for her professionalism and keen editorial eye; and all the other members of the editorial and production team, for making this a handsome book.

Any collection of primary source documents would be impossible without the efforts of librarians and archivists, who identify and preserve the sources that we historians rely on in our work. I cannot recall the names of everyone who assisted me during research trips, and at any rate, listing them all here would appear tedious and run the risk of slighting the ones I forgot. Instead I will simply thank the staffs of the following institutions, and rely on the folks working at them to remember helping me, and the gratitude I showed them at the time: the Abraham Lincoln Presidential Library; the Chicago History Museum; Eastern Illinois University's Booth Library; the Library of Congress; Morris Library's Special Collections Research Center, Southern Illinois University, Carbondale; the History, Philosophy, and Newspaper room at the University of Illinois, Urbana-Champaign; the Illinois History and Lincoln Collections, University of Illinois, Urbana-Champaign; and the Department of Archives and Manuscripts, Urbana Free Library.

I am grateful to Eastern Illinois University, my home institution, for help along the way. There was a Summer Research Grant that defrayed the costs of research trips around the state. There were also all those graduate student assistants, who pored over microfilmed newspapers in search of obscure editorials or stories: I thank Bryant Davis, Nancy Lurkins, Jason Miller, Adam Morrisette, and Krishna

Thomas. I am also indebted to Michael Kleen, another of our recent M.A. graduates and a budding historian in his own right, for making the election maps that appear in this book.

Finally, I thank my immediate family: Kim Hubbard, Max Hubbard, and Pierre Viallant. They may not understand my curious obsession with history; in fact, most of the time they think I'm downright strange. But their love and support makes everything worth it, and that is all I could ever ask for.

The luckiest day in my life was the day I met my wife, Kim. Ever since, she has filled my days with love and laughter, as only a soul mate can. Her stunning beauty, sharp wit, and genuine zest for life never fail to take my breath away. This book is but a small down payment on everything I owe to her.

Introduction

ILLINOIS WAS AT the heart of the national crisis over slavery. Many Northerners saw Illinois, with its booming city on the lake, its rich agricultural fields and growing industries, as a model of what the West should be: a dynamic, enterprising society that fairly rewarded free white labor. The state's geography was also pivotal. Bordered by two slave states—Missouri and Kentucky—and three major commercial arteries—the Mississippi, Ohio, and Wabash Rivers—Illinois was an entry point for countless runaway slaves. As slaves acted to free themselves, river towns such as Alton, East St. Louis, and Cairo became the scene of dramatic escapes, and equally dramatic rescue efforts by Illinoisans operating a loose network that stretched into Canada—the famous Underground Railroad—set up to aid fugitives in their flight to freedom. Illinois statesmen played starring roles in the crisis. Its leading U.S. senator, Democrat Stephen A. Douglas, attained national prominence by shepherding the Compromise of 1850 through a bitterly divided Congress. Four years later he sent shockwaves across the nation by authoring the Kansas-Nebraska Act. In 1860 the election of Republican Abraham Lincoln to the White House precipitated secession and civil war.

As the war unfolded, Illinois proved essential to the Union cause. Only the more populous states of New York, Pennsylvania, and Ohio sent more troops into battle on the Union side. Most of the 259,000 Illinoisans who served did so in the western theater, where Union troops outfought the Confederates early and built momentum toward ultimate victory. The state was home to several of the Union's best field commanders, including Ulysses S. Grant, the chief architect of those successful western campaigns. Illinois supplied key resources, such as coal and foodstuffs that fueled the Union's wartime industries and fed its massive armies. Illinois's largest city, Chicago, itself played a significant role in Union victory. The city's diverse residents responded enthusiastically to the calls for volunteers. Camp Douglas, located on the city's south side, was a major training site for troops and later a notorious prison for captured Confederates. Chicago's industries answered the demand for war resources, while its superior railroad and canal connections made it a hub for the collection and transport of supplies and men into battle.

Illinois underwent sweeping changes in the middle decades of the nineteenth century. But amid the multitude of issues that Illinoisans confronted, certain broad themes stand out. First, the deep political divisions that beset Illinois in these years—over the expansion of slavery, the place of blacks in society, and the policies of the federal government both during and after the Civil War—grew out of the state's demographic transformation. Throughout the antebellum decades

migrants from Kentucky, Tennessee, Virginia, and other slave states settled southern and central Illinois. Overwhelmingly rural in economic orientation, these
"upland Southerners" brought with them a socially and politically conservative
culture that emphasized limited government and personal autonomy. Beginning
in the 1830s, however, Illinois's population slowly diversified with the arrival of
newcomers attracted to the availability of cheap land and an abundance of new
jobs linked to the steady growth of the state's economy. Midwesterners from
Indiana and Ohio, immigrants from Germany, Ireland, and Scandinavia, and Yankees from the Mid-Atlantic and the Northeast poured into Illinois in search of
economic opportunity. Between 1850 and 1870, Illinois's population nearly tripled,
growing to over 2.5 million, as diverse settlers found irresistible Illinois's verdant
prairies and burgeoning cities. Most of the newcomers settled across central and
northern Illinois, and the Yankees in particular brought a moralizing, progres-
sive outlook that clashed significantly with the conservative worldview of upland
Southerners. The era's intense political battles reflected the growing influence of
those segments of Illinois society who differed, sometimes sharply so, from the
state's initial upland Southern majority.

The influx of new settler groups redefined the state's political geography. As
Illinois became more cosmopolitan, the center of gravity in state politics tilted
steadily northward, giving rise to a new generation of political leadership. Initially
it was Stephen Douglas who capitalized on the new demographic and economic
currents shaping the Prairie State. Born in 1813 in Vermont, Douglas migrated
to Illinois at age twenty, part of the Yankee diaspora then spreading out toward
the frontier West. Settling at first in Jacksonville, Douglas studied law and soon
entered into his lifelong passion, politics. Later Douglas moved to Chicago, in-
vested heavily in lakefront property, and became one the city's greatest boosters
and political assets. Douglas compiled a distinguished record of public service in
Illinois, at various times serving as secretary of state of Illinois, justice on the
Illinois Supreme Court, state representative, U.S. congressman, and, by the 1850s,
as a U.S. senator battling with Abraham Lincoln for the hearts and minds of the
Illinois electorate. Douglas's enormous popularity in Illinois owed to his political ideology, forged in what Douglas self-consciously described as his "Western
feelings[,] principles and interests."[1] Douglas linked traditional Jacksonian ideals—
especially white supremacy and democratic self-rule, popular among the state's
upland Southerners—with an aggressive nationalism that served the interests of
newer, more affluent settler groups. These were the principles of a new generation of Democratic Party leaders calling themselves Young America, and Douglas
was their chieftain. Douglas and his Young America allies knew that the key to the
nation's greatness lay in western expansion. Sowing the seeds of civilization across
the vast continental expanse was nothing less than America's manifest destiny.

Fulfilling that destiny would assure his adopted home state's continued growth and prosperity, for Illinois was best poised to profit from the vast territorial riches that lay across the Mississippi. Combining traditional Jacksonian themes with a nationalist-expansionist agenda, by the 1840s Douglas's Democratic Party enjoyed unrivaled strength and support across the entire state.

It is easy to forget that before 1860 it was largely Douglas's vision—not Lincoln's—that provided a measure of political coherence to the state's staggering economic and social development, a second major theme of Illinois's history in these years. In the decades surrounding the Civil War, Illinois transitioned from a comparatively homogenous, rural society to an increasingly heterogeneous, commercial, and industrializing one. Chicago led the way, but cities such as Galena, Moline, Peoria, Quincy, and Springfield grew impressively as well. Meanwhile new towns sprung up along the Illinois Central Railroad, which had commenced in early 1851, after Douglas, an avid promoter, crafted the land-grant scheme in Congress that funded its construction. Soon after, the Illinois General Assembly began authorizing secondary trunk lines to serve other towns across the state. By the eve of the Civil War, Illinois had over 2,800 miles of railroad, nearly all of which had been laid during the 1850s, a decade of frenzied investment and growth.

The state's railroads connected increasing numbers of people to markets and launched Illinois's economic transformation. Agriculture and livestock, shipping and warehousing, real estate and construction, mining and industry—all sectors of Illinois's economy flourished in the new age of cheaper and faster transport of goods. Springfield's Milton Hay, uncle of Lincoln's wartime secretary, John Hay, later remembered the coming of the railroad "as the dividing line in point of time between the new and the old. Not only our homemade manufactures, but our homemade life and habits to a great measure disappeared. . . . We began to build houses of a different style and with different materials. We farmed not only with different implements but in a different mode. Then we began to inquire what the markets were and what product of the farm we could raise and sell to the best advantage."[2] A new economic order had dawned.

Illinois's river and railroad connections positioned its people to take full advantage of the Civil War's economic stimulus. The coming of war enlarged the scope of the social and economic transformation that had begun in the antebellum era. Illinois farmers prospered during the war years, purchasing labor-saving machinery that increased the output of crops and livestock. The expansion of the state's industrial workforce during the 1860s also registered the war's effect, as did the rising value of the state's industrial output, which by 1870 for the first time nearly equaled that of its agricultural sector. By the 1870s the changes wrought in the lives of ordinary Illinoisans were scarcely imaginable just a generation before. For much of the antebellum era Illinois was a rural frontier. Now the state stood at

the center of trade and communication networks that spanned an entire continent. The Prairie State emerged in the postwar years as the nation's doorway to
the trans-Mississippi West, a principal beneficiary of the subsequent growth and
development of that region.

Inevitably Illinois's transformation caused tensions and anxieties among its
people. The first signs appeared in the mid 1850s when many native-born Illinoisans,
distrustful of immigrants, joined the anti-immigrant Know Nothing movement.
Chicago especially witnessed clashes between native-born Protestants and recently arrived German and Irish Catholics that reshaped the city's politics. Then during
and after the war, workers and farmers grew restless over the course of economic
change. In general, Illinoisans hailed their state's economic progress, seeing it as
proof of the superiority of free labor over slave labor. But as a practical matter not
everyone shared equally in Illinois's bounty. During these crucial decades it became clear that Illinois's ongoing economic transformation concentrated wealth
and power in the hands of those with capital to invest, goods to sell, and property
to let.

Of the many changes that Illinoisans experienced in these years, the end of
American slavery was by far the most dramatic. The unfolding of new racial politics in the wake of emancipation was a third major theme of the state's history in
this era. Illinois had always been a free state (though throughout its early history
there were efforts to introduce slavery within its borders), because it was territory
organized by the 1787 Northwest Ordinance, which had explicitly banned slavery. In fact many of those upland Southerners who initially settled Illinois did so
because they disliked living and working among black slaves. Nevertheless, the
movement against slavery proceeded very slowly in Illinois because nearly all residents shared an abiding faith in white supremacy. Any proposal to free the South's
slaves necessarily raised difficult questions: What would become of them? If free,
might they follow the example set by so many whites and settle on the Illinois
prairie? Might they take the choicest lands, the best jobs? Indeed, might the American birthrights of democratic equality and economic freedom be tainted by their
extension to black slaves? The related questions of race and slavery had powerful
economic and psychological dimensions in a state that began its steady growth
and social diversification at precisely the moment when radical abolitionism first
appeared on the scene. From the 1830s onward Douglas's Democratic Party pur-
posefully exploited the racial fears of ordinary Illinoisans jealously guarding their
social and economic privileges against the "threat" of black incursion. The power
of those fears was made plain in 1837 when the general assembly, by a vote of 77
to 6, passed a resolution condemning abolitionism and affirming slaveholding "a
sacred right" of the Southern states. Later that year an enraged mob in Alton set
fire to the warehouse where the abolitionist newspaper editor Elijah P. Lovejoy,

who had recently migrated to Illinois from Maine, kept his printing press. Lovejoy escaped the fire only to be gunned down by the mob.

If Illinoisans would not permit racial slavery to efface the prairie, neither would they risk a flood of imbruted ex-bondsmen into their prospering white utopia. Hence the violent fury directed at the abolitionist Lovejoy. The political economy and social psychology of white supremacy imprisoned the minds of nearly all Illinoisans before the Civil War, Lovejoy and his tiny band of followers notwithstanding. Illinois would be a white state (in fact almost entirely so) in a white republic; the state's Democratic leadership all but promised that the freedoms and opportunities enjoyed by white Illinoisans would never be extended to people of color. It would take decades of political strife and a bloody civil war before this way of thinking gave way, if only grudgingly and incompletely, to something different. In complex ways the long struggle against Southern slavery, the wartime origins of emancipation, and the postwar efforts to define the status of blacks in America all profoundly impacted Illinois and set its people on a new course. Illinoisans, like Americans everywhere, believed theirs was a special nation founded on the self-evident truths of freedom and equality among men. The Civil War era raised those questions anew and made those truths appear anything but self-evident.

~

The problems of race and slavery were uppermost in the mind of Abraham Lincoln as he prepared to give an address at Peoria in October 1854. Much had changed in Lincoln's life as he rose to speak that evening. Born in 1809 in Kentucky, nine years before Illinois became a state, the young Lincoln and his family relocated many times in the face of hardship and poverty. These early years filled Lincoln with a burning ambition for something more than rural farm life. At age twenty-two he left his family, now residing in Coles County, Illinois, to pursue a legal and political career, eventually settling in Springfield. By 1840, a year after it was made Illinois's state capital (replacing downstate Vandalia), Springfield was a bustling commercial town full of opportunity for young lawyers and rising politicos like Lincoln. Throughout his early political career, which included four stints in the Illinois General Assembly, Lincoln cultivated a following among the more affluent and upwardly mobile people settling central and northern Illinois. Like Lincoln, these Illinoisans identified with the Whig Party, which rose in the 1830s to challenge Democratic supremacy in the state. Whigs often aligned themselves with the moral reform movements of the era, including Christian missionary work, temperance, and even antislavery. But their core program—and Lincoln's primary concern before 1854—was the promotion of a national economy through improved transportation networks, protective tariffs, and the proliferation of banks and industrial enterprises. The idea of using government in systematic and positive ways to improve the nation's commercial and industrial position dated back to Founding Fathers like Alexander Hamilton. More recently it was the grand design of the Kentucky slaveholder and Whig Party founder Henry Clay, whom Lincoln idolized. This was an agenda suited to the aspirations of a new generation of Illinoisans who most welcomed and benefited from the state's economic transformation.

And yet by the time of Lincoln's Peoria speech, tariffs, banks, and the like no longer animated Illinoisans as they once did. The sole subject of Lincoln's address that evening was Stephen Douglas's recently enacted Kansas-Nebraska Act. Douglas had long envisioned Illinois, and Chicago in particular, as the chief beneficiary of western expansion. After all, his own real estate investments would boom in value should Chicago become the central link in a chain of railroad communications connecting East with West. In order for Douglas's vision to be realized, however, Nebraska Territory had to be opened to settlement. The problem was that this land was part of the old Louisiana Purchase, and slavery had been explicitly banned from it under the terms of the 1820 Missouri Compromise. Under pressure from Southern congressmen, Douglas, who also entertained presidential ambitions, included an explicit repeal of the Missouri Compromise in order to guarantee his bill's passage. With the slavery restriction now lifted, territorial settlers would decide the question of slavery themselves through democratic processes. The idea of letting settlers vote whether or not to have slavery, known as popular sovereignty, was a cardinal principle of Northern Democrats like Douglas, who sought to remain political partners with Southern Democrats without appearing to be pro-slavery to their own Northern constituents.

By repealing the Missouri Compromise, the Kansas-Nebraska Act thus opened new western territory to the prospect of slavery, and it was this issue—the potential expansion of slavery—that Lincoln's Peoria audience gathered that night to consider. In a sense those listening to Lincoln that evening could see both their past and future unfolding before them, all bound up in the question of whether or not slaveholders would be permitted to expand their system of unfree labor onto western soil. For many, the thought of an American West populated by arrogant slaveholders and their degraded black chattel was galling.

Lincoln lambasted Douglas for over three hours that night. When he wasn't assailing Douglas for betraying the interests of Illinoisans and the nation, Lincoln spoke philosophically about the larger issues of race and slavery in American life. He would not blame Southerners for slavery. Indeed Lincoln emphasized the inherent difficulty in freeing the slaves. "My first impulse," he said, "would be to free all the slaves, and send them to Liberia,—to their own native land." But Lincoln admitted that colonizing the nation's four million slaves out of the country was financially and logistically impractical. What then? Lincoln chose his words carefully:

Free them, and make them politically and socially our equals? My own feelings will not admit of this; and if mine would, we well know that those
of the great mass of white people will not. Whether this feeling accords
with justice and sound judgment, is not the sole question, if indeed, it is any
part of it. A universal feeling, whether well or ill-founded, cannot be safely
disregarded. We can not, then, make them equals. It does seem to me that
systems of gradual emancipation might be adopted; but for their tardiness in
this, I will not undertake to judge our brethren of the south.

Lincoln would never fully admit blacks as his equal, not that night in Peoria,
not throughout the remainder of his life. Lincoln's endorsement of gradual emancipation distinguished him from Illinois radicals like Owen Lovejoy, brother of the
martyred Alton abolitionist and champion of immediate emancipation. Nevertheless Lincoln always insisted that slavery was a "monstrous injustice." "The great
mass of mankind . . . consider slavery a great moral wrong," he declared at Peoria,
"and their feeling against it, is not evanescent, but eternal." Yet in Douglas's view,
the question of whether the American West "shall be slave or free, is a matter of
utter indifference."[3] Lincoln wanted Illinoisans to occupy a higher ground. He
wanted his listeners to recognize that the institution of slavery was incompatible
with America's moral fabric and traditions. In Lincoln's view, America, founded
on principles of democratic equality and economic freedom, was as much a moral
as it was a political and constitutional enterprise. When it came to slavery, all
Illinoisans must feel their own interest in preventing its spread.

If Lincoln understood slavery to be a moral wrong, he also understood the
limits of his own racial attitudes and those of his fellow citizens in the audience
that night in Peoria. As the nation divided, Illinoisans reached diverse answers to
the vexing problems of race and slavery that Lincoln had illuminated. No one listening to Lincoln that night could imagine how much their courage, their capacity
for sacrifice, and their values would be tested in the coming years. As their worlds
changed, Illinoisans learned much about themselves.

ONE

Illinois and the Politics of Slavery

*I*F NOT FOR the sectional crisis Illinois might well be known today as the Land of Douglas. For decades Stephen Douglas's Democratic Party forged solid state-wide majorities by emphasizing policy themes that had made Andrew Jackson, the party's national figurehead and Douglas's political hero, the most popular president since George Washington: low taxes, limited government, personal liberty, and white supremacy. These issues were well suited to a rural western state such as Illinois, especially in central and southern districts peopled by upland Southerners and midwesterners from Indiana or Ohio. The large number of immigrants entering the state by the late 1840s, fleeing economic exploitation and oligarchic rule in Europe, also found the Democratic message appealing. Indeed, on the eve of the Civil War, Jacksonian principles formed the basis of the state's organic law. In 1848 voters approved a new state constitution that reduced the size of the general assembly, limited lawmakers' ability to spend on internal improvements, required proposals for new bank charters to be submitted to popular referenda, and authorized the state legislature to prevent black settlement in Illinois. That latter article, submitted separately to voters for approval, won the support of seven out of ten Illinois voters.

The 1848 plebiscite to prevent black settlement in the state continued a long tradition of racial discrimination in Illinois. According to Illinois's numerous black laws, some of which dated back to the early nineteenth century, blacks could not vote, hold office, testify against whites in court, marry a white person, or serve on juries or in the state militia. Black Illinoisans, numbering fewer than 5,500 in 1850, or less than 1 percent of the state population, also faced residential, educational, and job discrimination from whites opposed to giving even the most meager opportunities to blacks. Then in 1853 Murphysboro's John A. Logan, Democratic leader of the Little Egypt region of southern Illinois, led the general assembly in enacting the Black Exclusion Law, which had been authorized by the 1848 constitution. The harsh terms of Logan's exclusion law held the black emigrant liable to a period of indentured servitude if he was unable to pay the associated fine and court costs. In defense of this draconian law Douglas said simply that his state refused to be "an asylum for all the old and decrepit and broken-down negroes that

8

may emigrate or be sent to it."[1] Within a year at least three blacks were arrested and "sold" under the terms of the exclusion law. Many black leaders emerged to challenge the state's black laws. In 1853, John Jones, Henry Waggoner, and William Robinson organized the first statewide black political convention, held in Chicago, to protest discrimination. Three years later black leaders gathered at Alton to form the State Repeal Association, which sponsored public lectures and circulated petitions against Illinois's black laws.

Over time, Illinois's embattled free black community gained support from white abolitionists who migrated from the Northeast and settled in northern Illinois. But before the 1850s to be an abolitionist in Illinois invited ostracism, or worse, violent reaction. This was a state where the vast majority of whites deemed abolitionists of any color dangerous fanatics, bent on endangering the Union with their radical antislavery agenda and revolutionizing society with their preposterous notions of racial equality. The first statewide antislavery society formed in Upper Alton in 1837 only to disappear soon after the murder of the martyred Lovejoy. The following year the Philadelphia Quaker Benjamin Lundy moved to Lowell, Illinois, and revived his famous abolitionist newspaper, the *Genius of Universal Emancipation*, but within months he fell ill and died. Nonetheless, as more Yankee settlers arrived from back east, abolitionism slowly took root on the inhospitable prairie. By 1842 abolitionists had established the state's Liberty Party devoted to using political means—voting and petitioning—to oppose slavery. Its official organ was the *Western Citizen*, a Chicago paper published by Zebina Eastman. In 1848, Eastman's colleagues, Owen Lovejoy and Charles Dyer, traveled to Buffalo, New York, as delegates to the national Free-Soil Party convention that nominated Martin Van Buren for president on a platform committed to preventing slavery's further expansion. The fall elections that year saw the Free-Soil Party attract modest pockets of support in the northern counties of Cook, DuPage, Lake, LaSalle, Lee, and Will.

What prompted the organization of the Free-Soil Party was the Mexican-American War (1846–48). As the war unfolded, Pennsylvania congressman David Wilmot introduced a controversial bill in 1846 proposing that all territory acquired as a result of the war with Mexico should be free soil. The political and constitutional debates over this so-called Wilmot Proviso proved protracted and divisive. Southerners responded that Congress had no constitutional authority to prevent slavery's expansion westward. Some Southern radicals even began to speak openly of secession—should Wilmot's proviso become law. Though never enacted, the Wilmot Proviso gained support from Northern Whigs, who were convinced that the Mexican war was part of a Southern plot to add new slave states to the Union, thus increasing the power of the South in national affairs. Though many Illinois Democratic leaders opposed the proviso because it threatened sectional harmony, a surprising number of rank-and-file Democrats supported it because, as Wilmot himself said, it "would preserve to free white labor a fair country . . . where the sons of toil, of my own race and own color, can live without the disgrace which association with negro slavery brings upon free labor."[2]

The controversy over slavery's expansion appeared to be resolved by the Compromise of 1850, the passage of which owed to Douglas's considerable influence and legislative skill. Under its terms California entered the Union as a free state, balancing the previous addition of Texas as a slave state. Slavery's fate in the remainder of the Mexican cession—the vast territories of Utah and New Mexico—however, would be decided by popular sovereignty. The compromise also made illegal the slave trade—but not slavery itself—in the District of Columbia. Finally, the Compromise of 1850 gave Southern congressmen what they had long wanted: a robust Fugitive Slave Law that committed federal and state authorities to assist slaveholders in the recapture of their fugitive property. By criminalizing the work of the Underground Railroad and obligating Northerners under penalty of law to participate in the rendition of runaway slaves, the Fugitive Slave Law was easily the most controversial of the compromise's measures. Chicago's city council protested the "cruel and unjust" law and labeled as traitors the Illinois congressmen who aided its passage—Douglas, John McClernand, and William Richardson. Douglas responded that the compromise had brought back the Union from the brink of civil war. Douglas's Union-saving themes, expressed in speeches at Chicago, Jacksonville, and Springfield, succeeded in turning public opinion in Illinois behind the compromise. By year's end the Democrat-controlled general assembly had officially endorsed it, and the majority of both Whigs and Democrats in Illinois made their peace with what President Millard Fillmore hailed as the nation's "final settlement" of the slavery issue.

The peace lasted about three years. In early 1854, Douglas produced his famous bill organizing the territories of Kansas and Nebraska under popular sovereignty. By overturning the Missouri Compromise and opening to slavery lands that for decades had been free soil, the Kansas-Nebraska Act ignited a firestorm of protest. Nonpartisan anti-Nebraska meetings, attracting Free-Soilers, antislavery Whigs, and anti-Nebraska Democrats, organized in northern and central Illinois towns. By fall some of these anti-Nebraska meetings were calling themselves Republican after similar movements began doing so in Wisconsin and Michigan. While Douglas himself survived the anti-Nebraska wave—he was not up for reelection in 1854—his once dominant party faced serious problems after the Kansas-Nebraska Act. Several key Democratic leaders, including Gustave Koerner, Lyman Trumbull, and John Wentworth, defected from the party. In November, Illinois voters elected only three of nine congressmen who openly favored the Nebraska bill. Pro-Douglas Democrats from northern Illinois were swept out of the state legislature, paving the way for the election of the anti-Nebraska Democrat Lyman Trumbull to the U.S. Senate.

The anti-Nebraska upheaval came at a crucial moment, for it furthered a process of political disruption already underway. Throughout the early and mid-1850s both the Whig and Democratic Parties faced major difficulties over two new issues: liquor and immigration. In 1851, Maine became the first state to pass a statewide prohibition law, prompting similar temperance agitation across the North. By 1855 the antiliquor crusade was strong enough in Illinois to force passage of a prohibition law, subject to voters' approval later that summer (Illinoisans narrowly defeated the measure in June). Meanwhile a wave of Irish and German immigration crested in the early 1850s, spawning a backlash among native-born Protestants, who feared both job competition and the impact that the immigrants, the vast majority of whom were Catholic, would have on America's Protestant culture and institutions. In fact the two issues of liquor and immigration were closely linked. The Irish and German working classes had strong traditions of drinking both on and off the job. Many native-born Protestants saw in this lifestyle choice a threat to American traditions of social and moral order. Significantly, since neither the Whigs nor the Democrats took a clear stance on these issues (Free-Soilers, in contrast, often combined antislavery with support for temperance), voters concerned with these issues grew increasingly alienated from the two major parties.

The joined impulses of nativism and temperance exploded onto the political scene in 1853 and 1854 when a secret anti-immigrant fraternal society—the Order of the Star Spangled Banner—began to influence elections in several eastern seaboard cities. Commonly called the Know Nothings (because members vowed to say "I know nothing" if asked about the organization's designs), this anti-Catholic, anti-immigrant political movement soon swept across the country. In Illinois the Know Nothings were a significant political force in some northern and central cities and towns along the state's railroads, built in part by cheap labor supplied by the Irish. No community in Illinois experienced the Know Nothings' rise quite so explosively as did Chicago. Chicago boomed during the 1850s; its population spiked from 30,000 to 109,000 in just ten years. The Windy City teemed with fresh arrivals from Europe, working at a variety of skilled trades and menial service jobs or industrial occupations. The German and Irish alone made up half the city's adult male population. In March 1855, Chicago's native-born Protestant middle and upper classes struck back, electing a coalition of antiliquor moral crusaders and anti-immigrant Know Nothings to run the city. Their man was mayor-elect and former Whig Levi Boone, great-nephew of Daniel Boone, and their slogan was Law and Order. When Boone and the city council moved to enforce new antiliquor ordinances aimed at Chicago's saloons, centers of immigrant working-class sociability and political organization, the charged atmosphere exploded. In April the city's native-born police force clashed violently with a mob of mostly German immigrants in what became known as the Lager Beer Riot.

The combined effect of temperance, nativist, and anti-Nebraska political mobilization from 1853 to 1855 was to upend the original Jacksonian two-party system. The Whig Party disintegrated as its supporters moved into either the Know Nothing or Republican movements. The Democratic Party survived this political crisis, as historians have termed it, but its composition was seriously altered.[3] In the wake of Nebraska some Democrats left the party and took up antislavery politics. Some anti-immigrant or antiliquor Democrats left for the Know Nothings (soon officially renamed the American Party). But these defections were offset by the growing numbers of naturalized immigrants who identified with the Democratic Party's unvarnished racism, opposition to Protestant moral reform, and support for relaxed naturalization laws. The political clout of immigrants was registered in Chicago's 1856 municipal elections, when the city's German and Irish working classes joined with Democrats to oust Mayor Boone and his polarizing law-and-order administration.

By now nativist politics was receding in the face of events in Kansas and in Washington. In Kansas Territory settlers from slave states battled for political supremacy with free-state settlers. By the spring of 1856 the conflict had devolved into violence—the tainted fruit of popular sovereignty. Proslavery settlers ransacked the free-soil settlement of Lawrence, destroying printing presses and several private homes. In response the abolitionist John Brown led a midnight raid near Pottawatomie Creek, murdering five proslavery settlers. In the bloody aftermath vengeance begot vengeance as the territory spiraled off into a quasi civil war. Meanwhile in Washington an enraged South Carolina congressman, Preston Brooks, brutally caned Massachusetts senator Charles Sumner on the floor of the U.S. Senate after Sumner had delivered an inflammatory antislavery, anti-Southern speech. Brooks's violent act earned him praise across the South. But in the North, the bloodletting in Kansas and the caning of Sumner crystallized the Republican campaign against the so-called Slave Power, now held liable for Bleeding Kansas and for trampling on Northerners' freedom of speech. Anti-Nebraska Democrats and Know Nothings, many of whom initially had believed the Republican movement too radical, were now ready to join with the Republicans for the upcoming 1856 elections. The effort to unite all antislavery factions in Illinois culminated in the anti-Nebraska state convention, held in Bloomington in May 1856. In effect this meeting founded the statewide Republican Party. Moderate and conservative Whig leaders Orville Browning, David Davis, and Lincoln were there. Anti-Douglas Democrats Trumbull, Wentworth, and John M. Palmer likewise attended. Reflecting the crucial role that German voters were now playing in Illinois politics, German leaders Gustave Koerner and Adolph Mayer traveled to Bloomington and threw their support to the new organization. This was highly significant, since

Jesse Dubois, Oziah Hatch, and other Know Nothing leaders were also conspicuous on that day. The diverse convention united behind a former Democrat for governor from southern Illinois, William Bissell, and put forward a statewide ticket balanced among former Whig, Democratic, and Know Nothing notables.

The election of 1856 was "a victorious defeat" for the fledgling party in Illinois.[4] Republicans won four of eight congressional races in a state that for decades had sent overwhelmingly Democratic delegations to Congress. In the governor's race Bissell rolled up huge numbers in northern Illinois, and his Democratic antecedents and popularity in southern and central Illinois—he hailed from Monroe

The presidential election of 1856: percent of Republican vote

County—earned him enough votes to defeat William Richardson in a major upset. On the other hand Republican presidential candidate John C. Frémont lost Illinois to Democrat James Buchanan in a three-way race that also included the nativist American Party candidate Millard Fillmore. Buchanan's victory in Illinois was crucial to his winning the White House that year, for Illinois was one of only five free states to go for the Democrat (joining California, Indiana, Pennsylvania, and New Jersey). Looking forward, the lessons were clear. Fremont polled well (40 percent) in Illinois, but not nearly well enough in central and southern districts (see map). Yet his statewide vote, when added to Fillmore's (15 percent), constituted a majority of the Illinois electorate. With the right candidate and the right message, Illinois could move to the Republican column in 1860.

A FUGITIVE SLAVE IS SEIZED IN ALTON

Geography brought the Fugitive Slave Law—and hence the ethical questions associated with human bondage—directly into Illinois communities. Bordered by two slave states, Illinois was a relatively easy destination for runaway slaves seeking freedom. Slave owners, in search of their escaped property, often followed close behind. No one knows how many instances of recapture—or of successful escape—occurred in Illinois. One thing is clear, however: By the early 1850s hostility to the Fugitive Slave Law was growing in Illinois, no doubt aided by publicity of alleged fugitives being recaptured and summarily returned to slavery. A typical account appeared in the Alton Telegraph. *Such coverage suggests the complexities of Illinoisans' attitudes toward slavery on the one hand and their own obligations under civil law on the other.*

"About noon on Thursday, Marshal Felps was advised that a gentleman living in this city had lost a valuable young male slave, and that the fugitive was probably secreted in Alton. With his usual promptitude, Felps despatched officers Doban and Clemmer on the Altoona, which left about four o'clock in the afternoon. The officers reached Alton shortly after six o'clock, and before they were ten minutes in town they came upon the runaway, whom they found engaged in opening oysters at Skinner's saloon. The poor fellow attempted to resist, and swore that he was 'nobody's nigger but his own.' Doban and Clemmer slipped on him a pair of handcuffs, and the Robert Campbell being, very opportunely, at the wharf, he was rushed aboard before even an effort at rescue could be attempted, and arrived here at nine o'clock—as at that hour he was safely locked up in the calaboose."

We clip the above paragraph from the St. Louis *Union*, of Saturday, and if the facts are as they are set forth, we must say it is as high-handed an outrage as has been perpetrated in this city in many a day.—We are willing that the citizens of Missouri, and of every other Slave State, should be protected in all the rights they are entitled to, under the laws of Congress, or of this State; but when they go to the length of kidnapping by force, and removing beyond our limits, without any trial or warrant of court, whomever they may suspect as a runaway slave, we enter our most emphatic protest. The authorities of St. Louis have for a long time been acting on the assumption that their jurisdiction was as complete in Illinois as within the limits of their own city; and we have frequently noticed the little respect they pay to the law and legal sanctions of this State. . . .

. . . We should remember that under the laws of this State, human servitude is not recognized, or known, and that until the contrary is proved before the proper officer, all men are regarded as freemen, and entitled to their natural liberty. Until this is done, in the manner provided for under the Fugitive Slave Law, every man, who attempts to carry away into servitude an inhabitant of this State, is liable to prosecution, fine, and imprisonment.

The high-handed manner in which persons, purporting to be fugitive slaves are arrested and carried away, under our eyes, is an insult to our city and to our State. If such things are to be permitted, no free colored man in our midst is safe in the enjoyment of his natural liberty. We hope our citizens will be more careful and circumspect in [the] future, and while they are willing to accord to the fugitive slave owner all the rights he is entitled to, under the laws of Congress, that they will let no man be carried away from their midst until this proof of ownership is adduced before the proper tribunal.

Alton Telegraph, reprinted in *Chicago Western Citizen,* December 21, 1852.

MARY RICHARDSON JONES RECALLS JOHN BROWN
AND THE UNDERGROUND RAILROAD

Mary Richardson Jones and her husband John Jones were leaders of Chicago's free black community before the Civil War. John, a tailor by trade, spearheaded efforts to repeal the state's discriminatory black laws, while Mary was active in Chicago's Quinn Chapel African Methodist Episcopal Church. Both worked closely with Chicago's abolitionist community. In this account, Mary remembers her antislavery work in Chicago after passage of the Fugitive Slave Law.

The fugitive slave law was passed on a Saturday night, and on Sunday, after the law had been passed, the friends of freedom chartered cars enough to send every fugitive slave from here [Chicago] and around the country, out of this country into Canada. They went out and loaded up the cars at what I believe was then called the Sherman street station, and I remember at that time, a man came along who looked as if he might do a great deal of fighting, and he told the slave owners and friends, "if they would bring one man at a time he would not leave one of them." . . .

The first time I [ever] met John Brown he came to our house one afternoon with Fred Douglas, and they sat up until late and John Brown stayed all night. Mr. Douglas said he was a nice man, and Mr. Jones wanted to know if I could make some provision for him to stay all night, that he did not want to send him away, and he remained all night. I told Mr. Jones I thought he was a little off on the slavery question, and that I did not think he was right, and that I did not believe he could ever do what he wanted to do, and that somebody would have to give up his life before it was done. The next morning I asked him if he had any family. He said: "Yes madam, I have quite a large family, besides over a million other people I am looking out for, and some of these days I am going to free them, if I live long enough." I thought to myself, How are you going to free them? Well then, after that time, until he went to Kansas, he dropped into our house most any time, generally in the morning, and stayed until long in the afternoon.

He would talk about the slavery question, about war, and say what might be done in the hills and mountains of Pennsylvania; and Mr. Jones would say: "Why, Mr. Brown, that is all wind, and there is nothing to it; and besides, you would lose your life if you undertook to carry out your plans." And I remember how Mr. Brown looked when he snapped his finger and said: "What do I care for my life?" He spoke low and distinctly, and said, with a snap of his finger: "What do I care for my life, if I can do what I want to do—if I can free these negroes?" But Mr. Jones told him that he did not believe his ideas would ever be carried out. . . .

After being in Kansas awhile, he came on here with thirteen slaves. One morning some one rang the bell, and Mr. Jones went down and answered the bell, about daylight, and I heard several men talking. I had been reading about how many men he had around him, and I said to my husband: "I do not want John Brown's fighters. I am willing to take care of him, but not his fighters," and told him that he would lay himself liable, but he said: "They are here, and I am going to let them in." I don't know how many, but four or five of the roughest looking men I ever saw. They had boots up to their knees, and their pants down in their boots, and they looked like they were ready to fight, but they behaved very nicely, and I came downstairs right away. But Mr. Brown said: "Now, Mr. Jones, if you will give my men a little bite, as they have had nothing to eat, we will go away from you, and won't be heard of any more to-day; and just give them a little bite of something." So we did, and Mr. Jones came downstairs and we all had breakfast. . . . [B]y and by I answered the door again, and there was Mr. [Allan] Pinkerton, whom I had met before, and I began a conversation with him. And just at that time the fugitive slave law was in force, and altogether it made me feel a little nervous, as I did not know whether he was on the right side or not. But he spoke, and said: "This is Mrs. Jones, I believe," and said: "Is John Brown stopping with you?" I thought the truth was the best, anyhow, and asked him to come in, and did not know what the result might be. But as soon as he saw John Brown I knew they were friends, and Mr. Pinkerton was on the right side; and so they were very friendly together and were very glad to see each other. Mr. Pinkerton said he had been to see the slaves Mr. Brown had brought in, and he said they were going to be looked after. "I am going to get money enough to send these negroes out of the city," he said; "Mrs. Jones will take good care of you to-day," and of course I said "Yes." And then their anti-slavery friends came up to see John Brown, and Dr. [Charles V.] Dyer suggested giving him a suit of clothes and said that would be a good disguise for him. Dr. Dyer, Mr. [Lemuel Covell Paine] Freer, and I do not know how many, were there; and one man, whose name I cannot remember, was about the same size as John Brown, and he went down in town and fitted the clothes on himself, because they did not want to send John Brown down in town. He brought them to John Brown, and I guess John Brown was hung in these same clothes.

Rufus Blanchard, *Discovery and Conquests of the North-west, with the History of Chicago*, 2 vols. (Chicago: R. Blanchard and Co., 1900), 2:298–302.

THE 1853 BLACK EXCLUSION LAW

In 1853 the Democrat-controlled general assembly passed an "act to prevent the immigration of free negroes into this state." At a time when opposition to the Fugitive Slave Law was growing in Illinois, the passage of the 1853 Black Exclusion Law simultaneously registered Illinoisans' racial attitudes.

AN ACT TO PREVENT THE IMMIGRATION OF FREE NEGROES INTO THIS STATE.

Be it enacted by the people of the state of Illinois, represented in the General Assembly, That if any person or persons shall bring, or cause to be brought into this state, any negro or mulatto slave, whether said slave is set free or not, shall be liable to an indictment, and, upon conviction thereof, be fined for every such negro or mulatto, a sum not less than one hundred dollars, nor more than five hundred dollars, and imprisoned in the county jail not more than one year, and shall stand committed until said fine and costs are paid. . . .

If any negro, or mulatto, bond or free, shall hereafter come into this state and remain ten days, with the evident intention of residing in the same, every such negro or mulatto shall be deemed guilty of a high misdemeanor, and for the first offence shall be fined the sum of fifty dollars, to be recovered before any justice of the peace in the county where said negro or mulatto may be found. Said proceedings shall be in the name of the people of the state of Illinois, and shall be tried by a jury of twelve men. The person making the information or complaint shall not be a competent witness upon said trial.

If said negro or mulatto shall be found guilty, and the fine assessed be not paid forthwith to the justice of the peace . . . it shall be the duty of said justice to commit said negro or mulatto to the custody of the sheriff of said county, or otherwise keep him, her or them in custody; and said justice shall forthwith advertise said negro or mulatto, by posting up notices thereof in at least three of the most public places in his district, which said notices shall be posted up for ten days, and on the day and at the time and place mentioned in said advertisement, the said justice shall, at public auction, proceed to sell said negro or mulatto to any person or persons who will pay said fine and costs, for the shortest time; and said purchaser shall have the right to compel said negro or mulatto to work for and serve out said time, and he shall furnish said negro or mulatto with comfortable food, clothing and lodging during said servitude.

If said negro or mulatto shall not within ten days after the expiration of his, her or their time of service as aforesaid, leave the state, he, she or they shall be liable to a second prosecution, in which the penalty to be inflicted shall be one hundred dollars, and so on for every subsequent offence the penalty shall be increased fifty dollars over and above the last penalty inflicted. . . .

In all cases arising under the provisions of this act, the prosecuting witness, or person making the complaint and prosecuting the same, shall be entitled to one half of the fine so imposed and collected, and the residue of said fine shall be paid into the county treasury . . . as a distinct and separate fund, to be called the "charity fund," and said fund shall be used for the express and only purpose of relieving the poor of said county. . . .

If any justice of the peace shall refuse to issue any writ of process necessary for the arrest and prosecution of any negro or mulatto, under the provisions of this act . . . said justice . . . shall be deemed guilty of nonfeasance in office, and upon conviction thereof punished accordingly. . . .

Every person who shall have one-fourth negro blood shall be deemed a mulatto. . . .

APPROVED February 12, 1853

Illinois, *General Laws of the State of Illinois, Passed by the Eighteenth General Assembly, Convened January 3, 1853* (Springfield: Lanphier and Walker, Printers, 1853), 57–60.

THE ADDRESS OF THE COLORED STATE CONVENTION

In October 1853 blacks from across the state met in Chicago to organize the Convention of Colored Citizens, the first statewide political convention held by blacks in Illinois. In the convention's official address, excerpted here, the delegates appeal to Illinoisans to eliminate the black laws.

Fellow Citizens:—We have here assembled as delegates representing the colored people of the State of Illinois, in the capacity of a State Convention, to confer together and to deliberate upon our intellectual, moral, industrial, civil, and political condition, and particularly our condition, as effected by the "Black Law" of the State,—to declare our sentiments, and to devise ways and means which may, through the blessing of God, tend to our improvement, elevation, and progress—fully believing that our cause is one that commends itself to all good men throughout the civilized world—that it is the sacred cause of truth and righteousness,—and that it particularly appeals to those professing to be governed by that religion which teacheth to "do unto all men as you would that all men should do unto to you." . . .

We are Americans by birth, and we assure you that we are Americans in feeling; and in spite of all the wrongs which we have long and *silently* endured in this country, we would yet exclaim, "with a full heart, Oh, America! with all thy *faults*, we *love* thee still." . . .

. . . We ask for no special privileges or peculiar favors—we ask only for *even handed Justice,* or for the removal of such positive obstructions and disabilities as past legislators have seen fit to throw in our way, and heap upon us. Without any rational cause or provocation on our part, of which we are conscious we as a people, have been virtually, and with very few exceptions, practically excluded from the schools of this State, (notwithstanding we are tax-payers,) thereby denying our children the most sacred right of a national being, namely, the cultivation of that intellect which the Creator has endowed them.

We are denied the right of giving our testimony in like manner with that of or white fellow-countrymen, in the courts of the State, by which our persons and property, are subject to every species of violence, insult, and fraud, without any redress, even from the common law.

We are also, by law, not only denied the right of citizenship, the inestimable right of voting for those who rule over us in the land of our birth, but, by the so-called *"Black Law,"* we are denied the right enjoyed by the *meanest rebel* that treads surface on the earth, the right to live and possess a peaceful home on the broad and beautiful prairies of this noble state.

We would particularly remind you of the late enactment of your Legislature, which was an attempt to strike down at a single blow, the rights of all persons having African blood in their veins, who shall come into the State to seek a peaceful home, and an honorable employment. And yet you invite all others to come freely into the State and possess it, and they shall be protected by your Republican laws. But if any colored person shall come into the State, for the *very same* purpose which you commend as praiseworthy in others, your Legislators have seen fit to condemn such colored persons as having committed a high crime against the State for which they shall be punished, not with death, but with that which Patrick Henry declared to be worse than death, namely, SLAVERY.

. . . We have still faith to believe that our present political disabilities are not the result of the well understood wishes of you, the people; and we, therefore, appeal distinctly to you, who, are, in truth the rightful sovereigns of the State, to instruct your Legislators to vote for the repeal of those enactments of which we so justly complain. And last, though not least, we appeal to the *Press*, that mighty engine and swift-winged intelligencer, to use its great power and influence in behalf of the oppressed and downtrodden of Illinois in particular, and of the country in general.

Frederick Douglass' Paper (Rochester, NY), October 28, 1853.

ICHABOD CODDING REPLIES TO DOUGLAS

In 1854 Stephen Douglas was forced to defend the Kansas-Nebraska Act in a tour across northern and central Illinois, where angry crowds denounced him. Seeing their opportunity, Illinois abolitionists like Ichabod Codding followed Douglas, dogging him with blistering indictments. The following excerpts are from speeches Codding delivered at Joliet and Geneva.

. . . The question now is, slavery or liberty, shall a slave policy or a free policy control the nation? Shall the 300,000 slaveholders, be made to keep their fated curse at home, or shall they force twenty millions of freemen to nationalize it and spread it over the entire American continent? . . .

We hold that, in the Declaration of American Independence, our fathers proclaimed the *natural* rights of men, the rights of *human* nature to protect which, Governments are or should be instituted.

Douglas declared in his 4th of July speech at Philadelphia, and here this afternoon, that the declaration simply proclaims the right of States to govern themselves; a declaration of popular Sovereignty.

We hold that the Constitution does not regard the principle of property in man. . . .

And therefore neither the Constitution nor those who framed it, ever contemplated the extension of slavery, but regarded it as a local institution. Slavery was considered sectional, local, temporary,—Liberty, *National*, limitless, *eternal*. But Douglas declares virtually that Slavery and Liberty were alike protected,—were to move on *pari passu* [on equal footing], under the ægis of the Constitution.

We hold that it is in keeping with the spirit of the Constitution, for Congress to pass prohibitory laws shutting Slavery from all our Territory. *He* declares such a law would be a violation of the Constitution. In a word, practically we hold the right of Congress to abolish Slavery in the District of Columbia, or in any territory owned by the United States. That there should be no more Slave States and *no* Slave Territory. That the whole policy of the government should be to FOSTER LIBERTY and DISCOURAGE SLAVERY. . . .

"All men are created equal, and are endowed by their Creator with certain unalienable rights, among which are *life, liberty, and the pursuit of happiness.*" This was an *inspiration,* a political EVANGEL, a GOSPEL!! *which the nations of the earth must understand and receive in order to be politically saved.*

ALL MEN—*not* all the men of the Colonies, not all Anglo-Saxon men—not all white men, not all rich men, not all men of royal blood, not all *American* born; but ALL MEN! It was no matter whether the cold, oblique rays of the north had paled a man's face into the standard of Anglo-Saxon beauty, or whether the vertical rays of the South had darkened it into the hue of the raven's wing; "a man's a man for a' that." *This* was the spirit of '76, the spirit that inspired the revolution. . . .

. . . The truth is too apparent to every one familiar with the history of his country, that at the time of the formation of the Constitution, the whole nation was instinct with the breath of liberty. IT WAS LIBERTY TOO, FOR THE HUMAN RACE. All the States save one, were Slave States; yet the incongruity of Slavery with the principles upon which the war of the revolution was waged, was most keenly felt throughout the nation. There is not a word in the history of that period which can be so construed as to show that the great men of the time in any way designed to guarantee or perpetuate the curse of human bondage. But Slavery existed as a fact. It could not be immediately destroyed. In this state of things the Constitution was framed and adopted, and though a document instinct with Liberty, it was so framed as not to interfere directly with the original States, but so as to leave each to sustain its own Sovereignty over this special and unnatural institution. But beyond the limits of that State Sovereignty, which existed prior to its formation—the Constitution *carries only Liberty.* Slavery cannot be made national except in violation of the Spirit of the Constitution. . . .

Ichabod Codding, *Codding's Reply to Douglas. Substantially Codding's Speech, in Reply to Douglas, at Joliet and Geneva, in the Fall of '54, on the Kansas-Nebraska Bill, and Slavery Extension. Reported at the Time for the [Chicago] "Free West"* (Chicago, n.d.), 1–15.

PRACTICAL ABOLITIONISM AND ITS TENDENCIES

Despite opposition to the Kansas-Nebraska Act, Stephen Douglas's Democratic Party remained powerful in Illinois. In this editorial, DeWitt County Democrat Burrel T. Jones expresses positions common among Illinois Democrats in the 1850s.

PRACTICAL ABOLITIONISM AND ITS TENDENCIES

No political party since the days of Washington, has created so much disturbance and excitement in our Union, as the abolition or free-soil party. The very institution that the abolition party is an avowed enemy to, that of slavery, compared with the principles of these negro-loving fanatics, is as far superior to them as Paradise is to Pandemonium. The abolitionists are the REAL disunionists of the present day, and until they are utterly exterminated, will continue to be the great political agitators. The principles and doctrines of this faction are so inconsistent, silly and totally at variance with the views of the founders of this republic, that no sensible man will for one moment notice them. The party has for its leaders men who are perfect lunatics upon the slavery question, but who are also men of unquestionable abilities as far as other subjects are concerned, aside from the god they worship, viz: the abolishment of slavery in the United States. These leaders are aided in their pernicious duties by philanthropic women, who deliver public discourses in favor of the freedom of the blacks. We will point to you the once notorious Abbey Kelley [Foster, a well-known Boston abolitionist] as one of these feminine philanthropists. What did she gain in this public career but notoriety, shouts of derision and rotten eggs? Hundreds of females are laboring as strenuously as Abbey did for the "amelioration of the condition of the suffering blacks of the south!" Midnight finds them delivering abolition curtain lectures to their weary, henpecked husbands; men who are naturally reserved, meddling with public affairs being farthest from their thoughts; but they are domineered over by their self-willed wives, and offer entire obedience to them rather than stand the shower of abuse and ridicule which certainly would oppose their resistance. These men argue in favor of abolitionism, but their arguments are only the expressions of sentiments dictated to them by their wives. . . . [T]he primary leaders of the abolition party, belch forth their detestable and Union-hating doctrines, interspersed with the most inflammatory appeals for the rescue of the slaves, thereby inciting their weak-minded followers to the most aggravated acts of disobedience towards the laws of the United States, often terminating with riot and bloodshed. Instances have occurred where slaves were under the protection of their masters in free cities, expressing themselves publicly that they would suffer anything rather than be parted from their kind owners; yet they have been actually forced from under the care of these owners by the hirelings and hangers-on of this negro-loving gang, hurried by the underground railway across into Canada, where they were perfect strangers, and the people strangers to them. They had nothing to depend upon for a living; no home of their own containing the cherished wife and little ones, then far at the south, and in a few weeks they literally starved to death! Does this treatment of the blacks tally with the widely preached doctrines of the abolitionists? Does the sympathy of these latter extend farther than to defraud the unsuspecting southerner of his slaves, and, then to desert them in the most trying hour, when sympathy is most needed? and lastly, are the abolitionists lovers of our Union, when they endeavor by every means to create an open hostility between the north and south, and seek to array these two grand sections in opposition to each other by their encroachments upon the institutions of the south, in the hopes of erecting a confederacy of the free states, to be ruled entirely by themselves? They will be sadly mistaken if they think to build up an abolition government, as the dissolution of this glorious Union can never take place, so long as ruled by men of honor, truth and sound judgment, who know no north nor south, and who glory in the perpetuity of the pure principles laid down for their use in Revolutionary days. . . .

DeWitt Courier (Clinton, IL), September 28, 1855.

CHICAGO'S FERMENT: THE 1855 LAGER BEER RIOT

Tensions between Chicago's Know Nothing–led municipal government and the city's Irish and German immigrants erupted in bloody violence on April 21, 1855. The so-called Lager Beer Riot was the Windy City's first civil disorder, resulting in sixty arrests and one death. In March a coalition of temperance reformers and anti-immigrant Know Nothings swept into office and their newly elected mayor, Levi Boone, along with a majority on the city council, moved swiftly to enact their law-and-order agenda. The council steeply raised liquor license fees and cut the term of the license from one year to three months. Mayor Boone, anticipating resistance from the city's working-class Irish and Germans, tripled the size of the city's police force, refused to hire immigrants into its ranks, required the police to wear uniforms for the first time, and ordered them to enforce an ordinance closing saloons on Sundays. Soon Boone's beefed-up "American" police force was arresting tavern keepers for violating the Sunday ban, antagonizing the city's working-class ethnics. Meanwhile German liquor interests organized a legal defense to resist the new license regime, and a trial was set for April 21. The Chicago Tribune *published this account of the riot that ensued on that day.*

THE MOB AND RIOT OF SATURDAY

It is well understood here, that the ring leaders in the organized opposition to our new License Law, existing and perfected among the lower portion of the German population of this city . . . have for several days past sadly engaged in facilitating a disorderly and mob spirit throughout the ranks of their followers. . . . [On] Saturday . . . these ring leaders mounted themselves on horseback and visited every lager beer saloon in the city, rallying their degraded and besotted [followers] and commanding them to assemble in force before the Court House. . . . The Dutch [i.e., Deutsch, or Germans] obeyed the summons and by half past nine o'clock Randolph street was crowded with a multitude of the most desperate and savage characters in the city, ready for any blood, rapine or murder, [illegible] to follow the programme laid down to them by their chiefs, and determined to vindicate the right of one portion of the community to openly violate and disregard a law to which we all owe allegiance. . . .

Here was indeed a strange spectacle! A body of men, foreigners by birth, speaking a foreign tongue, covered over with no panoply of citizenship, owing to this country gratitude for having afforded them a free home, a refuge from tyranny and oppression and an opportunity of proving themselves to be men and not beasts . . . [all believing] that an ordinance requiring them to close their Lager Beer Halls on the Sabbath, and restrain their Bacchanalian revels for one day [was an] infringement upon their Rights! . . . [The mob was determined] to overawe and intimidate a Court of Justice, to force it to decide according to their prejudices, or to revenge themselves by rapine and murder if justice did not yield to their audacious demand! A more outrageous, bold, flagrant and provoking act of insolence and mobism has never occurred within our knowledge.

The greatest bulk of the crowd had collected in the street and upon the sidewalk in front of the Lager Beer Saloons immediately west of the [illegible] Shoe Store on Randolph street, and about 11 o'clock became so dense as to form a perfect blockade of the street. Police officers were sent to disperse the crowd, and made one or two arrests of Germans who would not "move on" without much difficulty, when some three or four of the ringleaders came up and urged the crowd to stand their ground, to rescue the prisoners who had been taken into custody, and to kill the police if they persisted in endeavoring to disperse the assemblage. A [illegible] fight immediately ensued, the officers holding on to their prisoners, arresting others, and knocking down those who assaulted them. . . . The Germans fought savagely and resisted the officers with that obstinacy so peculiar to that race of people. Many of the police were very roughly handled, and some of them considerably injured. Marshal Knights was pounded brutally, but he fought most nobly, dropping the Dutchmen around him in every direction. Officer Teebruck arrested a German who was in the very act of drawing a pistol from his pocket, and after a desperate struggle succeeded in disarming him and taking him to the watch house. . . . We have never seen men fight more bravely and with better affect. They never let go their hold of a man. They were knocked down time and again—were pounded, bruised, kicked and mauled, but they stood up to their work and did it as American policemen only can. . . .

The fight, severe as it was, lasted but a few moments. Some dozen persons were taken into custody, several of whom were very badly injured. . . .

THE BATTLE AT THE CORNER OF CLARK AND RANDOLPH STS.
THE FIRST BLOOD SHED.
AMERICAN POLICEMAN SHOT DOWN

In Defense of the Laws.

[A large crowd of mostly German residents gathered on the north side of the Chicago River; authorities raised the Clark Street drawbridge to prevent the crowd from returning to the courthouse.]

At 4 o'clock P.M., the crowd of wagons and other vehicles on each side of Clark St. Bridge became so dense that it was deemed actually necessary to close the Bridge [lower the drawbridge] in order to allow them to pass. . . . [B]efore the last team had commenced crossing, the crowd on the North side rushed on the bridge, overpowered the officer whose duty it is to open the Bridge, before he could perform that duty, and filled the bridge in a moment.—Word was instantly carried to the Mayor that the crowd was approaching. A police force was sent to meet them. They marched out to the sidewalk at the north east gate of the Court House, at the corner of Clark and Randolph Sts. By this time the crowd had approached. . . . headed by a party of twelve or fifteen men, ten of whom carried muskets and the rest swords, knives and pistols. There were some two hundred persons in the crowd some of whom were armed with the heavy clubs or bludgeons. . . .

On arriving at the corner of Randolph street the crowd halted for a moment, gave a terrific yell, and leveled their muskets at the police who were drawn up at the opposite corner of the street. A detachment of the police force ran over to them, the officer in command ordering them to give up their muskets. Their reply was a *ball,* fired by a Dutchman named Peter Martin, who stood behind a hackney coach. It took effect in the arm of policeman Hunt, who was advancing towards the crowd. Hunt drew his revolver and fired at his assailant who dodged and ran down Clark street towards Washington, pursued by Hunt. As Hunt reached the corner of the street, near the Court House gate, he received another shot in the side, and fell. A well-known citizen immediately stepped up to him, seized his revolver, and continued the chase of the flying Dutchman. On coming within range of him, near Washington street, he fired and the Dutchman dropped. He was immediately arrested and taken to jail, where he will probably die of his wounds. . . .

. . . In the meantime the fight was raging on the corner. Probably a dozen shots had been fired by the crowd and nearly all the persons who fired them had been arrested by the police, though not without a severe and bloody struggle. Marshal Knights, Capt. Nichols, Lieut Cutler, officers Weston, Noyes, Chubb, Mr. Allan Pinkerton and many others, were engaged in the thicket of the fight, and performed prodigies of valor. Mr. Weston was brutally pounded on the head by three Dutch-men at once, who attacked him in front while two more came up behind and struck him several blows on the side of the head. Officer Chubb was also severely pounded about the head. At one time it seemed as if the small police force was on the point of being overpowered by the crowd of infuriated savages around them. But American policemen, although they may be killed at their posts, will never give up. By dint of exertions that seemed almost incredible, they extricated themselves from their peril and arrested ten or twelve of the ringleaders of the mob. A reinforcement of police were now seen approaching (for the whole affair was over in a very few moments) and the rest of the crowd dispersed [but not before still more arrests].

. . . Every man captured was heavily armed, either with swords or long, sharp knives, or pistols, in addition to their clubs. . . .

Chicago Tribune, April 23, 1855.

THE ILLINOIS AMERICAN PARTY PLATFORM

In June 1855 Illinois's Know Nothing leadership met in Springfield to declare an end to secrecy within the organization and to adopt a formal "American Party platform." The principles excerpted here reflect, of course, the movement's anti-immigrant and anti-Catholic agenda. But the platform also reflects the influence of the slavery expansion controversy. Slavery, it seemed, was fast becoming the controlling political issue, even for committed Know Nothings.

We are opposed to all political associations of men composed exclusively of persons of foreign birth, and to the formation of foreign military companies in our country.

The cultivation and development of a purely American sentiment and feeling—a passionate attachment our country, and its government—of admiration of the purer days of our national existence—of veneration of our national fathers, and of emulation of the virtue, wisdom and patriotism that framed our constitution.

That the time has arrived when the American Party of the United States are called upon to take open, fearless and unreserved ground upon the great question of slavery, that is now agitating the people of every section of this Union; and that the intense excitement and agitation which at the present time are distracting our country upon the subject of slavery have been caused by the repeal of the Missouri Compromise; and that that repeal was uncalled for, a gross violation and disregard of a sacred compact, entered into between the two great sections of this confederacy, and in the highest degree destructive to the peace and welfare of this Union.—That a restoration of the Missouri Compromise, as it will restore the ter-ritory for which it was originally made to the same situation in which it was before that line was unnecessarily destroyed, so it will restore the peace and harmony to the country, without injury or injustice to any portion of the Union. . . .

The essential modification of the naturalization laws by extending the time of residence required of those of foreign birth to entitle them to citizenship. A total repeal of all state laws allowing any but citizens of the United States the right of suffrage. . . .

Resistance to the corruptive influences and aggressive policy of the Romish Church, unswerving opposition to all foreign influence, or interference of foreign emissaries, whether civil or ecclesiastical.

A radical improvement in the present system of executive patronage, which unsparingly confers rewards for political subserviancy, and punishes for manly independence in political opinion. . . .

The education of the youth of our land in the schools of our country, which should be open to all, without regard to condition or creed, and which shall be free from all influences of a denominational or partizan character,—but in which the Holy Bible shall ever be freely introduced and read, as the book which contains the best system of morals, and the only system of pure religion, and from which every true Christian must derive the rule of his faith and practice.

The just and proper protection of American labor and American enterprise and genius, against the adverse policy of foreign nations; asserting also, that it is both within the power and duty of the general government to aid and facilitate internal commerce by an improvement of our rivers and the harbors upon our lakes.

We declare our attachment to the Union of these States, and while we do not partake of the fears so often entertained of its dissolution, we will endeavor to promote its perpetuity by a firm adherence to all the principles, as well of the constitution as the declaration of American independence.

We disclaim all right of the general government to interfere with the institution of slavery as it exists in any of the States of this Union; but we distinctly assert that Congress has full power, under the Constitution, to legislate upon the subject [of slavery] in the Territories of the United States.

Such a radical modification of the laws in reference to emigration as will effectually prevent the sending to our shores the paupers and felons of other nations.

We condemn, in the most positive manner, the assaults upon the elective franchise in Kansas, and the efforts to control the free exercise of the right of suffrage, to which every American citizen is entitled.

Resolved, That the principles of the American party shall hereafter be every where distinctly and openly avowed and published . . . and we will cheerfully cooperate with any party as a national party, whose object it will be to carry into effect the above sentiments.

"THE POLITICAL ATMOSPHERE IS SUCH . . . THAT I FEAR TO DO ANY THING"

In the following letters Abraham Lincoln conveys the fluidity of Illinois politics in the mid-1850s. Passage of the Kansas-Nebraska Act had reignited Lincoln's interest in state and national politics, but his beloved Whig Party had crumbled in the face of temperance, nativist, and antislavery agitation. By 1855 Lincoln was unsure what to do. In many ways Lincoln's uncertainty reflected the political confusion statewide. Nevertheless Lincoln's own principles are clear in these excerpts.

Springfield, August 11—1855

Hon: Owen Lovejoy:

My dear Sir:

Yours of the 7th. was received the day before yesterday. Not even *you* are more anxious to prevent the extension of slavery than I; and yet the political atmosphere is such, just now, that I fear to do any thing, lest I do wrong. Knownothingism has not yet entirely tumbled to pieces—nay, it is even a little encouraged by the late elections in Tennessee, Kentucky & Alabama. Until we can get the elements of this organization, there is not sufficient materials to successfully combat the Nebraska democracy with. We can not get [Illinois Know Nothings] so long as they cling to a hope of success under their own organization; and I fear an open push by us now, may offend them, and tend to prevent our ever getting them. About us here, they are mostly my old political and personal friends; and I have hoped their organization would die out without the painful necessity of my taking an open stand against them. Of their principles I think little better than I do of those of the slavery extentionists. Indeed I do not perceive how any one professing to be sensitive to the wrongs of the negroes, can join in a league to degrade a class of white men.

I have no object to "fuse" with any body provided I can fuse on ground which I think is right; and I believe the opponents of slavery extension could now do this, if it were not for the K.N.ism. . . .

Yours truly
A. Lincoln—

Abraham Lincoln, *Abraham Lincoln: His Speeches and Writings,* ed. Roy P. Basler (Cleveland: World Publishing, 1946), 328–29.

~

Springfield, Aug: 24, 1855

Dear [Joshua] Speed:

    You know what a poor correspondent I am. Ever since I have received your
very agreeable letter of the 22nd. of May I have been intending to write you in
answer to it. You suggest that in political action now, you and I would differ. I
suppose we would; not quite as much, however, as you may think. You know I
dislike slavery; and you fully admit the abstract wrong of it. So far there is no
cause of difference. But you say that sooner than yield your legal right to the
slave—especially at the bidding of those who are not themselves interested, you
would see the Union dissolved. I am not aware that *any one* is bidding you to
yield that right; very certainly *I* am not. I leave that matter entirely to yourself.
I also acknowledge *your* rights and *my* obligations, under the constitution, in
regard to your slaves. I confess I hate to see the poor creatures hunted down,
and caught, and carried back to their stripes, and unrewarded toils; but I bite my
lip and keep quiet. In 1841 you and I had together a tedious low-water trip, on a
Steam Boat from Louisville to St. Louis. You may remember, I well do, that from
Louisville to the mouth of the Ohio, there were, on board, ten or a dozen slaves,
shackled together with irons. That sight was a continued torment to me; and I
see something like it every time I touch the Ohio, or any other slave-border. It
is hardly fair for you to assume, that I have no interest in a thing which has, and
continually exercises, the power of making me miserable. You ought rather to
appreciate how much the great body of the Northern people do crucify their
feelings, in order to maintain their loyalty to the Constitution and the Union.

    I do oppose the extension of slavery, because my judgment and feelings so
prompt me; and I am under no obligation to the contrary. If for this you and I
must differ, differ we must. You say if you were President, you would send an
army and hang the leaders of the Missouri outrages upon the Kansas elections;
still, if Kansas fairly votes herself a slave state, she must be admitted, or the
Union must be dissolved. But how if she votes herself a slave state *unfairly*—that
is, by the very means for which you say you would hang men? Must she still
be admitted, or the Union be dissolved? That will be the phase of the question
when it first becomes a practical one. In your assumption that there may be
a *fair* decision of the slavery question in Kansas, I plainly see you and I would
differ about the Nebraska-law. I look upon that enactment not as a *law,* but as
violence from the beginning. It was conceived in violence, passed in violence, is
maintained in violence, and is being executed in violence. I say it was *conceived*
in violence, because the destruction of the Missouri Compromise, under the
circumstances, was nothing less than violence. It was *passed* in violence, because it

could not have passed at all but for the votes of many members in violence of the known will of their constituents. It is *maintained* in violence because the elections since, clearly demand its repeal, and this demand is openly disregarded. . . .

. . . You inquire where I now stand. That is a disputed point—I think I am a whig; but others say there are no whigs, and that I am an abolitionist. When I was at Washington I voted for the Wilmot Proviso as good as forty times, and I never heard of any one attempting to unwhig me for that. I now do no more than oppose the *extension* of slavery.

I am not a Know-Nothing. That is certain. How could I be? How can anyone who abhors the oppression of negroes, be in favor of degrading classes of white people? Our progress in degeneracy appears to me to be pretty rapid. As a nation, we began by declaring that *"all men are created equal."* We now practically read it "all men are created equal, *except negroes.*" When the Know-Nothings get control, it will read "all men are created equal, except negroes, *and foreigners, and Catholics."* When it comes to this I should prefer emigrating to some country where they make no pretense of loving liberty—to Russia, for instance, where despotism can be taken pure, and without the base alloy of hypocracy. . . .

Your friend forever
A. Lincoln.

Abraham Lincoln, *Abraham Lincoln: His Speeches and Writings,* ed. Roy P. Basler (Cleveland: World Publishing, 1946), 332–36.

THE 1856 ANTI-NEBRASKA STATE CONVENTION

The 1856 Anti-Nebraska State Convention was a defining moment in Illinois's political history. Held in Bloomington, the convention paved the way for antislavery men of all parties to unite in a single organization. Within two years the anti-Nebraska organization founded on that day would be known throughout the state as the Republican Party. The resolutions of the 1856 Bloomington convention provide insight into the nature of the Republican Party's early appeal in Illinois.

WHEREAS—The present administration has prostituted its powers, and devoted all its energies to the propagation of slavery, and to its extension into territories heretofore dedicated to freedom, against the known wishes of the people of such territories, to the suppression of the freedom of speech, and of the press; and to the revival of the odious doctrine of constructive treason, which has always been the resort of tyrants, and their most powerful engines of injustice and oppression; *and whereas,* we are convinced that an effort is making to subvert the principles, and ultimately to change the form of our government, and which it becomes all patriots, all who love their country and the cause of human freedom to resist: Therefore,

Resolved, That foregoing all former differences of opinion upon other questions, we pledge ourselves to unite in opposition to the present administration, and to the party which upholds and supports it, and to use all honorable and constitutional means to wrest the government from the unworthy hands which now control it, and to bring it back in its administration to the principles and practices of Washington, Jefferson and their great and good compatriots of the revolution.

Resolved, That we hold, in accordance with the principles and practices of all the great statesmen of all parties, for the first sixty years of the administration of the government, that, under the constitution, Congress possesses full power to prohibit slavery in the territories; and that whilst we will maintain all constitutional rights of the South, we also hold that justice, humanity, the principles of freedom as expressed in our declaration of independence, and our national constitution, and the purity and perpetuity of our government require that that power should be exerted to prevent the extension of slavery into territories heretofore free.

Resolved, That the repeal of the Missouri Compromise was unwise, unjust and injurious; in open and aggravated violation of the plighted faith of the States, and that the attempt of the present administration to force slavery into Kansas against the known wishes of the legal voters of that territory, is an arbitrary and tyrannous violation of the rights of the people to govern themselves, and that we will strive by all constitutional means, to secure to Kansas and Nebraska the legal guaranty against slavery of which they were deprived at the cost of the violation of the plighted faith of the nation.

Resolved, That we are devoted to the Union, and will, to the last extremity, defend it against the efforts now being made by the disunionists of this administration to compass its dissolution; and that we will support the Constitution of the United States in all its provisions; regarding it as the sacred bond of our Union, and the only safeguard for the preservation of the rights of ourselves and our posterity.

Resolved, That we are in favor of the immediate admission of Kansas as a member of this Confederacy, under the Constitution adopted by the people of said Territory.

Resolved, That the spirit of our institutions, as well as our constitution of our country, guarantees the liberty of conscience as well as political freedom, and that we will proscribe no one, by legislation or otherwise, on account of religious opinions, or in consequence of place of birth. . . .

Reprinted in *Illinois State Journal* (Springfield), May 30, 1856.

THE RISE OF CHICAGO

The Windy City was destined to play a central role in the Civil War. Yet Chicago's importance to Illinois and the expanding nation was already evident before men marched off to battle. During the 1850s Chicago's astonishing physical and social transformation awed everyone who experienced it. One such witness was Gustaf Unonius, a Scandinavian immigrant who settled in Wisconsin in the 1840s, and who occasionally visited Chicago before returning to Sweden in 1858. Here Unonius describes what he saw during a two-week visit to Chicago in 1857.

This will give the reader an idea of what Chicago was like [ca. 1845], when it was estimated that its population was something like 20,000. Twelve years have passed, and what a change in its appearance as well as its population, which is now 120,000! The formerly low, swampy streets have been raised several feet and paved with planks or stone. The river has been dredged and widened; its shore have been supported with piles, evened off, raised well above the water level, and are now occupied by loading piers or used as foundations for gigantic warehouses or factories. . . .

The growth of the city during the last sixteen years seems almost miraculous—even for America. In 1848 a canal was completed, a hundred miles long, by which Chicago secured direct communications with the Mississippi River, and consequently also with the Mississippi valley, all the way down to New Orleans, and all the way up to the land around the source of the giant river with its three thousand miles of navigable water. Through this canal the state of Illinois, which in fertility is surpassed by no other state in the Union, became commercially the most important state in the West, and the city of Chicago became the center of trade in products of America and other countries. The canal became the first powerful force leading to the present greatness and is still the artery through which rejuvenating strength flows into the constantly growing city.

However, the web of railroads which Chicago has spun around itself during the last ten years is the thing that more than anything else has contributed to its wealth and progress. In 1851 the first locomotive was to be seen rolling along on a track that extended only a few miles outside the city. Now Chicago is the terminus of more than a dozen trunk lines from which almost twice as many branch lines extend in every direction. Thereby the city has communication with the rich copper districts and other mining regions around Lake Superior, with Canada, with all the Atlantic states, with the rich grain-producing lands beyond the Mississippi, and with the cotton states around the Gulf of Mexico. While a few years ago it took eight to ten days to travel from New York to Chicago, the traveler may now make his choice among three different railroads and cover that distance in thirty to thirty-six hours. More than one hundred twenty trains, some of them consisting of up to forty fully loaded freight cars, arrive and depart each day from the railroad stations in various parts of the city. . . .

In addition to what has already been mentioned, Chicago has a great number of establishments, all of which testify to the speedy and constant development in all kinds of industries and business undertakings. Great locomotive works, car shops, foundries, and all kinds of machine shops employing thousands of workmen receive orders from almost every state for manufactures that a few years ago could be secured only from the eastern states. Among factories, [Cyrus] McCormick's establishment for the manufacture of agricultural machinery deserves mention. Among other things, it annually produces several thousand harvesting machines—Mr. McCormick's invention which is now being used almost everywhere in Europe. . . .

All of these things will give the reader an idea of how the city has grown from practically nothing during the last twenty years, and he will therefore realize that it is not an exaggeration to predict that within another score of years, when it is likely that the electric spark, crossing the Rocky Mountains, will bring messages from one ocean's shore to the other, and the locomotives which roll across the land from San Francisco and New York will meet in Chicago—that this city will become the central metropolis of the great North American continent, an emporium for the products of Asia, Europe, and America.

Gustaf Unionus, *A Pioneer in Northwest America, 1841–1858: The Memoirs of Gustaf Unonius*, trans. Jonas Oscar Backlund, ed. Nils William Olsson, 2 vols. (Minneapolis: University of Minnesota Press, 1960), 2:175, 179–80, 186–87.

TWO

The Emergence of Lincoln and the Secession Crisis

$\mathscr{S}$ECTIONAL TENSIONS MOUNTED following the election of President James Buchanan. In 1857 the Supreme Court rendered its decision in a case involving the slave Dred Scott, who had sued for his freedom on the basis of prolonged residence in free territory. In *Dred Scott v. Sandford* the court not only upheld Scott's status as a slave—as Chief Justice Roger Taney put it, a black man "had no rights which a white man was bound to respect"—it also held that under the Constitution slavery could not be excluded, either by Congress *or* a territorial legislature. The following year Buchanan, under pressure from Southerners, endorsed the fraudulent proslavery constitution drafted at Lecompton, Kansas. This was too much for Douglas, who saw immediately that Lecompton made a mockery of popular sovereignty. Accordingly he threw his energy against Kansas statehood, a stand that earned him admiration from some Republicans and bitter contempt from Southern Democrats. A deep rift emerged in the Democratic Party between Douglas men and Buchanan loyalists.

The stage was almost set for the greatest political confrontation in American history, the Lincoln-Douglas debates. Despite rumors that Illinois Republicans might let Douglas return to the U.S. Senate unopposed, instead they turned to Lincoln. In an unusual act the 1858 Republican state convention formally endorsed Lincoln—unusual because before 1913 state legislators, not the people directly, elected U.S. senators. Since the office would go to the man whose party controlled the general assembly, both Lincoln and Douglas campaigned vigorously. Oddsmakers pegged Douglas a clear favorite. The charismatic Little Giant commanded a formidable party machine with strength across the entire state, while Lincoln's experience on the national stage, a single term as U.S. congressman, seemed unimpressive alongside Douglas. But those familiar with Lincoln knew him to be clear thinking and quick witted. The factional infighting in Illinois between Douglas and Buchanan forces also did not hurt Lincoln's chances. Most important, as a moderate, former antislavery Whig from Springfield, Lincoln's political ideas were popular in central districts, the decisive battleground in Illinois politics.

Sensing his disadvantage Lincoln proposed, and Douglas accepted, a series of seven debates that commenced in August at Ottawa and climaxed in October at Alton. The epic clash turned on the related questions of slavery and race in America. With regard to slavery, two points logically followed the *Dred Scott* decision. First, the Republican opposition to slavery's further expansion now appeared unconstitutional. Lincoln had to somehow square his antislavery position with America's founding principles. Second, popular sovereignty also appeared untenable in the wake of *Dred Scott*. Thus Douglas too had to show his principles were consistent with the nation's traditions of constitutional liberty and self-government; only popular sovereignty, he maintained, could keep the Union together. Unquestionably it was Douglas who interjected the race issue into the debates. He poured forth a relentless volley of race-baiting rhetoric and imagery that many times forced Lincoln on the defensive. When the votes were finally tallied Democrats retained slim control of the general assembly and duly sent the Little Giant back to Washington. But the returns showed the Republicans had gained more strength in Illinois, and Lincoln had earned a national reputation, impressively matching the iconic Democratic statesman point for point.

In order to cement his status as a leader of western Republicanism, Lincoln set off in 1859 and again in 1860 on speaking tours of several western, mid-Atlantic, and Eastern Seaboard states. Soon more and more Illinois Republicans were resolving to support Lincoln for president, movements that Lincoln did nothing to discourage. Meanwhile, John Brown's raid on the federal arsenal at Harpers Ferry, Virginia, inflamed Southern fears of abolitionist-inspired slave rebellion. By now few Illinois Democrats troubled themselves with the finer distinctions between abolitionists and Republicans; both were fanatics whose mad counsels portended violence and disunion. In Illinois the Brown raid coincided with a case that refocused attention on the Fugitive Slave Law. In 1860, Ottawa's John Hossack and six others were tried in a U.S. district court in Chicago for violating the Fugitive Slave Law after having assisted the Missouri runaway slave Jim Gray in his flight to freedom. The closely followed trial provided Hossack, a charismatic Scottish immigrant, with a platform to denounce the law. It also provided compelling political theater in the weeks before the 1860 election. Chicago's Republican mayor, John Wentworth, seized on the trial to reinforce his antislavery credentials, at one point taking Hossack out of jail for a drive about the city, where approving crowds celebrated their new hero. Scandalized by the apparent approval of mob law by Hossack's defenders, Democrats vowed to defeat the "black Republicans" at the polls.

But such vows were empty now. Douglas's apostasy over Lecompton and his Freeport Doctrine alienated Southern Democrats, who sought firm guarantees for slavery's perpetuity. In the absence of such guarantees, warned Southerners, secession was the only honorable course. The South refused to back Douglas for president in 1860, turning instead to Kentucky's John C. Breckinridge, who ran on a proslavery platform. Northern Democrats stayed loyal to Douglas and his policy of popular sovereignty, but the split in the party assured the defeat of both Douglas and Breckinridge in November.

The man who benefited was, of course, the son of a Kentucky dirt farmer who had risen to become the undisputed leader of the Illinois Republican Party. Indeed, Lincoln's backers made the most of his humble, pioneer origins, for the "rail-splitter" seemed to personify western free-labor values. But in the end the two keys to Lincoln's emergence lay in his reputation as an antislavery moderate and the fact that the national Republican convention was held in Chicago. Lincoln's friends and managers at the convention—David Davis, Norman Judd, Gustave Koerner, and Orville Browning—made the most of their home-field advantage, working behind the scenes to convince delegates that Lincoln possessed none of the negatives of the frontrunners. New York's William Seward would lose the pivotal western battlegrounds of Illinois and Indiana; the Ohio radical Salmon P. Chase would frighten away conservative voters that Republicans needed to put them over the top in the swing states. Other potential candidates faced similar impediments; only Lincoln, the Illinoisans maintained, could unite all the disparate elements that Republicans needed for victory. On the convention's third ballot, Lincoln won the nomination.

Seeking to broaden the party's appeal, the Republicans also expanded their platform at Chicago. Aware of the crucial role of immigrant voters in states like Illinois and Pennsylvania, the Republicans renounced the old Know Nothing idea to lengthen the naturalization period for citizenship. The 1860 platform also reflected the full maturation of the party's free-labor vision for the nation. At the core of that vision lay the Republican commitment to preventing slavery's further expansion into the western territories. The West, Republicans insisted, must remain closed to the institution of slavery and its retrograde social ethics. Beyond that, the platform committed the party to using the federal government's power to develop the trans-Mississippi West and to further the nation's industrial and commercial capacity in direct, purposeful ways. Republicans declared their support for a new tariff to raise revenue and to protect American manufacturing from European competition; appropriations to improve the nation's rivers and harbors for commercial trade; free homesteads to individual settlers on the vast public domain (much of which was currently occupied by various American Indian tribes); and a transcontinental railroad built at the public's expense. In one of the Civil War's great ironies, Southern secession enabled Republican majorities in Congress to easily enact these and other nation-building projects, while eventual Union victory assured the triumph of the Republican vision of the nation and government's role in it.

On this platform Lincoln carried every Northern state in 1860, giving him a comfortable majority in the Electoral College. Douglas's diminished machine still made it close in Illinois, but Lincoln won by increasing the Republican vote in central and southern districts (see map). Republican gubernatorial candidate Richard Yates rolled to victory, and Republicans won control of the general assembly, assuring Lyman Trumbull's reelection to the U.S. Senate. "Well, boys," Lincoln allegedly quipped to reporters the morning after his election, "your troubles are over now, but mine have just begun."[1]

The presidential election of 1860: percent of Republican vote

Lincoln's humor understated the matter; secession came with a rapidity that astonished even the most seasoned observers. As Lincoln put together his cabinet— masterfully composed of leaders of all the contending factions in the Republican coalition—Illinoisans took stock of the ominous clouds of war on the horizon. By February 1861 seven Deep South states had declared themselves out of the Union. While Illinois Republicans stood firmly behind the president-elect, Illinois Democrats bemoaned Lincoln and congressional Republicans for refusing any compromise that might undermine their bedrock principle of no more slave states. Southern sympathizers in Marion openly contemplated ways to join the secessionists. The *Cairo City Gazette* declared that the "sympathies of our people are mainly with the South," denouncing anyone who would save the Union through force of arms.[2] The silence of southern Illinois leader John Logan fueled rumors of widespread disloyalty in Little Egypt. As the war came, it seemed that the New Testament metaphor in Lincoln's famous House Divided speech might apply equally to Illinois.

SLAVERY BLIGHTS THE WHITE MAN

Illinois Republicans stood firmly against slavery's spread, but their views on race were more complex. In the following letter Charles Wilson, Republican editor of the Chicago Daily Evening Journal, *writes Illinois's Republican Senator Lyman Trumbull to explain his view of the relationship between the Republican Party and African Americans.*

Daily Evening Journal Office,
Chicago, May 12th, 1858.

Hon. Lyman Trumbull

Dear Sir

Your letter enclosing a copy of your speech upon the admission of Oregon, together with an article cut from the Journal is at hand. . . .

Opposing the admission of Oregon because she had incorporated an article into her Constitution [a black exclusion provision similar to Illinois's] which was voted into our own by so large a majority, I at once foresaw would be a source from which we might derive defeat in this State and I am glad to find that you did not base your opposition on that ground.

Our friends in Kansas have jeopardized our cause there, by allowing negroes to vote on the adoption of their State Constitution and it is only necessary to win it in the States, by giving color to the charge so industriously circulated by Douglas and others, that we are a nigger-worshipping equality-advocating organization.

For myself I am opposed to Slavery not only because it is a wrong to the downtrodden and oppressed but that it blights and mildews the white man whose lot is toil, and whose capital is his labor. With this view only can we carry our standard into the Slave states. I am resolutely opposed to the "equalizing of the races" and it no more necessarily follows that we should fellowship with negroes because our policy strikes off their shackles, than it would to take felons to our embraces, because we might remonstrate against cruelty to them in our penitentiaries. So long as the prejudice exists against negroes, and the clause in State Constitutions forbidding free negroes to come into them is a dead letter, I think it foolish to combat it. . . .

Hoping to hear from you often, and with the assurance that you may always find the Journal opposing the policy of "putting too much nigger in our platform," I am very truly

Charles Wilson

Lyman Trumbull Papers, Library of Congress, Washington, DC.

A HOUSE DIVIDED

In June 1858, Illinois Republicans met in Springfield and chose Abraham Lincoln to run against Stephen Douglas for the U.S. Senate. At the close of the convention Lincoln launched the prolonged campaign with his famous House Divided speech, excerpted here.

We are now far into the *fifth* year, since a policy was initiated, with the *avowed* object, and *confident* promise, of putting an end to slavery agitation. Under the operation of that policy, that agitation has not only, *not ceased*, but has *constantly augmented*. In my opinion, it *will* not cease, until a *crisis* shall have been reached, and passed—

"A house divided against itself cannot stand." I believe this government cannot endure, permanently half *slave* and half *free*. I do not expect the Union to be *dissolved*—I do not expect the house to *fall*—but I *do* expect it will cease to be divided. It will become *all* one thing, or *all* the other. Either the *opponents* of slavery, will arrest the further spread of it, and place it where the public mind shall rest in the belief that it is in [the] course of ultimate extinction; or its *advocates* will push it forward, till it shall become alike lawful in *all* the States, *old* as well as *new*—*North* as well as *South*.

Have we no *tendency* to the latter condition? Let any one who doubts, carefully contemplate that now almost complete legal combination—piece of *machinery* so to speak—compounded of the Nebraska doctrine, and the Dred Scott decision. Let him consider not only *what work* the machinery is adapted to do, and *how well* adapted; but also, let him study the history of its construction, and trace, if he can, or rather *fail*, if he can, to trace the evidences of design, and concert of action, among its chief bosses, from the beginning.

The new year of 1854 found slavery excluded from more than half the States by State Constitutions, and from most of the national territory by congressional prohibition. Four days later, commenced the struggle, which ended in repealing that congressional prohibition. This opened all the national territory to slavery; and was the first point gained. . . . While the opinion of the Court, by Chief Justice Taney, in the Dred Scott case, and the separate opinions of all the concurring Judges, expressly declare that the Constitution of the United States neither permits Congress nor a territorial legislature to exclude slavery from any United States territory, they all *omit* to declare whether or not the same Constitution permits a state, or the people of a State, to exclude it. . . . Such a decision is all that slavery now lacks of being alike lawful in all the States.

Welcome or unwelcome, such decision *is* probably coming, and will soon be upon us, unless the power of the present political dynasty shall be met and overthrown. We shall *lie down* pleasantly dreaming that the people of *Missouri* are on the verge of making their State *free;* and we shall *awake* to the *reality*, instead, that the *Supreme* Court has made *Illinois* a *slave* State.

To meet and overthrow the power of that dynasty, is the work now before all those who would prevent its consummation.

Abraham Lincoln, *Abraham Lincoln: His Speeches and Writings*, ed. Roy P. Basler (Cleveland: World Publishing, 1946), 372–73, 378–79.

THE LINCOLN-DOUGLAS DEBATES

The following excerpts of the famous Lincoln-Douglas debates convey the strategies employed and principles held by each man. Meeting face to face in open-air venues before immense crowds—upward of twenty-five thousand at Galesburg; twenty thousand at Charleston—the two combatants debated seven times, each debate lasting three hours. In between the debates, both candidates maintained a demanding schedule of campaign appearances that left each exhausted; according to Gustave Koerner, Douglas had all but lost his voice by the time the campaign reached Alton. Those who did not witness the debates firsthand followed them closely in the press from as far away as Maine. Indeed, the most significant effect of the debates was to introduce the country to Lincoln, who to this point had been an obscure figure outside Illinois.

[Douglas at Ottawa, August, 21, 1858]

We are told by Lincoln that he is utterly opposed to the Dred Scott decision and will not submit to it for the reason that he says it deprives the negro of the rights and privileges of citizenship. *[Laughter, applause]* That is the first and main reason which he assigns for his warfare on the Supreme Court of the United States and its decision. I ask you, are you in favor of conferring upon the negro the rights and privileges of citizenship? *[Cries of "no"]* Do you desire to strike out of our state's constitution that clause which keeps slaves and free negroes out of the state, and allow the free negroes to flow in, and cover your prairies with black settlements? Do you desire to turn this beautiful state into a free negro colony? *[Cries of "no"]*, in order that when Missouri abolishes slavery, she can send one hundred thousand emancipated slaves into Illinois to become citizens and voters on an equality with yourselves? *[Cries of "never," "no"]* If you desire negro citizenship, if you desire to allow them to come into the state and settle with the white man, if you desire them to vote on an equality with yourselves, and to make them eligible to office, to serve on juries, and to judge your rights, then support Mr. Lincoln and the Black Republican party, who are in favor of the citizenship of the negro. *[Cries of "never"]* For one, I am opposed to negro citizenship in any and every form. *[Cheers]* I believe this government was made on the white basis. I believe it was made by white men, for the benefit of white men and their posterity forever, and I am in favor of confining citizenship to white men, men of European birth and descent, instead of conferring it upon negroes, Indians, and other inferior races. *[Cheers]*

Abraham Lincoln and Stephen A. Douglas, *The Lincoln-Douglas Debates*, ed. Rodney O. Davis and Douglas L. Wilson (Urbana: University of Illinois Press/Knox College Lincoln Studies Center, 2008), 13–14.

[Lincoln at Ottawa, August 21, 1858]

[T]his is the true complexion of all I have ever said in regard to the institution of slavery and the black race. This is the whole of it, and anything that argues me into his [Douglas's] idea of perfect social and political equality with the negro is but a specious and fantastic arrangement of words, by which a man can prove a horse chestnut to be a chestnut horse. *[Laughter, applause]* I will say here, while upon this subject, that I have no purpose directly or indirectly to interfere with the institution of slavery in the states where it exists. I believe I have no lawful right to do so, and I have no inclination to do so. I have no purpose to introduce political and social equality between the white and the black races. There is a physical difference between the two, which in my judgment will probably forever forbid their living together upon the footing of perfect equality, and inasmuch as it becomes a necessity that there must be a difference, I, as well as Judge Douglas, am in favor of the race to which I belong having the superior position. I have never said anything to the contrary, but I hold that notwithstanding all this, there is no reason in the world why the negro is not entitled to all the natural rights enumerated in the Declaration of Independence—the right to life, liberty, and the pursuit of happiness. *[Cheers, applause]* I hold that he is as much entitled to these as the white man. I agree with Judge Douglas he is not my equal in many respects—certainly not in color, perhaps not in moral or intellectual endowment. But in the right to eat the bread, without leave of anybody else, which his own hand earns, *he is my equal and the equal of Judge Douglas, and the equal of every living man. [Applause]* . . .

And when the Judge reminds me that I have often said to him that the institution of slavery has existed for eighty years in some states, and yet it does not exist in some others, I agree to the fact, and I account for it by looking at the position in which our fathers originally placed it—restricting it from the new territories where it had not gone, and legislating to cut off its source by the abrogation of the slave trade, thus putting the seal of legislation *against its spread.* The public mind *did* rest in the belief that it was in the course of ultimate extinction. *[Cheers, applause]*

But lately, I think—and in this I charge nothing on the Judge's motives—lately, I think, that he and those acting with him have placed that institution on a new basis, which looks to the *perpetuity and nationalization of slavery. [Cheers]* . . . [W]hat is necessary to make the institution national? Not war. There is no danger that the people of Kentucky will shoulder their muskets and, with a young nigger stuck on every bayonet, march into Illinois and force them upon us. There is no danger of our going over there and making war upon them. Then what is necessary for the nationalization of slavery? It is simply the next Dred Scott decision. It is merely for the Supreme Court to decide that no *state,* under the Constitution, can exclude it, just as they have already decided that, under the Constitution, neither Congress nor the territorial legislature can do it. When that is decided and acquiesced in, the whole thing is done.

Lincoln and Douglas, *Lincoln-Douglas Debates,* 20–22, 31–32.

[Douglas at Freeport, August 27, 1858]

The next question propounded to me by Mr. Lincoln is, "Can the people of a territory, in any lawful way, against the wishes of any citizen of the United States, exclude slavery from their limits prior to the formation of a state constitution?" I answer emphatically, as Mr. Lincoln has heard me answer a hundred times from every stump in Illinois, that in my opinion the people of a territory can, by lawful means, exclude slavery from their limits prior to the formation of a state constitution. *[Applause]* . . .

It matters not what way the Supreme Court may hereafter decide as to the abstract question whether slavery may or may not go into a territory under the Constitution. The people have the lawful means to introduce it or exclude it as they please, for the reason that slavery cannot exist a day or an hour anywhere, unless it is supported by local police regulations, furnishing remedies and means of enforcing the right to hold slaves. Those police regulations can only be established by the local legislature, and if the people are opposed to slavery, they will elect representatives to that body who will, by unfriendly legislation, effectually prevent the introduction of it into their midst. If, on the contrary, they are for it, their legislation will favor its extension. Hence, no matter what the decision of the Supreme Court may be on that abstract question, still the right of the people to make a slave territory or a free territory is perfect and complete under the Nebraska bill. . . .

Lincoln and Douglas, *Lincoln-Douglas Debates*, 58.

[Douglas at Charleston, September 18, 1858]

Mr. Lincoln tells you, in his speech at Springfield, that a house divided against itself cannot stand; that this government, divided into free and slave states, cannot endure permanently; that they must either be all free or all slave—all one thing or all the other. Why cannot this government endure divided into free and slave states, as our fathers made it? When this government was established by Washington, Jefferson, Madison, Jay, Hamilton, Franklin, and the other sages and patriots of that day, it was composed of free states and slave states, bound together by one common constitution. We have existed and prospered from that day to this thus divided, and have increased with a rapidity never before equaled in wealth, the extension of territory, and all the elements of power and greatness, until we have become the first nation on the face of the globe. Why can we not thus continue to prosper? We can if we will live up to and execute the government upon those principles upon which our fathers established it.

Lincoln and Douglas, *Lincoln-Douglas Debates*, 163.

[Lincoln at Alton, October 15, 1858]

I entertain the opinion, upon evidence sufficient to my mind, that the fathers of this government placed [slavery] where the public mind *did* rest in the belief that it was in the course of ultimate extinction. Let me ask why they made provision that the source of slavery—the African slave trade—should be cut off at the end of twenty years? Why did they make provision that, in all the new territory we owned at that time, slavery should be forever inhibited? Why stop its spread in one direction and cut off its source in another, if they did not look to its being placed in the course of ultimate extinction? . . . And when I say that I desire to see the further spread of it arrested, I only say I desire to see that done which the fathers have first done. . . .

Judge Douglas assumes that we have no interest in [the western territories], that we have no right whatever to interfere. I think we have some interest. I think that as white men we have. Do we not wish for an outlet for our surplus population, if I may so express myself? Do we not feel an interest in getting to that outlet with such institutions as we would like to have prevail there? . . .

I have stated upon former occasions, and I may as well state again, what I understand to be the real issue in this controversy between Judge Douglas and myself. On the point of my wanting to make war between the free and the slave states, there has been no issue between us. So, too, when he assumes that I am in favor of introducing a perfect social and political equality between the white and black races. These are false issues upon which Judge Douglas has tried to force the controversy. There is no foundation in truth for the charge that I maintain either of these propositions. The real issue in this controversy—the one pressing upon every mind—is the sentiment on the part of one class that looks upon the institution of slavery *as a wrong*, and of another class that *does not* look upon it as a wrong. The sentiment that contemplates the institution of slavery in this country as a wrong is the sentiment of the Republican party. It is the sentiment around which all their actions, all their arguments, circle, from which all their propositions radiate. They look upon it as being a moral, social, and political wrong, and while they contemplate it as such, they nevertheless have due regard for its actual existence among us, and the difficulties of getting rid of it in any satisfactory way, and to all the constitutional obligations thrown about it. Yet having a due regard for these, they desire a policy in regard to it that looks to its not creating any more danger. They insist that it should, as far as may be, *be treated* as a wrong, and one of the methods of treating it as a wrong is to *make provision that it shall grow no larger. [Applause]* . . .

[Douglas] contends that whatever community wants slaves has a right to have them. So they have, if it is not a wrong. But if it is a wrong, he cannot say people have a right to do wrong. He says that upon the score of equality, slaves should be allowed to go in a new territory like other property. This is strictly logical if there is no difference between [slavery] and other property. . . . But if you insist that one is wrong and the other right, there is no use to institute a comparison between right and wrong. You may turn over everything in the Democratic policy from beginning to end, whether in the shape it takes on the statute book, in the shape it takes in the Dred Scott decision, in the shape it takes in conversation, or the shape it takes in short maxim-like arguments. It everywhere carefully excludes the idea that there is anything wrong in [slavery].

That is the real issue. That is the issue that will continue in this country when these poor tongues of Judge Douglas and myself shall be silent. It is the eternal struggle between these two principles, right and wrong, throughout the world. They are the two principles that have stood face to face from the beginning of time, and will ever continue to struggle. The one is the common right of humanity, and the other the divine right of kings. It is the same principle in whatever shape it develops itself. It is the same old serpent that says, "You work and toil and earn bread, and I'll eat it." *[Applause]* No matter in what shape it comes, whether from the mouth of a king who seeks to bestride the people of his own nation and live by the fruit of their labor, or from one race of men as an apology for enslaving another race, it is the same tyrannical principle.

Lincoln and Douglas, *Lincoln-Douglas Debates*, 277–78, 281–82, 284–85.

[Douglas at Alton, October 15, 1858]

I have said everywhere, and now repeat it to you, that if the people of Kansas want a slave state they have a right, under the Constitution of the United States, to form such a state, and I will let them come into the Union with slavery or without, as they determine. . . . I say to you that there is but one hope, one safety for this country, and that is to stand immovably by that principle which declares the right of each state and each territory to decide these questions for themselves. This government was founded on that principle and must be administered in the same sense in which it was founded.

But the abolition party really think that under the Declaration of Independence the negro is equal to the white man, and that negro equality is an inalienable right conferred by the Almighty, and hence, that all human laws in violation of it are null and void. With such men, it is no use for me to argue. I hold that the signers of the Declaration of Independence had no reference to negroes at all when they declared all men to be created equal. They did not mean negro, nor the savage Indians, nor the Feejee Islanders, nor any other barbarous race. They were speaking of white men. *[Cheers]* They alluded to men of European birth and European descent, to white men and to none others, when they declared that doctrine. I hold that this government was established on the white basis. It was established by white men for the benefit of white men and their posterity forever, and should be administered by white men, and none others. But it does not follow, by any means, that merely because the negro is not a citizen, and merely because he is not our equal, that therefore he should be a slave. On the contrary, it does follow that we ought to extend to the negro race, and to all other dependent races, all the rights, all the privileges, and all the immunities which they can exercise consistently with the safety of society. . . .

The question then arises, what are those privileges, and what is the nature and extent of them? My answer is that that is a question which each state must answer for itself. We in Illinois have decided it for ourselves. We tried slavery, kept it up for twelve years, and finding that it was not profitable, we abolished it for that reason and became a free state. We adopted in its stead the policy that a negro in this state shall not be a slave and shall not be a citizen. We have a right to adopt that policy. For my part I think it is a wise and sound policy for us. You in Missouri must judge for yourselves whether it is a wise policy for you. If you choose to follow our example, very good; if you reject it, still well. It is your business, not ours. . . . If the people of all the states will act on that great principle, and each state mind its own business, attend to its own affairs, take care of its own negroes, and not meddle with its neighbors, then there will be peace between the North and the South, the East and the West, throughout the whole Union. *[Cheers]*

Lincoln and Douglas, *Lincoln-Douglas Debates,* 259, 265–67.

ILLINOIS REACTS TO JOHN BROWN

The documents that follow illustrate the divisions in Illinois over John Brown's 1859 raid at Harpers Ferry, Virginia, and his subsequent execution by hanging. First, Democratic editor and future wartime Democratic congressman John Eden offers his opinion of Brown. The second document reprints the resolves of a special meeting of the Millburn Congregational Church, held on the day of Brown's execution.

THE FOOTPRINTS OF BLACK REPUBLICANISM.

The Harper's Ferry tragedy is but the legitimate fruit of the teachings of the higher-law men. The leaders of the Republican party, especially in New England and New York, have, from the first inception of that party, taught their followers to believe that the slaveholders of the South have no rights "that the Abolition fanatics are bound to respect." . . .

The bold, bad men of the party, like old Ossawattomie Brown, having been taught that it was right and proper and commendable to kill slaveholders with Sharp's rifles, and to make war upon slavery in general, would naturally follow out the doctrines taught them by invading the slave States, stealing negroes, and murdering their masters. Old Brown, having been upheld in all his murders in Kansas, and all his negro stealing in Missouri, by the Republican party in the East and many of them in the West, would naturally conclude, that when he raised the standard of revolt in old Virginia, for the purpose of destroying slavery there, that the same men would again rush to his assistance. We do not wish to be understood as charging the masses of the Republican party in the West with any complicity with old Brown in his deeds of rapine and murder. But we do hold that he is only acting out the teachings of Seward, Lincoln, Greeley and the leaders of the party, and that this foray upon Harper's Ferry, in which the blood of our fellow-citizens has been wantonly shed by midnight assassins and marauders, is but the beginning of the irrepressible conflict, urged on by Seward, and is the mode by which the ultra men of the Republican party propose to carry out Lincoln's policy, "of the ultimate extinction of slavery."

Sullivan Express, November 3, 1859.

～

At a special meeting of the 1st. Congregational Church of Millburn, held on the 2d. day of Dec. 1859, after spending an hour in prayer with particular reference to the tragedy to be acted this day at Charleston Va. The following preamble and resolutions were adopted.

Whereas, the slaveholders of this country are making desperate efforts to extend and perpetuate the atrocious system of slavery which now exists in nearly one half of the states and exerts a baleful influence upon the prosperity of the nation; and are using the most base and unjustifiable means to accomplish their ends—repudiating the doctrine of our fathers, that all men are created free and equal;—disregarding the most sacred compromises and agreements of the patriots who founded the government;—and have revived the nefarious slave trade in defiance of the government, and the law of the land; and are this day inebri[ating] their hands in the blood of a Christian patriot, who, inspired by the spirit of our fathers, sought the liberty of the oppressed and enslaved. Therefore

Resolved, That henceforth we will redouble our efforts for the abolition of slavery, by all means justified by the word of God and a good conscience.

Resolved, That we will do good to those who have escaped from bondage as we have opportunity, by supplying their present wants and aiding them in their flight.

Resolved, That in future we will devote special attention to the subject of emancipation on the 2nd of Dec, annually, in grateful remembrance of John Brown, who fell a sacrifice to slaveholding vengeance, for his efforts peacefully to liberate the down-trodden slaves of Virginia.

Millburn Congregational Church minute book, December 2, 1859, facsimile reprinted in Glennette Tilley Turner, *The Underground Railroad in Illinois* (Glen Ellyn, IL: Newman Educational Publishing, 2001), 222–23.

THE OTTAWA RESCUE CASE

In September 1859 the slave Jim Gray escaped from Missouri and fled to Illinois. He got as far Union County, where local authorities apprehended him. As Gray sat in a courtroom, a group of abolitionists led by the Scottish immigrant John Hossack, from Ottawa, interrupted the proceedings, and amid the confusion sped Gray into a waiting carriage. Eventually Gray joined countless others who, assisted by Illinois's Underground Railroad, reached freedom in Canada. Determined to make an example of the abolitionists, in 1860 authorities tried Hossack and six others in a Chicago district court for violating the Fugitive Slave Law. Hossack and Joseph Stout were found guilty, fined $100, and sentenced to ten days in jail. Hossack's remarks prior to sentencing are excerpted here.

I have a few words to say why sentence should not be pronounced against me. I am found guilty of a violation of the Fugitive Slave Law, and it may appear strange to your Honor that I have no sense of guilt. I came, Sir, from the tyranny of the Old World, when but a lad, and landed upon the American shores, having left my kindred and native land in pursuit of some place where men of toil would not be crushed by the property-holding class. . . .

Twenty-two years ago, I landed in this city. I immediately engaged on the public works, on the canal then building that connects this city with the great

river of the West. In the process of time, the State failed to procure money to
carry on the public works. I then opened a prairie farm to get bread for my family, and I am one of the men who have made Chicago what it is to-day, having
shipped some of the first grain that was exported from this city. I am, Sir, one
of the pioneers of Illinois, who have gone through the many hardships of the
settlement of a new country.

. . . I would call the attention of your Honor to the partiality of the [Fugitive
Slave] law, which is so at variance with the designs of the Fathers in organizing this
Government. No man can read the Constitution—in which the word slave cannot
be found; from which the idea that a man could be reduced to a thing, and held as
property, was carefully excluded—no man, I say, can read that Constitution, and
come to the conclusion that slavery was to be *fostered, guaranteed,* and *protected* far
beyond every thing else in the country. Admit that Jim Gray was [Richard] Phillips's property, how comes it that that particular property is more sacred than any
other property? Phillips's horse escapes from him, and is found in a distant State;
but the President of the United States, and every department of Government, are
not put on the track to find the horse, and return him to Phillips's stable, and then
pay the whole bill from the National Treasury. No, Sir. But his slave escapes—he
runs away, and, for some reason, his property in man is so much more holy and
sacred, that the whole Government is bound to take the track and hunt the poor
panting fugitive down, and carry him back to his chains and bondage at the Government's expense. . . .

But, Sir, I have one consideration more that I will urge why sentence ought
not to be pronounced against me. This law, which I think I have proved outrageous to the rights of man, is so obviously at variance with the law of that God
who commands me to love Him with all my soul, mind, might and strength,
and my neighbor as myself, and the Redeemer who took upon him my nature
and the nature of poor Jim Gray has been so particular in telling me who my
neighbor is, that the path of duty is plain to me. This law so plainly tramples
upon the divine law, that it cannot be binding upon any human being under any
circumstances to obey it. . . . Send me a law bidding me rob or murder my neighbor, I must decline to obey it. I can suffer, but I must not do wrong. Send me a
law bidding me join hands in robbing my fellow-men of their freedom, I cannot
do so great a wrong. Yea, send me a law bidding me stop my ears to the cry of
the poor, I can suffer the loss of all these hands have earned, I can suffer bonds
and imprisonment—yes, God helping me, I can give up my life—but I cannot
knowingly trample upon the law of my God, nor upon the bleeding, prostrate
form of my fellow-man. I go not to Missouri to relieve oppressed humanity, for
my duty has called me nearer home; but when He that directs the steps of man
conducts a poor, oppressed, panting fugitive to my door, and there I hear his

bitter cry, I dare not close my ear against it, lest in my extremity I cry for mercy, and shall not be heard. Sir, this law so flagrantly outrages the divine law, that I ought not to be sentenced under it.

John Hossack, *Speech of John Hossack, convicted of a violation of the Fugitive slave law, before Judge Drummond, of the United States district court, Chicago, Ill.* (New York: American Anti-Slavery Society, 1860), 3–4, 9–11.

THE 1860 NATIONAL REPUBLICAN CONVENTION

In May 1860, Republicans from across the country arrived in Chicago and met in a hastily constructed wooden structure—the Wigwam—to nominate their presidential ticket. One writer estimated that over twenty-five thousand visitors descended upon the city to attend, report on, or simply indulge in the hoopla and spectacle of the convention. In an age without cable television or YouTube, nineteenth-century political campaigns functioned as mass entertainment, and few contests matched the intensity and excitement of this one. Much was at stake, especially for Illinoisans, who hoped and prayed that one of their favorite sons—Lincoln or Douglas—might become the next president of the United States. Following are reports that convey the festive atmosphere that attended the nomination of Lincoln in Chicago.

It was my good fortune to be present at the National Convention in Chicago, in 1860, which nominated Mr. Lincoln to the Presidency. It was held in an immense building erected for the occasion, and known as the "Wigwam." I had undertaken to report the proceedings for an editor friend, and a seat was assigned me near the platform, where the electors from the several states were seated, and where not one word could escape me. My place was in the midst of the great reportorial army collected from all parts of the country. I was fortunate above all women on that occasion, for the far-away gallery was assigned them, and they were strictly forbidden the enclosed and guarded lower floor, which was sacred to men exclusively. From the immensity of the "Wigwam," the proceedings could not be heard in the gallery, and seemed there like gigantic pantomime.

. . . Women reporters were then almost unheard of; and inconspicuous as I had endeavored to make myself by dressing in black, like my brethren of the press, the marshal of the day spied me, after the lower floor was densely packed with masculinity. In stentorian tones that rang through the building, while his extended arm and forefinger pointed me out, and made me the target for thousands of eyes, he ordered me to withdraw my profane womanhood from the sacred enclosure provided for men, and "go up higher," among the women. I rose mechanically to obey, but the crowd rendered this impossible. My husband beside me, reporting for his own paper, undertook to explain, but was not allowed. The reporters about me then took the matter into their own hands, and in a tumult of voices cavalierly bade me "Sit still!" and the marshal "Dry up!" A momentary battle of words was waged over my head, between my husband and the reporters, the police and the marshal, and then I was left in peace. . . .

I was well repaid for the annoyance, by being a near witness of the electric scenes which followed the nomination of Mr. Lincoln to the Presidency, on the third ballot. Who that saw the tumultuous rapture of that occasion could ever forget it! Men embraced each other, and fell on one another's neck, and wept out their repressed feeling. They threw their hats in the air, and almost rent the roof with huzzahs. Thousands and thousands were packed in the streets outside, who stood patiently receiving accounts of the proceedings within, from reporters posted on the roof, listening at the numerous open skylights, and shouting them in detail to the crowd below.

Mary A. Livermore, *My Story of the War* (Hartford, CT: A. D. Worthington and Company, 1889), 550–51.

〜

I cannot undertake to narrate the demonstrations consequent on the nominations of to-day; it would require the services of a score of active reporters to do so, and even then language would fail to convey a just appreciation of the exuberance of joy and enthusiasm with which they have been greeted. Everybody seems to have, for the time, laid aside their gravity and become again boys. The city is wild with excitement, and apparently, in the language of one of Sangamon's sons, the political millennium has arrived. . . .

At the Illinois head-quarters in the Tremont [Hotel] was assembled a set of the craziest men I ever saw. Their demonstrations were such as to defy competition from the inmate of any Lunatic Asylum. Screeches were made, embraces were exchanged, and songs were sung at the point, and sometimes accompanied with cheers which almost raised the roof.

To-night the population is in the field, with triumphal processions, and the streets are lighted with bonfires and fire works, while the cannon is thundering from the east of the Tremont, where many public buildings are illuminated; and as I write, I hear the cheers of the multitude who are listening to the eloquence of Corwin in the wigwam.

Illinois State Journal (Springfield), May 19, 1860.

RICHARD YATES DEFINES REPUBLICAN PRINCIPLES

Richard Yates, of Jacksonville, first rose to prominence as a Whig, serving several terms in the Illinois General Assembly and two terms in the U.S. Congress (1851–55). As the Whig Party disappeared, Yates emerged as a leader of the state's Republican Party. Excerpted here is a speech Yates delivered at Springfield while campaigning for governor in 1860. During a time of tremendous economic growth and social change for Illinois, Yates describes Republican principles in ways that move well beyond the antislavery themes present at the party's birth.

The great idea and basis of the Republican party, as I understand it, is free labor. It is all in that word, to elevate, to dignify, to advance, to reward, to ennoble labor—to make labor honorable is the object, end and aim of the Republican party. Fellow citizens, labor is the foundation of all our prosperity—every blow of honest labor is a part of our national wealth; and he is no statesman who does not give to labor its highest rewards—who does not open to it the broadest fields— who does not make labor as honorable as he possibly can.

Thirty-five years ago, . . . [Illinois] . . . was in the possession of Black Hawk, Keokuk, Shabonee and their wild warrior tribes. But, what a change! Look at our mighty cities, magnificent with the temples of art, and the crowded thoroughfares of commerce—look at these vast sunny prairies, blooming with orchards, and gardens, and broad green fields. Behold the beautiful homes, scattered thickly all over the country—the manufacturing establishments on your rivers—the long trains of cars, trooping in procession along your railroads—the splendid steamers which ply day by day along your magnificent streams, carrying the products of your labor, and creating a commerce whose influence extends throughout the world. [Tremendous applause.]

And what produces all this wealth and prosperity? Labor, hard handed labor— the labor of millions of patient hands—the humblest as well as the most exalted.

Now the question comes, how shall we advance this labor? As presented in our politics, the question is, whether unpaid, unwilling slave labor is better than voluntary, intelligent, free labor? I was not so young when I left Kentucky, but that I recollect the time when a poor man toiled all day, with a hod upon his shoulder, up the scaffold of a rich man's edifice for three shillings a day, because a slave could be hired for seventy-five dollars a year. Do you recollect what Senator [James Henry] Hammond said of the free white population of South Carolina? That a majority of that unhappy class subsisted by hunting and fishing, and trading with the negroes for what they were stealing from their masters and they cannot live and prosper in competition with unpaid slave labor. . . .

How shall we advance this labor? In the first place, we have, as a part of our platform, a tariff resolution. . . . I believe, that we should have a revenue tariff—thus fulfilling [Andrew] Jackson's notion, with incidental protection, which secured [Henry] Clay's object, that is, . . . discriminating in favor of articles [for] the growth and manufacturing of our own country. We propose to elevate labor by these principles; by upturning the concealed riches of the earth; by opening the beds of iron that rest in our mountains; by affording in every way in which we can, a better market for farmers and mechanics. . . .

Another portion of our platform is in favor of a free homestead upon the public lands to any actual settler, whether an American born citizen or one of the poor wanderers from foreign lands who may come upon this soil and settle, improve and occupy it for a limited period. . . . Look at the vast Utah territory, at Minnesota, Kansas, Nebraska, Washington, Oregon, containing hundreds and hundreds of millions of acres—a territory more extended and magnificent than Rome commanded in her greatest power and pride, when her imperial eagles swept in their irresistible course over the ancient world. And is there anything wrong in giving a home from all this bounty to the poor laboring man? Shall he breathe this pure air free? Shall he enjoy God's glorious sunlight *free?* Shall he drink the waters of our lakes and rivers free? . . . Let the poor laborer go there, and by the blessing of God we will keep that territory free from the clank of a chain. [Loud Applause.] We will let no slave be taken to that territory. We will preserve it free, as God made it, for the poor white people of the South and of the North, and for their children and their children's children [applause.] We will keep it for the Anglo-Saxon race— that giant race which God designed should stamp the impress of their genius, and plant their free institutions upon this land. [Applause.] We will send our poor laborers there with the Bible and the ax, bearing with them the independence which our fathers achieved, and all the thousand improvements of an enlightened and Christian civilization. We will build up cities upon those broad plains, and scatter homesteads upon their thousand hills, until you can hear the rattle of machinery by every stream from the granite hills of New England to the rocky ramparts of the Pacific. Yea to the golden gates of the West there shall be a line of witnesses of the onward majestic march of free American labor. [Tremendous applause.] . . .

We are in favor of the construction of the Pacific Railroad. Do you say the Democrats are also for it? Have you seen many of their speeches in favor of it? . . . Why can we not build this road, spanning the continent? You say the country is uninhabited. So once was the country through which the great trunk lines of railroad across the Alleghenies have been built. Give to the people homesteads. Let every actual settler have one hundred and sixty acres free, for his home, on the public lands; and as the railroad is constructed, settlements will spring up at the stations and nestle along the track, until from New York to San Francisco . . . we will have an unbroken cordon of free, powerful commonwealths, stretching from ocean to ocean.

Richard Yates, *Speech of Hon. Richard Yates, Delivered at the Republican Ratification Meeting, of the Citizens of Sangamon County, in the Hall of the House of Representatives, Springfield, June 7th, 1860* (Springfield, [1860]), 6–8.

ILLINOIS RESPONDS TO SECESSION

Before Lincoln even took office, the lower South, beginning with South Carolina, seceded from the Union. Following are examples of how Illinoisans interpreted the beginning of secession in December 1860.

THE UNION, IT MUST BE PRESERVED.

There are not a few who seem to think that the Union will be dissolved whenever the South Carolina Secession Convention passes a resolution to that effect. The Union cannot be dissolved by the passage of resolutions. South Carolina may resolve that she is no longer a part of this Union. She may hold secession meetings, mount disunion cockades, plant palmetto trees, make palmetto flags, trample under foot the glorious flag of our country, and proclaim from the housetops her treason and her shame, but all this will not dissolve the Union. She may compel her citizens to resign [her] official place held under the Federal Government—she may close her courts and post offices, and put her own people to a great deal of inconvenience and trouble, but she will still be in the Union, unmolested. She cannot get out of this Union until she conquers this Government. The revenues must and will be collected at her ports, and any resistance on her part will lead to war. At the close of that war we can tell with certainty whether she [is] in or out of the Union. While this Government endures there can be no disunion. . . . The laws of the United States must be executed—the President has no discretionary power on the subject—his duty is emphatically pronounced in the Constitution. Mr. Lincoln will perform that duty. Disunion, by armed force, is TREASON, and treason must and will be put down at all hazards. This Union is not, will not, and cannot be dissolved until this Government is overthrown by the traitors who have raised the disunion flag. Can they overthrow it? We think not. . . . Let the secessionists understand it—let the press proclaim it—let it fly on the wings of the lightning, and fall like a thunderbolt among those now plotting treason in Convention, that the Republican party, that the great North, aided by hundreds of thousands of patriotic men in the slave States, have determined to preserve the Union—peaceably if they can, forcibly if they must.

Illinois State Journal (Springfield), December 20, 1860.

~

. . . We envy no man his feelings who can contemplate as an object of desire the disruption of the American union. We have no sympathy, no feelings in common with that man, whoever he is or wherever he is located, who is not willing to sacrifice his prejudices, or to forego almost any cherished judgment, rather than see our glorious union of hallowed memories and magnificent achievement, blotted from the world's map. Do the abolitionists fancy that they are extending the arc of human freedom, by their war upon southern institutions? Will the shackles fall from a single slave, because South Carolina and Georgia and Mississippi are driven out of a union where those feelings of fraternity that once bound all hearts together, have ceased to exist?

For the first time in the history of the government, its highest officers are elected upon a purely sectional issue. They are chosen as the exponents of a line of policy which favors one part of the country and puts down another, which glorifies the north and debases the south, which declares that this nation must become entirely a free or a slaveholding people; and at the very threshold of their entrance into power, they find that the nation which they had proposed to subjugate to freedom is rending in twain. This is their hour to speak conciliatory words, and check the firestorm. This is their time to yield something of the fanaticism which has borne them into office, and save the country. Will they do it? Will Abraham Lincoln and [vice president–elect] Hannibal Hamlin speak for their country's peace, now throbbing with agitation as the result of their sectionalism? What kind words can arrest the angry tide which is threatening to engulf the republic, will they utter them? A million eyes look anxiously to them at this moment, and a million hearts are moved with intense emotion to learn how they regard this crisis, and what they will do to beat back the furious waves which are urging our noble bark onward to ruin.

Peoria Daily Democratic Union, December 22, 1860.

EGYPT CALLS FOR SEPARATE STATEHOOD

As secession unfolded, rumor spread of a similar movement afoot in southern Illinois. In this letter, the pseudonymous writer "Egypt" calls for separate southern Illinois statehood and highlights the political, cultural, and economic divisions that would plague Illinois throughout the war.

Mrssrs. Editors—In considering the policy of creating a new State, and welcoming it into the Union, among the family of sovereignties, under the name of "South Illinois," it will be taken as an admitted fact that the inhabitants who will compose that State are a distinct people, having their own independent and peculiar ideas and views of religion, government and social life. They are brave, generous and hospitable. The many pestilent *isms* of the day meet with but little favor with them. They countenance neither free-love societies, women's rights associations, Maine-liquor-lawism, nor abolitionism. They are essentially a religious people. Infidelity has made but little progress among them, and as long as they can shut out the other *isms*, skepticism will be in disrepute. They are more completely *westernized* than any other of the free States, and very much more so than North Illinois. . . .

Being, then, a distinct people, they are entitled to a separate government; and they should at once examine the country they inhabit and see if it is possessed of the material elements that are necessary to success in any political community.

South Illinois produces grain of every description in prolific abundance. In wheat growing it may take first rank.—Twice or thrice wheat grown in Union county has received the first prize at the Illinois State Fair, in competition with specimens from all the Western States, and the wheat of Union is not superior to that grown in at least twenty other Southern counties. As a fruit growing and wine making region its excellent qualities are beginning to be developed, and its superiority demonstrated. Its mineral resources, when fully developed, will be enough to enrich the State if there were no other element of wealth.—Iron, lead, salt, and coal are found in abundance and in close proximity. In a word the germ of commercial greatness would pre-eminently exist in the new State, and her people need not fear to launch their political bark. . . .

The destiny of south Illinois to be the manufacturing district for the south and west [of the United States] is "manifest." But as the derided and neglected end of a vast state with almost two million people, south Illinois will not accomplish that destiny inside of fifty years. The present generation will never see, but only dream of her great future. She is now under the ban of yankee landsharks and emigrant aid societies. The character of her population is misrepresented and her resources denied. Every one who knows of her admirable commercial position and great wealth wonders why she is behind in the race of greatness. She is the *tail end* of a state whose head is far to the north on the frozen lakes. That is the difficulty. Let us divide the state, and have a head nearer our heart.

"Egypt"

Cairo City Gazette, March 21, 1861.

THREE

Improvising War

*E*FFORTS IN WASHINGTON to avert war came to naught in Charleston harbor in April 1861, when South Carolina batteries opened fire on Fort Sumter, one of the last strongholds of federal property in the seceded states. The attack prompted Lincoln to order the mobilization of seventy-five thousand volunteers on ninety-day terms of service to put down rebellion. In response to Lincoln's call to arms four more slave states joined the Confederacy. The Civil War had begun.

Illinoisans from all walks of life and from every corner of the state reacted with enthusiastic bursts of patriotism. In the absence of a centralized recruitment system, Illinois communities raised troops ad hoc. Relying on private donations and in some cases direct tax assessments, local communities created war funds that paid out bounties to individual volunteers. The funds were also used as relief money in support of the families left behind. Community-based mobilization worked within five days to meet the War Department's initial quota for six Illinois regiments. Still thousands more continued to pour into Camp Yates, hastily organized on the Springfield fairgrounds and burdened to overflowing as the volunteers waited for enlistment. Amid fears that irregular Confederate units in Missouri might launch raids into southern Illinois, initially most Illinois troops were stationed at Camp Defiance, located at Cairo, or at smaller barracks at Alton and Caseyville. Resolving to sacrifice for their president—the first Illinoisan to occupy the White House—and their nation, Illinoisans naively believed that a firm demonstration of unity would quickly defeat secession. The *Chicago Tribune* proclaimed that Union victory would "take two to three months at the furthest." "Illinois," it boasted, "can whip the South by herself."[1] No one at the time had the remotest idea of the lengthy trials they were about to endure.

The state's Democratic leadership played a key role in building early unity on the home front. Stephen Douglas, who would die suddenly in June, and downstate Democratic congressman John McClernand quickly backed the administration's effort to put down the rebellion by force. Then in June, Little Egypt's leading Democrat, John Logan, emerged from prolonged silence to deliver a rousing pro-Union speech before troops gathered at Camp Yates. Soon Logan was raising Union regiments in southern Illinois, beginning a remarkable political odyssey that ultimately made him a staunch Republican. In return for their loyalty, McClernand, Logan, James Shields, and other Illinois Democrats received prominent military commissions. Following Sumter, Quincy's Orville Browning confided in his diary, "All men of all parties are now for the Government." For the time being he was right.[2]

It fell to Governor Richard Yates and the Republican-controlled legislature to meet the organizational and administrative challenges that war now thrust upon the state government. Improvisation marked Illinois's early war. In April, Yates called the general assembly into emergency session. The ten-day session produced legislation that enlarged and refurbished the state's outmoded militia system, raised a force of ten thousand (four thousand more than the War Department's initial authorization), authorized the state to issue $2 million in new bonds, and gave the governor broad authority to spend emergency funds on equipment and matériel. No state spent more on military procurement in 1861 than Illinois, and the spiraling expenditures—nearly $4 million between April and December—exceeded Illinois's debt limit under the 1848 constitution, something that soon became a political problem for Yates and the Republicans.

The paramount need for updated systems of supply and administration was underscored after Sumter when authorities in Washington, cognizant of Cairo's strategic significance, asked Yates to send troops to occupy the city and protect its railroads and port. The ragtag force made up of state militia companies and headed by General Richard K. Swift traveled to Cairo with arms supplied by Chicago dry goods stores. The dearth of arms in Illinois was solved quickly, however. In response to Sumter the Illinois State Arsenal, at Springfield, opened a munitions factory. The factory hands—mostly women and young children—churned out small-arms ammunition and light ordnance to meet Illinois's growing demand. To the chagrin of state authorities and the workers, the arsenal shut down the factory in November 1861 after the federal government assumed responsibility for munitions purchases. A more immediate influx of military hardware came in late April, when Captain James Stokes orchestrated a splendid midnight raid on the federal arsenal at St. Louis, stealthily moving twenty thousand stands of arms to Cairo for distribution to Illinois volunteers. A day later Colonel Benjamin Prentiss ordered the capture of the southbound steamers *C. E. Hillman* and *John D. Perry* near Cairo. The booty included a large stash of arms and munitions, soon redistributed to Illinois men.

Following the Union defeat at Bull Run, in July, President Lincoln issued another call for volunteers—this one for half a million on three-year terms. In response Governor Yates sent his aides on several trips to New York City and Washington to purchase arms, artillery, ammunition, and supplies for the new recruits. Recently erected facilities at Anna, Chicago, Freeport, Jacksonville, Joliet, Mattoon, Peoria, and Quincy now began processing and training the huge influx of Illinois volunteers, over fifty thousand by the end of 1861 (by this time at least ten thousand more Illinoisans were also serving in regiments from Iowa, Kansas, and Missouri). Throughout the war the largest and most significant of Illinois's military installations was Camp Butler, just east of Springfield. The fifty-acre site eventually trained or mustered out of service more than two-thirds of Illinois's 170 regiments of infantry, cavalry, and artillery. In addition to those regular units, Illinois also raised nearly a dozen independent units of cavalry and artillery, while over 2,200 Illinoisans also served in the navy. Many of the latter were stationed at Mound City, on the Ohio River, after the navy selected the site as one of its primary "brown water" depots. The state was also home to the Rock Island Prison, built in 1862 and located in the Mississippi River just south of Moline. By war's end Rock Island had earned infamy as one of the North's worst military prisons. About 16 percent of the twelve thousand Confederates who were housed at Rock Island perished there, victims of the highly unsanitary conditions that prevailed at the overcrowded barracks. The shocking conditions inspired a chorus of criticism from Southerners, who singled out Rock Island as evidence of Union callousness and barbarity. In reality, the mortality rate at Rock Island was only slightly higher than most large Civil War prisons and paled in comparison to Andersonville, the Confederate prison in Georgia where over 30 percent of Union inmates died.

Camp Butler. *Courtesy Abraham Lincoln Presidential Library, Springfield, Illinois*

As the war produced its first battles and casualties, women, denied the vote everywhere in the United States, found themselves at the center of wartime politics. Women's decisions to act (or not to act) on behalf of the Union cause would necessarily implicate them directly in this nation's greatest conflict. Beyond urging their husbands, brothers, and fathers to volunteer—itself a political act—loyal Illinois women engaged in activities that over time strengthened their own sense of citizenship and public purpose. An intrepid few women managed to pass as men and fought in the Union army. One of the most fascinating was Jennie Hodgers, an Irish immigrant living in Belvidere who in 1862 enlisted in the Ninety-Fifth Illinois Infantry under the pseudonym Albert Cashier. Cashier saw action throughout the rest of the war, including the decisive Vicksburg campaign. After the war Cashier settled in Saunemin and maintained his transgendered identity, voting in elections and working as a farmhand and other menial jobs. Cashier's secret was not discovered until a doctor examined him in 1910. Many more women, like Galesburg's Mary Bickerdyke and Cairo's Mary Jane Safford, served near Civil War battlefields as nurses in camp hospitals or on ambulance duty. Back on the home front, women were the shock troops of the Union war effort. They knitted socks, sewed uniforms, and gathered hospital supplies for the war effort. Some Illinois women gained valuable business experience founding and managing loyal leagues, soldier's aid societies, and soldier's rest homes.

Despite the local bases of women's public activism—Safford began her Civil War nursing career spontaneously one day at a Cairo hospital, Bickerdyke in response to a Sunday sermon in Galesburg—gradually the U. S. Sanitary Commission and its branch offices assumed greater coordination over women's war work. Founded in 1861 by the New York City Unitarian minister Henry Bellows, the USSC recognized the need for an organization that could investigate conditions and suggest improvements in army hospitals. Despite initial resistance from the Army Medical Bureau, the USSC expanded its mission into virtually all noncombat aspects of a soldier's life, including the creation of a paid nursing staff, the coordination of various ambulance corps, and the collection and distribution of food and medical supplies. The most important branch office, because of its proximity to the western theater of war, was the Chicago Sanitary Commission, established in October 1861. Chicagoans Mary Livermore and Jane Hoge assumed responsibility for its day-to-day operations after touring hospitals in St. Louis, Cairo, and Mound City. Their first great test came in early spring 1862 during Grant's western offensive. In response to the awful reports of casualties at Fort Donelson, Livermore and Hoge tapped into the state's network of soldier's aid societies, coordinating the delivery of nurses, food, and medical supplies for the makeshift field hospitals— some of them on riverboats—set up to care for the wounded. Governor Yates encouraged the relief effort and traveled to Fort Donelson with a shipment of supplies, earning him praise as the "soldier's friend." Not to be outdone the state's Democrat-controlled constitutional convention, then meeting in Springfield, appropriated half a million dollars for the relief effort. Every penny was needed in April after Shiloh, the Civil War's bloodiest battle up to that point and the one that generated the highest percentage of Illinois casualties.

Despite the unity displayed on behalf of the wounded at Donelson and Shiloh, Illinois politics was already mired in divisions that would plague the home front through the duration of the conflict. Union military reverses in 1861 generated impatience and finally growing criticism of the administration. The elections that year, which Republicans hoped would solidify the bipartisan unity that marked the very beginning of the war, ended with a surprise Democratic victory in Illinois. Ignoring offers to work alongside Republicans through the nomination of "Union" tickets, in most districts Democrats mounted a vigorous campaign of their own. As Wilbur Storey, influential Democratic editor of the *Chicago Times* proclaimed, "*Henceforth the two parties must be as distinct as oil and water*—as far apart as earth and sun."[3]

That fall Democrats won a decisive majority (better than two to one) of the delegates sent to a convention to produce a new state constitution, authorized by voters in 1860. Convening in January 1862 in Springfield, the delegates sought to enact long-standing Democratic policy goals, such as regulation of banks and railroads and a legislative apportionment scheme weighted to rural—and heavily Democratic—districts. But beneath the veil of economic and political reform lay the Democrats' dissatisfaction with Governor Yates and the direction of the war under Republican auspices. Democrats in the convention charged that Yates had abused his constitutional authority by spending money for troops and supplies that only the federal government had authority to spend. They proposed to reduce the governor's term to two years, and place wartime spending under the direction of a special commission. Meanwhile, amid the growing debate over emancipating the slaves, Democrats sought to write black exclusion and a ban on black voting directly into the new constitution.

After a bitter canvass, in June 1862, Illinois voters rejected what many Republicans decried as the "Secession Constitution."[4] On the other hand, the articles prohibiting black migration into Illinois and black voting, submitted separately to voters, won huge majorities. During the convention's deliberations Yates had written to Lyman Trumbull, "Secession is deeper and stronger here than you have any idea."[5] This was clearly an exaggeration; Yates had conflated opposition to his administration with support for the Southern cause. But in a general sense his alarming analysis was warranted: within a year the bipartisan cooperation that had marked the first months of Illinois's war seemed a distant memory.

"WAR IS NOW BEGUN"

Quincy's Orville Hickman Browning, elected U.S. senator in 1861, wrote to his friend Abraham Lincoln, describing scenes in Quincy after the fall of Sumter and offering insight into Illinois public opinion during the war's earliest days.

Quincy, Ills Apl. 18, 1861

My Friend

I sympathize deeply and profoundly with you in your present difficulties, but am proud to believe that you are adequate to the emergency; that you will meet it as it should be met, and bear yourself bravely through it.

Thinking it probable you might be glad to know something of public sentiment here I take the liberty of writing you.

The fall of Sumter carried bitterness to all Republican hearts, but despondency to none. The universal sentiment among Republicans is that they had rather Sumter should have been knocked into a thousand atoms, and every man in it killed, than that it should have been tamely surrendered, on the demand of traitors, without a blow.

. . . War is now begun. It has been causelessly inaugurated by the seceding states—and you have them so palpably in the wrong as to unite all men, of all parties, in the free states in support of the government.

Being, as we are, just upon the border; and the extreme western point on the Mississippi River, I have been very apprehensive that when the crisis came, and war was fairly upon us, we would have dangerous strifes and contentions among ourselves, and be compelled to fight traitors in our midst. But that fear is past. Our city has been full of insolent, traitorous sympathizers with the South, some of whom even dared to declare their purpose of taking part with the seceders, if coercion, as they term it, was attempted. But the tempest of patriotic indignation which burst forth upon the fall of Sumter has intimidated them. They have been compelled to face to the right about, and most of them are now loud in support of the government, and eager, by their zeal to wipe away suspicion of having ever been otherwise than loyal to their country. There may be, and probably are, a few traitors still among us, but they dare not let their sentiments be known. They dare not utter a word of sympathy with the South, nor a denunciation of the administration. They would be torn in pieces.

These were, and are all, of course, in the democratic ranks, and their democratic brethren are now loudest in execrating their treason.

We had an immense meeting last night, called without distinction of party, and composed of almost the entire mass of both parties.

I drew up, and presented resolutions pledging our undivided and ardent support to the administration in all measures it should adopt for the suppression of rebellion, preservation of the Union, chastisement of treason &c. They were adopted unanimously and enthusiastically. The meeting was addressed by both Republicans and Democrats. Among the democratic speakers were Ike Morris, Barney Arntzen & Dr Stahl. They all came fully up to the Republican standard. They are Union men, and for the government, and against treason and traitors, without a "but" or an "if." Other speeches were made by laboring men of the democratic party, some of whom said there were still a few amongst us who were against the stars and stripes, and for the [copperhead] "snake," but that they intended to hunt them out, and that no man who was disloyal to the government should remain as a spy in the camp. . . . [The meeting] has quieted all apprehension of trouble with our own people. It has, indeed, made treason here impossible. . . .

Problems of immense and oppressive difficulty affecting both races, will spring out of the present condition of things. I think I see their solution, but cannot enter upon that subject. God bless and prosper you. Truly your friend

O. H. Browning

Abraham Lincoln Papers, Manuscripts, Library of Congress, Washington, DC.

"THERE CAN BE NONE BUT PATRIOTS AND TRAITORS"

Following the fall of Fort Sumter, Stephen Douglas gave a series of speeches that called on Illinoisans to put party differences aside and rally behind the Lincoln administration. On May 1, 1861, Douglas, already weak and feverish from overexertion, delivered yet another address at National Hall in Chicago. It would be his last. A month later, at age forty-eight, Douglas succumbed to acute rheumatic fever and a series of throat and liver ailments that may have included typhoid. After his death many eulogized Douglas for doing more than any other leader in these days to unite Illinois. This excerpt is from his final speech.

What excuse can the disunionists give for breaking up the best government the sun ever shed its light upon? They are dissatisfied with the result of the last presidential election. Were they never beaten before? Are we to tolerate the idea that the defeated party is to resort to the sword? I understand it to be a fundamental principle that the voice of the people must command obedience. They assume that in the election of a party candidate their rights are not safe. What evidence have we of it? I defy any man to show a fact that will substantiate it. What one act has been omitted which they can complain of. . . . What specific grievance can they assign from the days of Washington to this moment? If they refer to the territorial question, it is an extraordinary fact that there is now no act on our statute books limiting slavery in any manner. If to the enforcement of laws, the only complaint is that too much has been done, that we have been to eager to enforce the fugitive slave law. Then I ask what excuse has the south for the scheme they have concocted to wind up the Union? . . . There are but two sides to the question. Every man must be on the side of the United States or against it. There can be none but patriots and traitors. Thank God, Illinois is not to be doubted on this question. [The South] conspired to produce a civil war among republicans and democrats, expecting to step in and accomplish an easy victory. The scheme will involve civil war and bloodshed in the United States, and the calamity is only to be averted by united action.

. . . [S]o long as there was a possibility of settling the troubles peacefully, every sacrifice was made and proposed, and now, when the question is to be transferred from the cotton states to the corn fields of Illinois, I say the farther off the better. War is a sad thing, but civil war must now be recognized as existing in the United States. We can no longer close our eyes to the solemn fact. In this exigency the government must be maintained, and the more stupendous and overwhelming are our preparations the shorter will be the struggle. But, my countrymen, we must remember that certain restrictions are to be observed. We must not forget that we are christians, and that war must be waged in a christian spirit—not against the rights of a people—not against the rights of women and children. Say that you will sanction no war on rights, and say that never will you lay down your arms until those which you claim as your own are recognized. We were born under the constitution of the United States, and its provisions are our birthright. Then be prepared to enforce the inalienable rights which it confers.

We have peculiar reasons why we cannot recognize the right to secede and break up the Union. Once recognize it and you not only destroy the government, but annihilate order, and inaugurate anarchy such as disgraced the history of the worst days of the French revolution. My friends, you have a solemn duty to perform. Use all your power to maintain the constitution and the government which our fathers gave us. The greater the unanimity, the less the loss of life and property, and the sooner the establishment of peace. I am aware that we have some prejudice to encounter, but that does not surprise me. It is but a few short months since we passed a stormy election, and it takes some little time to drive out the party contentions and substitute patriotism; and yet, he who would not sacrifice political differences does not deserve the support of his country. How, then, are we to present a united front? Cease to discuss, cease to criminate and recriminate. Indulge in no taunts as to who caused the trouble, but unite manfully now, and when the flag waves over every inch of our country, argue the point of authorship. . . . Illinois occupies a proud position before the nation, and let her sons unite in the determined resolve never to permit this government to be dissolved.

Reprinted in *Illinois State Register* (Springfield), June 7, 1861.

THE WAR SPIRIT IN CHICAGO

When the war came Chicago was already the Midwest's foremost "immigrant city." Roughly three of four residents were immigrants and their children. Chicago's North Division was home to one of the largest concentrations of Germans anywhere in the world except Germany itself; the Irish settled heavily around the bustling canal docks, stockyards, and meat-packing districts located south and west of downtown. Significant concentrations of Scandinavians, Bohemians, Canadians, and British also called Chicago home, settling across the urban landscape in kaleidoscope fashion. Taken together the foreign born comprised the bulk of the city's hard-pressed working class, but by the 1860s Chicago also had one of the highest percentages of immigrant home ownership of any city in the United States. Reports from the Chicago Tribune illuminate how the nationalism and patriotism so prominent at the outset of the war built upon immigrant neighborhood networks and ethnic identities.

THE SCANDINAVIANS RISING.

Pursuant to call a large number of our Scandinavian citizens assembled at West Market Hall last night, to deliberate and take action in regard to the present crisis.

After being called to order, the meeting was addressed in short but stirring speeches by Chas. M. Reese, Esq., Rev. A. C. Preus, Dr. G. C. Paoli, A. B. Johnson, J. Gittleson, A. S. Bergh, and others. A list for the signature of volunteers was presented, and there is every prospect of a good company being formed out of the hardy material from the Norwegian mountains. We say, as we have said before, "God protect the right!"

We are requested to state that the list will be at the store of Mr. Olson, on Desplaines street, between Kinzie and Hubbard, where any Scandinavian can have an opportunity of enrolling his name.

Chicago Tribune, April 19, 1861.

THE WAR SPIRIT IN CHICAGO.

Departure of More Troops.

To give the details of the incidents and excitements of yesterday would be but to repeat what we have already written in the preceeding issues. The same bustle and din in the streets; the same rush of eager spectators, and folding of hands in deserted stores; and closed ledgers at vacant desks of book-keepers and railroad clerks; and shops more than decimated by enlistments; and squeak of life and rattle of drum—the centre of dense crowds about the recruiting stations; the same flag everywhere, and the same devotion to it; the marching to and fro of newly formed companies; the bustle of Quartermaster's and Commissary's aids; the same rush of business in the foundries where round shot are being cast, and the lead works and upper rooms of the gunsmiths where the "tap, tap," of the moulds keeps pace to the increase of ounce bullets and wicked looking Minie balls; the same excited and ravenous quest of news, sought from all sources; the same scraps of street talk falling upon the ear in the kaleidoscopic conversation overheard, mingling war and volunteering, and rumor and fact, stiff canard, and doubtful report, in one ever changing tissue; the same eagerness and patriotic zeal; the same meagerness as to news from abroad—such made up yesterday in Chicago and its news. . . .

THE IRISH BRIGADE.

Editors Chicago Tribune:

Irishmen of Chicago, whilst at this trying moment, when the liberty and independence of this country are jeopardized by the unnatural and damnable treason of rebellion against the authority of the legitimate Government, all party feeling, and religious animosity are buried in oblivion, and men of all nations enthusiastically rush forward to defend the banner of freedom, beneath whose broad folds you have so often rallied and found shelter. The question is now asked, "What are the Irish doing? What will they do?" Irishmen I will say to the world for you that we are now as true to that old flag which found no abler defenders since it was first unfurled than Irishmen, whose bones now moulder beneath the sod of all our battle fields, as when Montgomery led you, to seal with his life's blood his devotion to the cause of freedom. And that we too of Chicago will not be found wanting now, when the independence of our country requires our aid. Rally then Irishmen, and let us speedily fill up the ranks of our brigade with such stout hearts as will strike terror into the souls of tyrants and the enemies of freedom. Let us show the world that we who have adored the freedom of this land, shall be now its boldest defenders against all its enemies, whether domestic or foreign, and that treason and traitors shall find no mercy or sympathy with us. . . .

Chas. D. B. O'Ryan, MD

Chicago Tribune, April 24, 1861.

THE IRISH BRIGADE.

A dispatch from Springfield, as we stated in our last issue, accepts the Irish Brigade now enrolling, over six hundred men, and nearly full. They will be the first called on the second requisition. Their drill-rooms show a vast amount of activity and they will turn out a regiment most creditable to our city.

The Secretary of the Executive Committee of the Irish Brigade acknowledges the receipt of [$667] to aid in the equipment of the Irish Regiment, and also for the support of families of those volunteering in the same. . . .

A Ladies' Association was lately organized for the purpose of assisting and encouraging the Regiment. The Committee appointed for the raising of funds to procure a Banner for the regiment, report the handsome sum of four hundred and seventy six dollars and ninety-two cents ($476 32) collected since they last met, which is alike creditable to the good ladies and the Union-loving citizens of Chicago. . . .

The Female patriots, not being satisfied with the noble work already accomplished, on motion of Mrs. Garrick, the above ladies were appointed a permanent collection-committee, to add to the fund already so generously subscribed to by our most prominent citizens, for the purpose of providing the necessary ways and means for the "Irish Brigade," the relief of their widows and orphans, &c. . . .

Chicago Tribune, April 29, 1861.

ACTION OF GERMAN CITIZENS.

The following are a series of Resolutions passed at a meeting of Germans, held April 28th, at the German House:

WHEREAS, Complaints have come to the officers of the German Society by German women on account of assistance having been refused by the Finance Committee of the War Fund, and

WHEREAS, There is in said Finance Committee no German representative of the families [of volunteers] . . . although the number of Germans in Chicago who have gone forth in the defense of the country far exceeds all other nationalities,

Resolved, That we deem it required by circumstances, and therefore ask, that the members of said Finance Committee add to their number one German, who shall be sided by one assistant from each division of this city.

Resolved, That the full support of the families of volunteers is not a matter of mere humane charity, but that it is a sacred duty, resting upon remaining citizens, a duty which, in case private subscriptions do not suffice, is to be carried out directly from the City and County Treasury.

Resolved, That we regard as highly improper and as showing an entire misconception of the extent of patriotism of married men, the opinion expressed by a member of the said Finance Committee as a pretext for refusal of an application for assistance of a German woman with two children near by "That there were plenty of young men to go out, that married men could have stayed at home.["]

Resolved, That the delivery of means of support to the respected families should be done in a manner and by such men, as will avoid any show as if the same were tendered by way of assistance to the poor, but as carrying out a necessary and ordinary duty towards the relatives of those who have marched in the field to shed their blood for those remaining at home in peace.

Resolved, That the Germans of Chicago are hereby earnestly called upon to contribute directly to the Finance Committee for the support of the families of volunteers. With the understanding that the requests above set forth, shall be complied with. . . .

Chicago Tribune, April 30, 1861.

GUSTAVE KOERNER DESCRIBES MOBILIZATION AND PREPAREDNESS

The Republican leader and lieutenant governor Gustave Koerner, of Belleville, was closely involved in the mobilization of Illinois Germans in St. Clair County and the surrounding areas near St. Louis. In this document, an excerpt of his postwar memoirs, Koerner remembers the rapid response of Illinois Germans to Lincoln's call to arms and provides an insider's perspective on the state government's preparation.

ILLINOIS ORGANIZING

. . . Governor Yates by proclamation convened the Legislature in special session for the 23d of April for the purpose of organizing troops and placing the State on the best footing to render assistance to the general government in preserving the Union. At the same time the Adjutant-General proclaimed that the quota of Illinois was six regiments of infantry. Then there was a perfect race as to who should volunteer first. Augustus Mersy, whom I have mentioned before as having been an officer in the Baden army and as having with that army joined the people's cause in 1849, after commanding as a colonel and brigadier-general in various actions against the Prussians, at once started a company [in Belleville] the day after the President's call. A second one was organized by Mr. Tiedemann. Word was sent from Mascoutah that one was getting up there, and from Lebanon came the same information. Henry Goedeking and Sharon Tyndale, then postmaster, were most active in getting these companies organized. They and some other patriotic citizens pledged their credit to furnish them at once with simple uniforms, blue blouses and military caps, and to provide for their support until they reached the camp designated at Springfield. Our ladies worked day and night for their outfit.

The same day the Governor issued his proclamation, he telegraphed me to come up at once, as he wanted to have me with him. I stayed two or three days in Belleville until I saw that everything relating to volunteers, consisting mostly of the best part of our youth, was going on right. Arrived at Springfield, I was at once overwhelmed with business. Fortunately I found Trumbull also there. Yates was overrun with people about volunteers, about appointments, and with visitors from curiosity. He did not know how to get rid of them, and left really most of the important business to us. [John A.] McClernand, a strong Democrat, but equally strong for the Union, came in often and gave us good counsel, particularly about Southern Illinois, where his influence was strong.

Our militia for years had existed only on paper. We had an adjutant-general, commissary and quartermaster-general, some brigadier-generals and their staff, but no privates. With the exception of some volunteer companies in some of the larger cities, we had no brigades, no regiments, no battalions. The adjutant-generals and quartermaster-generals were appointed by the Governor from his friends from civil life anxious to have a title but perfectly ignorant of the duties of their office. To assist Adjutant-General Colonel [Thomas S.] Mather, the Governor had appointed a gentleman from Massachusetts, who had been a high officer in the well-organized militia of that State, and seemed to understand the routine business, John B. Wyman, afterwards colonel of the 13th Illinois, who fell in battle. Governor Woods volunteered his services as assistant quartermaster, but everything was at first in great confusion. . . .

On the 23d of April the Belleville companies came up to Springfield under the command of Captain Mersy,—five large companies. They were the first that came from a distance. Many of the boys had been members of the various volunteer companies that had existed from time to time at Belleville. A large number were or had been Turners [members of male gymnastic and athletic clubs, founded in Germany, that also taught political liberalism and German nationalism], and understood marching to perfection, and some of the older men had been in the military service in Germany before they came here. . . .

WAR SESSION OF THE ILLINOIS LEGISLATURE

It was evident that the session of the Legislature would be a short one. Several of the members were already officers in the regiments. Others were desirous of entering the State military service, as recommended in the Governor's message; still others, interested in commercial and industrial pursuits, were anxious to return to their business at home. . . . A few days before, at the commencement of the session, all the bills thought necessary for the occasion were prepared in the Governor's office, and the Chairmen of the Committees on Military Affairs, on

Finance, and on Judiciary, were called in, the bills at once submitted to them, their opinions taken, and the amendments suggested by them adopted. Having agreed on all points, they on their part laid them before their committees, got them approved, reported them at once to their respective houses, where with very little opposition they passed under suspension of rules in a few days. No buncombe resolutions were discussed or passed, and in ten days the Legislature adjourned. By one law the organization of the six regiments was provided for in detail; by another entitled "An act to prepare the State of Illinois to protect its own territory, repel invasion, and render efficient and prompt aid to the United States, when demanded," ten regiments of infantry, one battalion of artillery, and one regiment of cavalry were authorized to be raised, one in each Congressional district, which were to repair to the camps of instruction for thirty days and to be ready to enter the United States service in case of a new call for soldiers being made on the State. By another law the militia of the State was organized upon an effective plan, dividing it into active or voluntary or reserve classes. A war-fund, by the issue of bonds for two millions, was provided for, and a commission created to audit and certify all accounts for supplies and munitions of war, clothing, etc., furnished for Illinois troops, and all accounts in any manner accruing for organizing the troops under the call of the President for volunteers. A severe law to prevent the giving of aid to the enemies of the United States, and also one against the obstruction of transportation of troops or military stores, were enacted, inflicting heavy penalties upon the offenders. Another law provided for the establishment of powder-magazines, for the purchase of arms, and still another to prevent the use of telegraph for illegal and revolutionary purposes. . . .

Gustave Koerner, *Memoirs of Gustave Koerner 1809–1896: Life-Sketches Written at the Suggestion of His Children*, ed. Thomas J. McCormack, 2 vols. (Cedar Rapids, IA: Torch Press, 1909), 2:120–21, 137–38.

"WE HAVE BEFORE US . . . A SERIOUS STRUGGLE"

The Union army's defeat at Bull Run, in July 1861, prompted Illinoisans to reassess the nature of the conflict between North and South. In the following reports, the Republican-affiliated Illinois State Journal *and the Democrat-affiliated* Chicago Times *react to this pivotal early battle.*

THE DISGRACE AT BULL RUN.

The news received yesterday afternoon of the precipitate retreat of our army under Gen. [Irvin] McDowell from Bull Run back to their entrenchments, fell with stunning effect upon our citizens. Our previous advices had been of so satisfactory character that such a repulse was the last thing they were looking for.

The fact that McDowell's army had just succeeded in storming three batteries of the enemy and driving them back two miles toward the [Manassas] Junction, that we had also finally outflanked them; and the further report that Col. Alexander was then busily engaged in throwing his pontoons over the Run for a last charge upon them, had prepared us to anticipate a successful issue of the engagement. Indeed our dispatches gave assurances of as much. The news, coming immediately upon the heels of all this, that our "grand army" were retreating in confusion and disorder back to Washington struck upon us like a clap of thunder. The full extent of the disaster which has thus befallen our arms is not at the time we write definitively ascertained. We are in hopes the telegraph has exaggerated the facts. It is almost incredible that an army of fifty thousand of the flower of the North could be so carried away by panic as to retreat in confusion to the distance of twenty-six miles. But bad as this business now appears, and unfortunate as the *morale* may be, let no one for a moment suppose that the disaster is either irreparable or disheartening. Indeed, we are not so certain but that it may in some measure be of service to our troops. The men composing our army are not of the kind of stuff to be demoralized by any such reverse. . . . That our reverse will speedily be more than repaired; and that treason and disunion will be crushed under the strong heel of the law, no one who will for a moment consider the resources and energies of the Federal Government can for a moment doubt. Instead of being disheartened or discouraged, our army will be only stimulated to further and more vigorous action. Be assured, the disaster at Bull Run WILL BE WIPED OUT.

Illinois State Journal (Springfield), July 23, 1861.

KNOW THE TRUTH.

While the disaster in Virginia is not so great as at first reported, it must in many ways prove injurious to the nation. It will, indeed has, inspired the rebels with new confidence, and complicates affairs in the border States which have not seceded. It will, then, embolden rebellion. We may expect, too, decisive effects from it in Europe—whether to the extent of a recognition of the Southern Confederacy by European powers or not we cannot foresee, but it will naturally strengthen the rebel cause there. Besides this, it must not be forgotten that the army has returned to Alexandria,—that the advance must be made over again, and that consequently, the time and money which have been expended upon it are lost, and must be repeated. These are serious evils, and must not be hidden from the public view by the mitigations which recent accounts lend to the defeat. The truth must be known, and whatever morals it teaches ought to be treasured by the nation.

Our people are undoubtedly influenced by a pure patriotism, but, in the exuberance of their devotion to the country, they have underrated the strength, resources and generalship of the rebels. So common has this been, that even to suggest a doubt of constant success to the Federal armies has been deemed treasonable. With all their enthusiasm, the nation have not been thoroughly aroused to the magnitude of the struggle before them,—but have systematically sung pæans to their own courage, and mental, numerical, and financial superiority. All this is natural—the result of human weakness, but of a commendable spirit of loyalty and bravery. . . .

The recent reverse to our arms affords opportunity to strip from the war the delusions which have surrounded it. We have a brave, vigilant, and cunning foe to contend with. Every retreat they have made was a stratagem to lead our army to the ground on which they chose to fight. Every place over whose abandonment by them our press and people have chuckled, as evidence of a short and easy war, has been a snare to entrap us to the reverse which has opened our eyes. We undoubtedly are more powerful in warlike elements than the revolted States; but we must not for that reason believe them weak and easily conquered.

We have before us, then, a serious struggle, which demands all the strength of mind and body of the nation. Flippant talk in the streets of cities about the superiority of the North, and abusive editorials against secession leaders, or misrepresentations of the rebel strength by newspapers, must be abandoned. . . . Let us now take it for granted that we have a stern, obstinate struggle to pass through, that impatience of the operations of our generals, incendiary stimulus to our armies, self-flattering praises of our own valor, and depreciation of the enemy, can never bear us through with success, and that the nation must now go on to the future impressed with the vast import of the events around them, and with a resolution henceforth to be calm and sagacious, as well as brave and patriotic—to be practical, as well as enthusiastic, in the conduct of hostilities.

Chicago Times, July 25, 1861.

THE AMBIGUITIES OF UNIONISM

What did it mean to support the Union in time of war? Could one be for the Union and critical of the administration at the same time? Before the war, Democrats and Republicans had offered sharply different conceptions of the Union, especially of government's role in both public and private life. When the war came, leaders of both parties suppressed those long-standing differences and presented a united home front. But in a prolonged war, how long could such unity be expected to last? Stories and editorials such as these from from the Champaign County Democrat, *published in Urbana, suggest the growing political tensions on Illinois's home front by the summer of 1861.*

ATTEMPT TO SUPPRESS FREE SPEECH

It is with extreme pain that we are obliged to chronicle an event which took place in this city last Saturday night, but which had been properly taken care of by our Union citizens. These are great times,—times when facts should be revealed. There are great ills in the country—terrible when manifested; but the Union democrats and republicans regard a local war as the total of all evils, and hence they have averted it by their prudence last Saturday night.

In the afternoon of the day in question a bulletin was issued from the Union printing-office, signed by "MANY CITIZENS," for the purpose of calling a meeting to appoint a vigilance committee to watch persons who may be so unfortunate as to give expression to sentiments against the administration, and to gag the mouths of freemen, against which democrats have ever recorded their voices. The bulletin, in large boldface letters, proclaimed that there were secessionists in this county who had raised a rattlesnake rag [flag with the motto Don't Tread on Me] on the east side of Big Grove, an assertion that proved to be a deliberate falsehood, got up for partisan purposes, and to gratify the evil passions of a few disgusting and unpopular abolitionists in this neighborhood. But they have mistaken the nature of the game for whom they set this trap. At about 7 o'clock in the evening our citizens assembled in Park's Hall. W. D. Somers, a democrat but a brave, energetic Union man, was called upon the floor, and requested to act as chairman of the meeting. He appeared on the floor, but confessed that he was opposed to a vigilance committee being appointed over the citizens of Urbana. He made some very judicious remarks in support of his opposition to the object of the meeting as he understood it, and did not believe there was one secessionist in Champaign county. He requested all in the house who were in favor of a vigorous prosecution of the war, and the maintainance of the Union, to make it manifest by rising from their seats. All presently assumed a perpendicular position, except a boy ten or twelve years old, whom certainly the abolitionists could not say was competent to commit treason. . . . Mr. W. D. Somers emphatically remarked that condemning partisan measures did not constitute secessionism; a secessionist, he said, was one who would thwart the enforcement of the laws either by aiding the enemy by a supply of men or provisions. He believed that the Chicago Tribune did more to help the reverse of our army at Manassas [Bull Run] and to aid the cause of the rebels, than did even the people of Champaign county. He did not want inquiry and free speech hushed into silence, or into timid whispers, for fear it would destroy the apathy which is now hurrying the country into ruin. . . .

The meeting, after repudiating the appointment of a vigilance committee, adjourned. This simulating zeal for the appointment of a committee was an abolition vision, calculated to produce partisan distinction. We now, more than ever, charge them with introducing partisan policies, and we ask our own party now, and every conservative republican in the county, if this is the right way to obliterate party lines and consolidate the people in support of the administration in prosecuting the war? If men of all parties, who wish to be fair in the present crisis, give this question deliberate reflection, they will honestly answer, NO! . . . We would consider ourselves unfit for freedom, and so should every American in the land, were we deprived of the liberty of thundering in the ears of the administration, or any other officer, civil or military, whenever they neglect their duty or act improperly. But this line of duty, the great prerogative of freemen, is called secessionism by abolitionists. . . . Let us, therefore, pronounce abolitionism as not only disagreeable, but dangerous. . . .

~

CONSTITUTIONAL CONVENTION.

The democrats of Champaign county should wake up to the importance of selecting delegates to this convention, and proclaim in tones that cannot be misunderstood that they are in earnest upon all matters absorbing State casualities at this particular time. We have a right to such vigor and prudence in the action of the convention as should characterize the democracy as independent in the fall election. The whip and spur of extreme abolition sentiment, and the efforts made to give the war a partisan character, should teach us the experience of sound legislation for the prosperity of Illinois. Unless we revive our partizan issues as far as regards State and local elections, and demand our rights in the State, it may be expected that we will have to witness in silence the overthrow and abhorrent defeat of democratic principles; principles, too, which have kept the government on foot for the last fifty or sixty years, safe and secure, in spite of despotism and partisan policies which threatened its subversion, and, more than once, racked the State Chair to and fro in dangerous proximity.—This question is one of great magnitude, and the democrats of the whole State should not be caught napping and careless over their interests, for the issue is to them one of great local importance. . . .

Champaign County Democrat (Urbana), August 24, 1861.

ORGANIZING THE CHICAGO SANITARY COMMISSION

Founded by men in fall 1861, the Chicago Sanitary Commission relied on women for its day-to-day operations. These two circulars, some of the first produced by the commission (later renamed the Northwest Sanitary Commission), suggest the range of relief work pursued by Illinois's premier relief agency, as well as the ways in which traditional ideologies of gender and newer ideologies of centralization and efficiency merged in the construction, organization, and delivery of Civil War relief.

Chicago, November 1, 1861

COUNTRYWOMEN: There is a service you owe to your country, which she now calls upon you to perform. It is to make full provision for the relief and comfort of our sick and wounded soldiers. From every city, and town, and neighborhood of the Northwest, these brave men have gone to defend our National honor, and we feel assured that you—their wives, mothers, sisters, daughters—will need no other appeal to awaken all your interest and activity than the simple statement that many of them are now lying sick and wounded in the military hospitals, enduring sufferings and privations which it is in your power to relieve. Our Government, although earnestly desiring to make ample provision for all her soldiers, both in health and in sickness, has thus far failed to accomplish fully this result. The United States Sanitary Commission at Washington, a volunteer and unpaid Bureau of the War Department, has been for months engaged in earnest efforts to supply these deficiencies, and with a success most encouraging for the future.

Such a Commission has been organized in Chicago as a Branch of the United States Sanitary Commission. We have already sent a Committee of two of our number to visit and thoroughly inspect the various camps and hospitals in and near our State—at Cairo, Bird's Point [Missouri], Fort Holt [Kentucky], Mound City [Illinois], Paducah [Kentucky], and in Missouri—and it is, therefore, from personal knowledge of the urgent necessities of our soldiers that we earnestly beg you to co-operate with us in affording them relief.

For the purpose of receiving and promptly distributing all articles sent to us from this city and from abroad, we have obtained, free of rent, a convenient and centrally located room at No. 41 Wabash Avenue. This room is well lighted and warmed, and will be used as our office and depot. We have secured the services of Mrs. Jeremiah Porter, as Directress, a lady who has the entire confidence of our community. She will be at the room every day, from 10 A.M. to 4 P.M, to receive letters and the calls of our citizens or of those from out of town who desire any information relative to this work. The room will be open all day, and a clerk will be always there to receive and register contributions, which will be carefully acknowledged each week in the Chicago DAILY TRIBUNE of Tuesday. Our supplies are especially intended for the soldiers who have gone from the Northwest, and from their distant and widely separated camps we are constantly in receipt of reliable information of the supplies needed; and, therefore, while we comply with the requests of those who desire their packages to be sent to any particular regiment, we would still respectfully suggest that it would ordinarily be better to leave their distribution to our judgment, assuring our friends that we will hold ourselves individually responsible for all contributions made, and will guarantee their prompt and judicious appropriation.

We append a list of articles needed for the hospitals, carefully drawn up, with plain directions for preparing them, and explicit directions for packing, marking and shipping; also, a few simple suggestions to aid in organizing and conducting Societies for accomplishing this object.

Very Respectfully,

HON. MARK SKINNER, PRESIDENT.

REV. W. W. PATTON,

O. H. TIFFANY, D. D.

JAMES WARD,

R. N. ISHAM, M. D.

COL JOHN W. FOSTER,

E. W. BLATCHFORD,

CORRESPONDING SECRETARY.

HENRY E. SEELYE,

SEC'Y AND TREASURER.

Chicago Sanitary Commission

[The List of Supplies included bedding, clothing, medical supplies, and edibles.]

DIRECTIONS FOR FORMING "SOLDIERS' RELIEF CIRCLES."

In order to make it perfectly easy in towns and villages where no Association exists to form a society to work for the benefit of the soldiers, in connection with the "Chicago Sanitary Commission," we here furnish some plain directions:

1. Let the first woman whose heart is stirred with yearnings to do something in her own town, or for the relief of the sufferings of the sick and wounded among our soldiers, go to two or three of her neighbors and take counsel.

2. Let them agree upon some convenient day and hour for a meeting of ladies in the lecture-room of some place of worship, or in the town-house or school house.

3. Let notices of this be written and carried to the pastors of all the churches in town, with a request that they be read, with comments by the Pastor, in each society.

4. Let the ladies meet, select a President and Secretary; then let such portions of this circular be read by the President as will explain the nature and workings of this society, and the immediate wants of our soldiers.

5. Then let the ladies present form themselves into a "Soldiers' Relief Circle," to meet once a week, from 1 to 4 p.m, the time to be spent in sewing or knitting for the soldier.

6. Let them, in addition to the President and Secretary already elected, choose a Treasurer and two committees, of three ladies each, one on supplies and work, and one on general business, as correspondence, forwarding, &c. . . .

Circulars of the Chicago Sanitary Commission, reprinted in *Chicago Tribune*, November 9, 1861

JANE HOGE ON WOMEN'S WAR EFFORTS

Chicago's Jane Hoge and Mary Livermore served as codirectors of the Chicago Sanitary Commission, in charge of coordinating the collection and distribution of relief supplies and the recruitment of women nurses. Initially the idea of female nurses generated controversy among men in the Army Medical Bureau, used to male-dominated hospitals and soldiers' care. In The Boys in Blue *(1867), Hoge describes her impressions of women's wartime sacrifice and recounts her experiences with Galesburg's famous Civil War nurse Mary Ann Bickerdyke.*

. . . The women of the land . . . counted the cost, paid the price, and with a sagacity and zeal that has turned a new leaf in woman's history and development, have created supplies by the work of their fingers, managed and controlled at the different branches of the Commission an amount of business heretofore considered impracticable for women. In the various departments of aid societies, soldiers' rests and homes, in hospitals and transports, they have performed a humane work, that may well challenge history for a parallel. . . .

Still another order of female army workers must not be omitted. I refer to the nurses in hospitals and transports. Most of these self-sacrificing women left homes of comfort, some of luxury, to administer to the sick and wounded soldiers. . . .

In the earlier organization of hospitals, great opposition to the introduction of these nurses existed among the medical staff of the army. The system was an untried experiment, and was suspiciously watched and severely criticized. Unfortunate failures were magnified and widely circulated. The misguided zeal of some benevolent individuals thrust large numbers of women into hospitals, without organization or consultation with surgeons. As a consequence, they were summarily dismissed by the surgeons. During the progress of the war, evils were corrected in this, as in other departments, and order more fully established. The most skillful and humane surgeons sought the assistance of women as nurses, in suitable numbers and for proper positions. . . . The linen-rooms and diet-kitchens were eventually placed entirely in the hands of women, and the improved condition of the beds, patients, and food, and the decreased per centum of deaths, attested the wisdom of the change. . . .

At the commencement of the war, Mrs. Bickerdyke was a widow, with two sons, residing in Galesburg, Illinois. Dr. Woodruff, surgeon of 22d Regiment

Illinois Volunteers, was from the same place, and wrote from below to his friends of the suffering of the army. The letter was read in church; she heard it. Being a famous nurse and housekeeper, with a tender, patriotic heart, Mrs. B. felt called upon to go. Her friends and neighbors agreed with her, and Mrs. [Emily] Colton, of Galesburg, placed at her disposal five hundred dollars' worth of sanitary stores to take to the hospitals.

Her first army work was at Bird's Point, where, for a time, there was a regimental hospital. From that place she went to Fort Holt, thence to the Brick Hospital of Cairo, keeping in the track of the most important and needy hospitals, and constantly receiving more or less assistance from the North-Western Sanitary Commission, and friends in Illinois; also from Mr. [Alfred] and Miss [Mary Jane] Safford, of Cairo.

She soon discovered a disposition to misappropriate sanitary stores, and raised her first *tempest* in the Brick Hospital at Cairo. A fine box of supplies had been consigned to her from Galesburg, conspicuously marked with the name of the society that sent them. She gave a certain number of shirts, socks, and slippers to a ward-master to distribute. The next morning, in going her rounds, she perceived this official wearing a sanitary shirt, broadly marked, while one of his sick patients was minus a clean one. "Where did you get that shirt?" she said, fiercely. "It's none of your business," he answered. "I'll see if it isn't," she replied; and seizing it, as he had no coat on, she drew it over the head of the unfortunate wight, stunned into silence. "Now let me see your feet" said she, stooping and taking one in her hand. Off came the socks and slippers in a twinkling, to the infinite delight of the patients. The denuded thief slunk off suddenly, a sadder and a wiser man, and Mrs. B. had no further trouble in this hospital concerning sanitary stores.

She took charge of the nursing in the amputation ward in the Brick Hospital, and astonished all, by her skill and endurance. The men, strange to say, were made comfortable. In retrospect, this is difficult to comprehend, when the paucity of supplies and conveniences in the earlier part of the war, are borne in mind. Mrs. Bickerdyke says they lived from day to day, and supplies came as manna in the wilderness. After the battle of Donelson, where many of the wounded men lay in the cold and storm more than twenty-four hours without relief, Mrs. B. went up to the fort on the hospital-boat, to take charge of them *in transitu*. She accompanied and attended five boat-loads of these freshly-wounded men to Paducah, Mound City, Cairo, Evansville, and Louisville. What superhuman strength and endurance, executive ability and fertile genius, such a work, at such a time, required, cannot be comprehended by any who have not witnessed such scenes and worked upon hospital transports. . . .

Mrs. A. H. [Jane] Hoge, *The Boys in Blue; or, Heroes of the "Rank and File"* (Chicago: C. W. Lilley, 1867), 107–10, 120–22.

THE POLITICS OF OPPOSITION:
THE 1862 CONSTITUTIONAL CONVENTION

*In November 1860, Illinois voters authorized a new constitutional convention, scheduled
to convene in January 1862. Initially the idea of a constitutional convention was
unrelated to the war. The state's population had doubled since 1850 (to 1.7 million),
and its economy had changed dramatically. By 1860 many Illinoisans considered
the state's old 1848 constitution to be inflexible and outdated. But by the time of
the fall 1861 elections, when voters elected a large majority of Democrats to serve
as convention delegates, it was clear that divisions over the course of the war had
fully intruded into state politics. Illinois Democrats politicized the constitutional
convention, using it to mount opposition to Governor Yates and to associate the
Republican Party with the "threat" of black freedom.*

TO THE CONSTITUTIONAL CONVENTION—PROTECT THE TREASURY OF THE STATE.

In common with thousands of others, I have learned with amazement and
regret, through the published reports of your proceedings, that the governor of
the state has expended some millions of the people's money without any color
of authority or law—nay more—that he boldly declares he will continue to so
misappropriate and expend other millions, if, in his august wisdom, the *necessity*
of the case shall seem to justify it. . . . And, in pursuance of this line of policy, I
am informed that further expenditures are daily being made without warrant of
law, and that, in fact, the governor's military machinery is still in motion, as briskly
as though the legislature had made the appropriations indefinite in amount, and
authorized the state executive to draw upon the treasury at will. . . .

Now, gentlemen of the convention, the people, whom you represent in their
sovereign capacity, expect that you will put a stop to this extravagant and unauthor-
ized use of their money. It is understood that the United States authorities prefer
to make all needed expenditures for military purposes here and elsewhere, and
the people of the state expect that *you will exercise your authority* to stop the useless
depletion of the treasury of the state. Be not alarmed, gentlemen, by the clap-trap
cries of "usurpation of power," "revolutionary proceedings," &c., with which the
governor and his adherents will assail you. The people will sustain you in any honest effort you may make to lessen the burden of taxation which, for years, must
grind them in the dust. *It is the governor who, in this case, is the usurper.* It is he, who,
by illegal and revolutionary means, seeks to set the executive above the legislative
authority, and to make the servant superior to his master, the people; and it is
your duty to protect the people, and their hard earned gatherings against these
dangerous usurpations of the executive. Act, then, gentlemen, while action will

be of some avail. Stop the wasteful outpourings from the public treasury. Protect the honest creditors of the state who have hitherto furnished supplies, but at the same time say with emphasis which cannot be misunderstood, that further illegal expenditures cannot be made.

Tax-Payer.

Illinois State Register (Springfield), February 4, 1862.

THE "NIGGER" IN THE CONVENTION.

The report of the legislative committee of the convention, proposing for adoption a clause almost identical with that of the present constitution, forbidding the immigration of negroes to this state, was the subject of warm debate yesterday. Messrs. Anthony and Ferry, on the republican side, considered it an outrage, a breach of courtesy and fair comity, to introduce what they termed "political" questions into the convention. Using the words "political" and "partisan" as convertible, they foamed, in true abolition style—told of their forbearance—that they had sat and witnessed the presentation of resolutions relative to the exclusion of the negro, with commendable meekness, but forbearance had ceased to be a virtue; hence they railed and told of the negro's wrongs, and of the cruelty and barbarism of Illinois white men forbidding their state to be made a receptacle for negro paupers from the south. . . .

The proposition presented, and the amendments proposed, are subjects involving the public policy of the state, and legitimately before the convention. Abolitionists alone, in their discussions, will give them a partisan hue, and, doubtless, before the people they will take partisan shape, as between negro-worshippers and those who have no taste for negro equality, political or social, and who believe it best for Illinois white men that negroes should be excluded from their midst. There are two parties in this convention, and we have faith that in Illinois at least the white man's party is largely in the ascendancy.

Illinois State Register (Springfield), March 5, 1862.

FOUR

Illinois and Emancipation

$\mathcal{E}$MANCIPATION BROUGHT UNPRECEDENTED change to all Illinoisans. For the state's white majority emancipation encouraged a broader reexamination of racial attitudes and policy on the home front. For if the slaves were to be freed, what did that mean for the place of blacks in Illinois? The question spawned intense debate and continued to shape Illinois politics and society for decades to come. For the slaves emancipation represented a new birth of freedom; by war's end nearly fifteen thousand had seized on that freedom to settle in Illinois in hope of a better life, an influx that tripled the state's black population and produced heightened racial tension. For free blacks already living in Illinois, emancipation suggested the dawn of a new era. That hopeful possibility is glimpsed in the life of the black Chicago abolitionist H. Ford Douglas. Before the war Douglas had urged blacks to migrate out of the country to escape racial oppression. During the election of 1860 he bitterly indicted Lincoln's Republican Party for doing nothing to end racism in the North. Scarcely two years later he was praising Lincoln and fighting in the Union army to vindicate black freedom.

Lincoln personified the position of many Illinoisans when it came to slavery's relationship to the war. Though he had long considered slavery a moral wrong, as president he was bound by the U.S. Constitution, which protected slavery where it already existed. Secession and civil war changed the relationship between the federal government and slavery in complex ways, yet well into the war's second year Lincoln disavowed any intention to strike at slavery. If slavery became a Union target, Lincoln reasoned, slaveholders in the loyal slave states of Kentucky, Missouri, and Maryland might initiate movements to join the Confederacy. Likewise a war to free the slaves might fortify the Confederate cause in the Deep South, prolonging the conflict. The whole purpose of the war, as far as Lincoln and most Illinoisans were concerned, was to restore the Union, not abolish slavery. In retrospect it is clear that Lincoln, like most Northerners, underestimated the strength, capacity, and sheer endurance of the Confederate cause. Union military reverses in 1861 and the stunning casualties of the spring of 1862 underscored the Confederacy's will to endure a long, bloody struggle.

From the start, abolitionists maintained that the war would never be won unless the Union struck at slavery. But as the war evolved, pressure to recognize slavery's essential relationship to the rebellion emanated from two new sources: Protestant churches on the home front and the slaves themselves. Following the attack on Fort Sumter, Illinois's Protestant leadership worked to sway public opinion behind emancipation. Mainstream Northern ministers, who had for decades opposed abolitionist extremism, quickly changed their minds, seeing in the war evidence of a divine plan to exorcise the evils of slavery. Their campaign culminated in an impressive interdenominational convention held at Chicago's Bryan Hall in September 1862. After the meeting the Congregationalist ministers William Weston Patton and John Dempster traveled to Washington to present the convention's Emancipation Memorial to Lincoln.[1]

The nation's nearly four million slaves offered another source of pressure. The slaves understood at once how deeply implicated they were in the Civil War's origins and progress. Wherever Union forces penetrated into Confederate territory, nearby slaves quickly flocked to Union lines. Runaways compelled the Union military to deal immediately with slavery's relationship to the war. Were runaways still slaves? Or, having reached the Union lines, were they now free? Many in the Union army quickly accepted the military rationale for allowing runaways—termed contrabands—to remain behind Union lines. Contrabands provided crucial support to the Union cause as paid orderlies, laundresses, cooks, and common laborers in Union encampments. Indeed, because the slaves' absence from the South deprived the Confederacy of labor, contrabands constituted a double gain for the Union, a fact driven home in the final two years of the conflict when the federal government opened the Union army to blacks, the large majority of whom had begun the war as slaves. Cairo became a major site for the temporary settlement of contrabands; by early 1862 the Union army had built a large camp there that eventually housed thousands of runaways. As the number of contrabands stationed at Cairo grew Democrats pointed out that their presence violated the state's ban on black migration into Illinois.

Yet while the slaves took the initial steps toward their own freedom, only the federal government had the authority to establish emancipation as official Union policy. Two weeks after the Union disaster at Bull Run, Republican congressmen took their own tentative steps in this direction, enacting the First Confiscation Act, which authorized Union forces to take rebel property—including slaves—used directly in the service of rebellion. But soon many Republicans came to believe that broader measures were necessary. In August 1861, General John C. Frémont, commander of Union forces in Missouri, ordered martial law across the state and declared the slaves of Confederate supporters free. Lincoln had not authorized this bold step; he revoked Frémont's order and relieved him of command. Lincoln's clash with Frémont caused consternation among many Illinois Republicans. Lincoln's longtime law partner William Herndon expressed shock at the revocation of Frémont's order. "Good God! If I were Lincoln," he wrote Illinois senator Lyman Trumbull, "I would declare that all slaves should be free. . . . What does Lincoln suppose[—]he can squelch out this rebellion while he and the North in common are fighting for the status of slavery?"[2] Then in December, Trumbull introduced the bill that became the Second Confiscation Act. This more radical proposal envisioned freeing any slave that managed to cross into Union lines—whether or not they had been used to aid the rebellion. The debate over Trumbull's bill proved difficult and long, for confiscation raised fundamental questions of individual property rights and the limits of federal power, even in time of war. As the debate in Congress over confiscation ground on, General Robert E. Lee scored a series of unlikely victories in Virginia on the York-James peninsula, thwarting Union commander George McClellan's much-anticipated campaign against Richmond, the Confederate capital. In the wake of McClellan's defeat Congress enacted Trumbull's Second Confiscation Act in July 1862.

By this time the idea of a general emancipation policy—one that also would include arming the freed slaves—attracted support from a broad coalition of civilians and military personnel. Still, Lincoln waited. Publicly he continued to back a plan to use government funds to compensate slave owners who voluntarily freed their slaves, and then to ship those freed blacks out of the country. Privately, however, he was more and more persuaded by the military rationale for freeing the slaves, a policy he would predicate on his war powers as commander-in-chief. In late July he stunned his cabinet by revealing his plan for a general emancipation proclamation. Secretary of State William Seward advised him to wait for a military victory before announcing the radical new policy, else emancipation might appear to be weak and desperate. Finally, in September 1862, that victory came at Antietam. Five days after Antietam, on September 22, Lincoln announced the preliminary emancipation proclamation.

It is often pointed out that Lincoln's famous proclamation did not free a single slave. It left untouched those slaves residing in the still-loyal slave states of Delaware, Kentucky, Maryland, and Missouri, and explicitly exempted occupied Tennessee and southern Louisiana. The proclamation thus declared only that the slaves in the rebellious states—where presumably Lincoln's edict had no legal standing—would be henceforth and forever free as of January 1, 1863. Yet despite its shortcomings the Emancipation Proclamation dramatically transformed the scope and purpose of the war. Lincoln had connected the progress of the Union military directly to the destruction of Southern slavery, for every inch of Confederate territory gained by

Union armies would be free soil. The Union army was now an army of liberation, and to underscore that point, Lincoln also authorized the wholesale enlistment of black troops. Lincoln had long resisted the idea that the Civil War would mark the beginning of a revolution in American life. His new policy of emancipation and the arming of black soldiers promised exactly that.

Predictably, Illinois Democrats howled in protest and mobilized to defeat the Republicans in the election of 1862. The Democrats' campaign received an unexpected boost from two ill-timed policies. First, on September 18, Secretary of War Edwin Stanton ordered the shipping of contrabands into Illinois (and other states in the Old Northwest) from their temporary housing at Cairo. Stanton reasoned that the contrabands were needed to help bring in the fall harvest. Pressured by Illinois Republicans, Stanton reversed the order in October, but that did little to prevent Democrats from capitalizing on the issue. Adding more fuel to the opposition fire was Lincoln's September 24 order suspending the writ of habeas corpus. Lincoln's suspension had become necessary as opposition to the enrollment provisions in the Militia Act, passed in 1862, mounted in Illinois. Democrats considered Lincoln's order a flagrant violation of constitutional power and a threat to individual liberty. Lincoln aimed "to liberate the millions of negroes and put the millions of white men in their places," screamed the *Macomb Eagle*.[3]

In the November elections Democrats rolled to victory. Weaving together opposition to emancipation, Lincoln's suspension of civil liberties, and the transportation of contrabands into Illinois communities, Democrats captured both houses of the state legislature, nine of fourteen congressional seats, and several state offices. The rout seemed to indicate overwhelming opposition to Lincoln's policies in his home state, yet Republicans also pointed to the absence of soldiers, who were not permitted to cast absentee ballots in the field. A large majority of those missing soldiers might well have cast a Republican vote. In any event Illinois Democrats interpreted the results as a mandate for opposing Lincoln and the "black Republican" war effort. The coming years would reveal the breadth and depth of that opposition.

LINCOLN OPPOSES GENERAL FRÉMONT'S EMANCIPATION ORDER

In September 1861, Lincoln revoked Union general John Frémont's order freeing the slaves in Missouri and relieved the popular leader of command. Many Illinois Republicans were dismayed, including Orville Browning, who wrote Lincoln that his actions toward Frémont would "demoralize our cause throughout the North West." In this letter Lincoln responds to Browning's criticisms and reveals how he conceptualized the complex relationship between slavery and federal authority during the war's first year.

Private & confidential
Washington, Sept 22, 1861.

My dear Sir:

Yours of the 17th is just received; and, coming from you, I confess it astonishes
me. That you should object to my adhering to a law [the First Confiscation Act]
which you had assisted in making and presenting to me less than a month before,
is odd enough. But this is a very small part. Gen. Fremont's proclamation as to
confiscation of property, and the liberation of slaves, is *purely political,* and not
within the range of *military* law, or necessity. If a commanding General finds a
necessity to seize the farm of a private owner, for a pasture, an encampment,
or a fortification, he has the right to do so, and to so hold it, as long as the
necessity lasts; and this is within military law, because within military necessity.
But to say the farm shall no longer belong to the owner, or his heirs, forever;
and this as well when the farm is *not* needed for military purposes, as when
it is, is purely political; without the savor of military law about it. And the
same is true of slaves. If the General needs them he can seize them, and use
them; but when the need is past, it is not for him to fix their permanent future
condition. That must be settled according to laws made by lawmakers, and not
by military proclamations. The proclamation, in the point in question, is simply
"dictatorship." It assumes that the General may do *anything* he pleases. . . . But
I cannot assume this reckless position; nor allow others to assume it on my
responsibility. You speak of it as being the only means of *saving* the government.
On the contrary, it is itself the surrender of the government. . . . I do not say
Congress might not with propriety, pass a law, on the point, just such as General
Fremont proclaimed. I do not say, I might not, as a member of Congress, vote
for it. What I object to, is, that I, as President, shall expressly or impliedly, seize
and exercise the permanent legislative functions of the government.

So much as to principle. Now as to policy. No doubt the thing was popular
in some quarters, and would have been more so, if it had been a general
declaration of emancipation. The Kentucky Legislature would not budge till that
proclamation was modified; and Gen. [Robert] Anderson telegraphed me that
on the news of Gen. Fremont having actually issued deeds of manumission, a
whole company of our volunteers threw down their arms and disbanded. I was
so assured as to think it probable that the very arms we had furnished Kentucky,
would be turned against us. I think to lose Kentucky is nearly the same as to the
lose the whole game. Kentucky gone, we can not hold Missouri, nor as I think,
Maryland. These all against us, and the job on our hands is too large for us. We
would as well consent to separation at once, including the surrender of this

capitol. On the contrary, if you will give up your restlessness for new positions, and back me manfully on the grounds upon which you and other kind friends gave me the election, and have approved in my public documents, we shall go through triumphantly. . . .

Your friend as ever
A. Lincoln

Abraham Lincoln to Orville Browning, September 22, 1861, Abraham Lincoln Papers, Library of Congress, Washington, DC.

THE ODYSSEY OF ANDREW SMITH, RUNAWAY SLAVE

Perhaps the greatest pressure for emancipation came from runaway slaves, or contrabands. One such runaway was Andrew Jackson Smith, a former Kentucky slave who gained his freedom in January 1862 and lived in Clinton, Illinois, before relocating to his home state after the war. In 2001, he was posthumously awarded the Medal of Honor for saving his regiment's colors at the battle of Honey Hill. Here Smith recounts his odyssey from bondage to freedom and service in the Union army.

My owner had been in the Confederate army since September, 1861. He came home on the 4th or 5th of January, 1862. I was in the field gathering corn with his two sons, William and Harrison. We looked down the road and thought we recognized him, and when we drove the wagon to the barn, sure enough, it was he. We all shook hands with him. There was another colored boy by the name of Alfred Bissell who was at the house. He had overheard a conversation between my owner and another man. Our owners had come to take us to the Confederate army. This occurred about 10 o'clock in the day.

Later my owner sent his two boys away and we suspected that he had sent them to get help to take us away. We left the wagon with the team hitched and climbed over the fence into the woods. We know that Smithlands Landing was about 25 miles away and we struck out for that point, where we expected to find the Union Army. Alf and I walked until about 2 o'clock the following morning before we reached the picket line of the Union Army.

We both had left home in our shirtsleeves. It was a bright, sunshiny morning when we left home, but about nightfall it began to rain a slow drizzle. With the constant rain there came a sudden change in temperature and our clothes, having become soaking wet by the rain, began to freeze upon us. All night we walked around the picket line half frozen. Near daybreak we approached the picket line and were taken in by the guards and warmed and fed. This outpost was held by a company of the 41st Ill. in charge of a Capt. Bacon. The company had been sent out to block the Cumberland and protect the Ohio. The company was afterward sent to Paducah, Ky., to join the rest of the regiment. This was about the last of January.

Other troops continued to come to Paducah to join the command. These troops were in Gen. [Andrew J.] Smith's division and we stayed there about two weeks. Gen. Grant then made up an expedition to go up the Tennessee River to Fort Henry. We landed in Tennessee below Fort Hyman, which was on the Tennessee. . . . There were four gunboats, two ironclad and two wooden, in this expedition. The two ironclad boats were sent to attack Fort Henry. The intention was, I suppose, to have the ironclad boats attack the fort, bombard it, and excite them so the land forces could capture them. The boats, however, attacked before the land forces arrived and captured all the men in the garrison. The rest retreated to Fort Donelson. . . .

The attacks [on Fort Donelson] were made on Thursday, Friday, and Saturday mornings from the 12th of February. Gen. Smith's division charged the fort on Friday evening. Seven regiments were selected for the charge and warned of their duty. On Saturday at daybreak he led them in a charge on 15,000 men. The enemy planned for them to retreat up the Cumberland River and go out at Dover, on the Tennessee, but the other men cut them off and they surrendered on Sunday morning, Feb. 16.

I shook hands with the captain of my master's company about 11 o'clock Sunday morning. Quite a number of the men had been reared around my home town of Eddyville, Ky. We lay around in camp about a week or so, then marched down the Tennessee River and took boats to Savannah, Tenn., just below Pittsburg Landing. . . .

Early in April a Confederate army came up from Corinth, Miss., under Gen. Albert Sidney Johnston. It was spoken of among us soldiers as an army of 150,000 men—an army, to my inexperienced eyes, which seemed so grand that it could hardly be beaten.

On Sunday morning early they were in our camps. It was said that they shot some of our men in their bunks before they could get out. The troop that I was with was about a half mile from the firing line. We heard the guns firing but did not know what it was. About sundown some messengers came to us and gave the news of the attack. Lieut. Col. Tuper of the [Forty-First Illinois] . . . ordered an attack. I was then only about 18 years old and not a regular soldier. I had gone out on the field just to look at the soldiers. Col. Tupper ordered the company to lie down behind a breastworks made of fence rails. [Major John] Warner asked me to take his horse to the rear, and as I was doing so I was knocked down by a minie ball. This was my first wound, though nothing serious.

After that Maj. Warner . . . saw he was in danger of being killed he told me where he lived and asked me to promise to take his trunk to Clinton, Ill., to his family, and assured me that I would be well taken care of. After much persuasion I took his horse and started to the rear. I was in full view of the whole southern army. When I had gone about 50 yards from him he called to me, "Hurry: don't stop, but go like hell!" I started again, but was struck by another ball over the left ear. The ball plowed its way under the skin and was taken out in the center of my forehead. I went back to the hospital and the doctor took the ball out and screwed a piece of sponge in my forehead.

The battle went on until night. Someone told me that Maj. Warner was wounded, and I was ordered to meet him Tuesday after the battle and give him his horse. He obtained a leave of absence and took me to Clinton. I stayed there until 1863 with the Warner family. . . .

[In 1863] I heard [Major Warner] reading about the 54th Mass. being formed. He learned that I was eager to join, so he wrote for transportation money for me and I then went to Chicago and joined some more recruits and went to Massachusetts. When I arrived at Boston the 54th Mass. had been formed, leaving five men to start the 55th Mass. . . . The noncommissioned officers were picked from the regiments. We drilled there about three months and then were sent to Port Royal, S.C. We stayed there and, under Gen. [Quincy] Gillmore, helped in the siege at Fort Wagner. . . .

The first time the regiment was ever in battle by themselves was there in the Battle of the Causeway. We were led by Capt. Charles E. Grant. We captured the intrenchments and two pieces of artillery. In July, 1864, it seemed that the war was getting near the end. The enemy moved about in squads. We had been in South Carolina, Florida, and Georgia. I do not know the purpose. It seemed to have been to run them down. We were supposed to tear down the railroads between Savannah, Ga., and Charleston, S.C., so the Confederate troops could not reinforce the armies in front of Sherman.

My regiment intended to take Honey Hill, S.C., but we found the enemy too strong. We made three charges and lost one-third of the men engaged, and were driven out. I had been placed in the color guard. My position was on the left of the sergeant, who was Robert King. He said to me: "Will you go with me? I am going to carry the flag into the fort or die." We had nearly reached the muzzles of the guns when he was killed. I caught him with one hand and the flag with the other when he staggered back. . . . [Smith carried the regimental flag for the remainder of the battle.]

I got my final discharge at Mt. Pleasant, S.C., in August, 1865. Shortly afterwards we sailed to Gallop[s] Island, near Boston, from whence we returned to Clinton in September or October. I stayed there until May, 1866, when I went to Kentucky to visit my mother and three sisters. Col. Warner and his daughter came to the train and told me to come back to Clinton whenever I was ready, as I had a lifetime home there.

I went down to Cairo and took a boat to Moses Ferry, a mile below Birmingham, about 8 or 10 miles from where I was born. Later I went to Eddyville and saw all my former playmates, who were ex-Confederate soldiers. I then saw my former owner, who came to me and gave me good advice. He told me that he was as poor as I.

"Adventures of a Colored Boy in War," *National Tribune*, March 21, 1929, reprinted in Noah Andre Trudeau, ed., *Voices of the 55th: Letters from the 55th Massachusetts Volunteers, 1861–1865* (Dayton: Morningside House, 1996), 187–91.

"THE CONSERVATIVE POLICY HAS UTTERLY FAILED"

In July 1862, Governor Richard Yates wrote President Lincoln to urge a decisive shift in Union strategy. Such a letter from the governor of the president's home state carried unusual weight. Reprinted widely across the North, the letter confirmed Yates's reputation as a forceful war governor and a leader in Illinois for those who now accepted the use of federal power—through measures such as the Confiscation Acts—to strike at slavery, a position at odds with the long-held view that the federal government had no jurisdiction over slavery in states where it already existed.

Executive Department, Springfield Illinois, July 11th, 1862.

President Lincoln, Washington, D.C.:

The crisis of the war and our national existence is upon us. The time has come for the adoption of more decisive measures. Greater vigor and earnestness must be infused into our military movements. Blows must be struck at the vital parts of the rebellion. The Government should employ every available means compatible with the rules of warfare to [subdue] the traitors. Summon to the standard of the Republic all men willing to fight for the Union. Let loyalty, and that alone, be the dividing line between the nation and its foes. Generals should not be permitted to fritter away the sinews of our brave men in guarding the property of traitors, and in driving back into their hands loyal blacks, who offer us their labor, and seek shelter beneath the Federal flag. Shall we sit supinely by, and see the war sweep off the youth and strength of the land, and refuse aid from that class of men, who are at least worthy foes of traitors and the murderers of our Government and of our children?

Our armies should be directed to forage on the enemy, and to cease paying traitors and their abettors exorbitant exactions for food needed by the sick or hungry soldier. Mild and conciliatory means have been tried in vain to recall the rebels to their allegiance. The conservative policy has utterly failed to reduce traitors to obedience and to restore the supremacy of the laws. They have, by means of sweeping conscriptions, gathered in countless hordes, and threaten to

Governor Richard Yates. *Courtesy Abraham Lincoln Presidential Library, Springfield, Illinois*

beat back and overwhelm the armies of the Union. With blood and treason in their hearts, they flaunt the black flag of rebellion in the face of the Government, and threaten to butcher our brave and loyal armies with foreign bayonets. They arm negroes and merciless savages in their behalf.

Mr. LINCOLN, the crisis demands greater and sterner measures. Proclaim anew the good old motto of the Republic, "Liberty and Union, now and forever, one and inseparable," and accept the services of *all loyal men*, and it will be in your power to stamp armies out of the earth—irresistible armies that will bear our banners to certain victory.

In any event, Illinois, already alive with beat of drum and resounding with the tramp of new recruits, will respond to your call. Adopt this policy and she will leap like a flaming giant into the fight.

This policy for the conduct of the war will render foreign intervention impossible, and the arms of the Republic invincible. It will bring the conflict to a speedy close, and secure peace on a permanent basis.

RICHARD YATES,
Governor of Illinois.

Richard Yates to Abraham Lincoln, July 11, 1862, Yates Family Papers, Abraham Lincoln Presidential Library, Springfield.

"TOO MUCH PROTECTION HAS BEEN GIVEN TO REBEL PROPERTY"

In this letter to his father, Clinton's George Hull, of the Twentieth Illinois Infantry, advocates emancipating and arming the slaves. The letter reveals the political sophistication of a common Union soldier during a crucial period in which Union strategy was shifting to embrace the very logic that Hull articulates. At the same time, Hull's letter illustrates a common soldier's appraisal—rather accurate, as it turns out—of Union generalship in the eastern as compared to the western theater.

Jackson, Tenn., July 22, 1862

Dear Father:—I was glad to hear you had such a good time on the Fourth, and would like to have enjoyed it with you; but it was not my privilege; so I am content to remain here.

Nothing particular transpired here on the Fourth. In the army, there is no difference in days—we use them all alike. We cannot lay work aside and go on a frolic. Nothing can interfere with a soldier's duty. It *must* be done, whether on the Fourth of July or the Sabbath; in sunshine or Storm; in heat or cold.

I am of your opinion about the war. Too much protection has been given to rebel property. We will never be free from trouble until slavery is annihilated. So arm the negroes, and let them help put down this wicked rebellion. Nothing will do it so quickly. The milk and water policy is about played out; and if McClellan and Halleck had paid more attention to the negroes who came into our camps, and not so much to rebel deserters, (most of whom were spies) matters would now be very different. Some folks say the negroes lack courage, and will not stand fire. They know better; so do the rebels, who dread the day when they will be armed and put to work.

I don't like the way our Generals are doing in the east. I wish Gen. Pope had been there, and think he would have led the grand army of the Potomac on a little faster scale than McClellan does. If Pope had been in command at Corinth, Beauregard would not have escaped.

McClellan has a good army. They fought bravely; but with their present leaders, they are more of a draw-back than anything else. They start to seize a place—go five miles the first day—then comes a big speech to the men—go three miles the next day—rest a week—go one mile further, and so on, till the rebels have time to fortify and reinforce. Gen. Grant, was only one day marching twelve miles and taking his position around Fort Donelson—and he took the place; and I will venture to say, that when Halleck was at Shiloh, and McClellan was at Yorktown, neither Corinth or Richmond was more strongly fortified, or more difficult to take, than Donelson; Corinth, I know, was not.

We will have to stay here twelve months longer, if not more. I am willing to stay just as long as any of them; but I want to be led by good generals; men who understand their business.

Tell all the boys you see, to come and help us. We have fought long and hard, and are willing to fight, until the h—l hounds that are trying to overthrow the best government man was ever blest with, are completely cleared out. Tell them that the blessings and privileges they are now enjoying are in danger, ask them how they can stand back, and see us do all. Tell them to come and join us, and we will give them a hearty welcome, and lead them on to victory.

George Hull.

Clinton Public, July 31, 1862.

THE EMANCIPATION MEMORIAL

On September 7, 1862, evangelical Protestants gathered in Chicago's Bryan Hall to rally public support for emancipation. Longtime antislavery activists from Illinois's Protestant establishment led the meeting, including Rev. J. M. Sturtevant, president of Illinois College; Rev. William Weston Patton of Chicago's First Congregationalist Church; the outspoken Methodist preacher Thomas M. Eddy; and Rev. John Dempster, president of the Garrett Biblical Institute (now Garrett-Evangelical Theological Seminary). The Emancipation Memorial, approved at the Bryan Hall meeting and excerpted here, captures the evangelical Protestant view of the war and its redemptive possibilities.

MEMORIAL.

To His Excellency, Abraham Lincoln, President of the United States;

Your memorialists of all Christian denominations in the city of Chicago, assembled in solemn meeting to consider the moral aspects of the war now waging, would utter their deepest convictions as to the present relation of our country & its rulers to the government & providence of Almighty God, & would respectfully ask a hearing for the principles & facts deemed fundamental to a right judgment of this appalling crisis. And to this we are encouraged by the frequency with which on various public occasions you have officially recognized the dependence of the country & its Chief Magistrate upon the divine favor.

We claim, then, that the war is a divine retribution upon our land for its manifold sins, & especially for the crime of oppression, against which the denunciations of God's word are so numerous & pointed. . . . The slave-oligarchy has organized the most unnatural, perfidious & formidable rebellion known to history. It has professedly established an independent government on the avowed basis of slavery, acknowledging that the Federal Union was constituted to conserve & promote liberty. All but four of the Slave States have seceded from the Union, & those four (with the exception of Delaware, in which slavery but nominally exists) have been kept in subjection only by overwhelming military force. Can we doubt that this is a divine retribution for national sin; in which our crime has justly shaped our punishment?

Proceeding upon this belief, which recent events have made it almost atheism to deny, your memorialists avow their solemn conviction, deepening every hour, that there can be no deliverance from divine judgements, *till Slavery ceases in the land!* We cannot expect God to save a nation that clings to its sin. This is too fearful an hour to insult God or to deceive ourselves. National existence is in peril: our sons & brothers are falling by tens of thousands on the battlefield: the war daily becomes more determined & destructive: while we speak, the enemy thunders at the gates of the capital: our acknowledged superiority of resources has availed little or nothing in the conflict. As Christian patriots we dare not conceal the truth, that these judgements mean what the divine judgements meant in Egypt. . . .

We urge you, therefore, as the Head of this Christian nation, from considerations of moral principle & as the only means of preserving the Union, to proclaim, without delay, [a decree] of *National Emancipation.*

However void of authority, in this respect, you might have been in time of peace, you are well aware, as a statesman, that the exigencies of war are the only limits of its powers, especially in a war to preserve the very life of the nation. . . .

In this view, of a change of power involving an equal change in duty, we will not conceal the fact, that gloom has filled our hearts at every indication that the war was regarded as simply an issue between the Federal authorities & the rebel States, & that therefore slavery was to be touched only to the extent that the pressure of rebel success might absolutely necessitate. Have we not reason to *expect* rebel success, on that policy? Are we to omit from our calculations, the necessary conditions of divine favor? Has the fact no moral force, that the war has suddenly placed within the power of the President the system that has provoked God's wrath? Is there not danger, that while we are waiting till the last, terrible exigency shall force us to liberate the slave, God may decide the contest against us, & the measure that we would not adopt on principle, prove too late for our salvation? We claim that justice, here as everywhere, is the highest expediency.

"Emancipation Memorial," Miscellaneous Civil War Papers of William Weston Patton, Chicago Historical Museum.

THE CAIRO CONTRABANDS

Located at the confluence of the Mississippi and Ohio Rivers, Cairo was also the site of Camp Defiance, a staging ground for Union forces in the western theater and site of a large contraband camp. In this letter to Frederick Douglass, H. Oscar describes the Cairo contrabands.

FREEDMEN AT CAIRO.

Well Friend Douglass:—Cairo now begins to look as though the jubilee sure enough [has] come in this country. Besides what are here already, filling the old barracks, from one end to the other, still they come. Every morning, when I go down to the "Ohio Levee," I find it literally dotted over with new arrivals of contrabands. Old men and young men, old women and young women, and children here. The town is literally alive with them. And they are like "Joseph's coat of many colors"—black, white, almost white, half white, "ring streaked and striped."—Many with whom I have talked appear buoyant and hopefull, and say, "God bless the Yankees." I have heard various accounts of what they thought and what they did when they heard *"dem big guns roar"*—how the men and women in the fields would prick up their ears and listen, and how they would begin to fall back upon their dignity and disregard the commands of the overseer, and rejoice and thank God that their friends had come. The overseers and the white folks generally had been telling them that the Yankees were their enemies, and they pretended to believe them until now. The overseers would tell them, "now, when you see the Yankees coming you must break for the woods or Cainbreaks." They would say, "no, we think the best way would be to run to the Yankees and throw ourselves on their mercies, and they will be less liable to hurt us."

I am constantly asked by both men and women whether they can get work in the North—what the *wages are,* and whether they *can make money there,* and whether it is very cold in the winter &c. &c.

Now it is a noticeable fact, to the most careless observer, that the prejudices of the common laborers, PARTICULARLY *the* Irish, are raging intensely and fiercely here against those poor unfortunate and innocent people. I believe the Irish would murder every man and woman of them if they thought they dare do it. Indeed, were it not for the military authorities here, you might not be surprised to hear a mob here any day—I have been informed by parties who are known to the facts—the attending physician on the poor mother and her two little daughters of a circumstance that took place here, recently, that would shock the *moral* sensibilities of any well regulated mind or community. I saw the mother and her two little outraged daughters while under the doctors' hands. No doubt the three white men who committed the outrage would "d— a nigger anyhow." But thank heaven there is a "higher Law" that rules the destinies of us all.

Your friend and brother,

H. OSCAR

Cairo, Illinois, Sept. 25th, 1862.

Douglass' Monthly (Rochester, NY), November 1862.

"THERE IS A DANGER IN THE ELECTION HERE"

In September 1862, Secretary of War Edwin Stanton ordered the shipment of the Cairo contrabands into the Illinois countryside. At the government's expense, the Illinois Central Railroad soon began transporting contrabands into communities across the state. These documents illustrate how the Cairo contraband issue shaped the 1862 campaign in Illinois. First, the Chicago Tribune *defends the policy. Second, the* Salem Advocate, *a Democratic mouthpiece, opines on what the presence of the Cairo contrabands might mean for Illinoisans. Finally, Lincoln's close friend David Davis advises the president on the political situation in Illinois.*

THE CONTRABANDS AT CAIRO.

These colored refugees have been driven North, like hundreds of loyal white persons, by the retreat of our army in Tennessee. They have left their homes unwillingly, and they will return to them gladly whenever they can do so without being again reduced to bondage. What shall be done with them? Each able bodied male is capable of gathering and husking corn, and preparing the ground for the winter wheat crop. At least sixty thousand farmers and farmers' sons and farm laborers have gone to the war from Illinois, leaving crops ungathered and land untilled. To refuse the labor of these contrabands for the time being, is little less than suicide. . . . The prejudice which would refuse them under such circumstances would also spurn the horse or ox that draws the wagon or plow across the field.

When President Lincoln's proclamation of freedom takes effect in the South, these contrabands will return to their homes and take with them nine tenths of the free colored population of the North. The laws of climate and production will draw them thither by an irresistible attraction. We have been told a thousand times by the pro-slavery organs that the cotton and rice fields are exactly adopted [sic] to the blacks, and the blacks to them; and this is about the only truth that they ever did tell. . . . The plantations must be cultivated and the blacks, if not the only ones who *can* do the work, are certainly the only class who can do it advantageously and profitably.

Chicago Tribune, September 23, 1862.

NEGROES OR WHITE MEN?

. . . . Accounts from Cairo show that nearly twenty-five hundred negroes have been landed at that point in our State and are seeking to lead the van in an ir-ruption upon the length and breadth of Illinois. Our readers will recollect that news of the incoming of these negroes into our State was dispatched to Secretary STANTON, at Washington, and an inquiry made of him as to how they should be enabled to go North. Whereupon Secretary STANTON answered that if places of refuge and domicil should be found for them, the Government would pay the expense of their transportation. Now Mr. Secretary STANTON ought to know that this is a violation of our laws. In the first place we can hardly perceive how the people's servants, at Washington, can expend the money of the tax payers in send-ing negroes into our State, especially as our laws forbid their coming amongst us. We might perhaps in extremity be willing to pay for their transportation out of the State in order to observe the law; but it seems extremely hard that we should pay for bringing them into our State in violation of our laws.

The people of Illinois are almost unanimously opposed to the ingress of ne-groes into the State. There is no other matter or thing upon which they have expressed by their votes, an opinion so decided as upon this subject. There can be no doubt of it. Even so late as last June, by a vote of the people upon subject, a majority of more than one hundred and seventy-six thousand in a vote of two hundred and eleven thousand or more than five-sixths declared their opposition to the introduction of negroes.

Is it not then a high affront of the people of this State for a servant of the Government to insist upon a violation of their will? . . .

It is not yet known what will be the further action in regard to the black man. Thousands, perhaps tens of thousands are crowding upon the border free States and unless the people are prepared for a perfect inundation of this black element, disturbing all our social relations and threatening the complete overthrow of white labor, and the almost utter destitution of thousands of white laboring people, we should insist that the laws of our State should be observed and respected.

Salem Advocate, October 2, 1862.

Lincoln, Logan Co. Ills—
Octo 14th 1862.

My Dear Sir—
I am satisfied that the spreading of negroes from Cairo, through the Central portion of Illinois, will work great harm in the coming election.
—They should not be moved from Cairo until after the election—I don't wish to discuss the question, of what should be done with them—I feel most earnestly the *necessity* of not bringing any into the State, or spreading any from Cairo, while this election is pending—Facts I could give, but it would lengthen this letter too much—I went to see the Govr. at Springfield last night on the subject, & he telegraphed you—
—He feels the *necessity*, as much as I do—There is a danger in the election here, growing out of the large number of Republican voters, who have gone to war under the last call & of the negroes, coming into the State Your friend,

David Davis

David Davis to Abraham Lincoln, October 14, 1862, Abraham Lincoln Papers, Manuscripts, Library of Congress, Washington, DC.

ILLINOIS REACTS TO THE EMANCIPATION PROCLAMATION

Samples from Illinois newspapers reveal the ideological divide that opened between Democrats and Republicans in the wake of Lincoln's fateful decision to free the slaves in the rebellious states.

THE NEGRO QUESTION IN ILLINOIS.

Its Influence Upon the Approaching Election.

The abolitionists have given the people too much nigger. The people have become tired of it. They are disgusted with it, and they will make that disgust most terribly manifest at the polls next Tuesday. The people will teach the abolition tories that there are other interests beside those of the negro, that should claim the attention of those who are selected to make and execute the laws. Since the republican party came into power the country has been convulsed from one extreme to the other with the most constant, unceasing and disgusting clamour about negroes. They were not satisfied that the war should be prosecuted for the white man, and the rights of the white man, but have persistently clamored for its prosecution for the interests of the inevitable negro. Having bullied the President into issuing an unconstitutional proclamation declaring the negroes all free, they couldn't rest satisfied with that, but must raise the howl for the emigration of these negroes into the northern States. They persist in forcing hundreds and thousands of these negroes into Illinois, in open, flagrant violation of the [U.S.] Constitution and laws of the State, and in utter contempt of the will of the people. When they wanted a proclamation freeing the negroes, they were told the President had no authority, under the [U.S.] Constitution, to issue such a proclamation, and what was their reply? They said, "d—n the Constitution—free the negroes!" They are now told that it is a violation of the Constitution of this State to bring these negroes here, and what is their reply? They continue to say, "d—n the Constitution." In short, they "d—n" and denounce everything that stands in the way of their cherished scheme of reducing the white man to a level with the negro, and conferring upon the black man all the rights and privileges that are enjoyed by the whites. The people of Illinois are not yet ready to tolerate these proceedings. They are not yet ready to have the Constitution trampled down by the abolitionists. Nor are they yet ready to permit the State to be overrun by these fugitive negroes from the south. They will therefore administer such a rebuke to the abolitionists next Tuesday as will make the heart of every true patriot in the land rejoice. . . .

Quincy Daily Herald, November 1, 1862.

NUMBER OF SLAVES FREED BY THE PROCLAMATION.

. . . It is impossible now to estimate fully the importance of that act which will make the first day of January, 1863, forever memorable. Its full significance can only be estimated by results which are to extend through coming ages. Only future ages can comprehend it in its full grandeur, and do its author entire justice.

The downfall of the institution of slavery is not an unexpected result of the war begun and prosecuted for its perpetuation. Many sagacious and far-seeing statesmen early foresaw that such must be the result of the rebellion.—Thousands of others who, at the beginning of the war, were zealous in defense of the peculiar institutions of the South, but whose attachment to the Union was still stronger than their attachment to slavery, have become convinced that there can be no permanent peace or security for the country so long as an institution so inconsistent with the spirit of free government shall continue to exert its malign influence upon the politics of the nation. Who shall say that they are not right, and that the nation can be cured of its terrible disease so long as the cause of it remains in full force and vigor. . . .

Illinois State Journal (Springfield), January 6, 1863.

~

In issuing his emancipation proclamation of January 1st, Lincoln, in the judgment of all unprejudiced men, committed a *crime* compared to which the peaceful secession of States was an act of justice and right. In so doing he has convinced the people, North as well as South, that the apprehensions of the latter upon his election—that the prime object of his administration would be to destroy their local institutions, were well founded. By this act he has, in the minds of the people, but verified the truth of the plea upon which was based the action of the southern people in severing their connection with the government. He has now done that which will go far to convince mankind everywhere that the withdrawal of the southern States was not without just cause. And what will be the judgment of the people, at home and abroad, upon him? What becomes of his oft repeated declarations expressed in his messages to Congress, in his proclamations to the people, and in his dispatches to foreign lands to the effect that the object of the war was to restore the Union, with the rights of the several States under the constitution unimpaired? Was it a willful misrepresentation made to conceal his intended great wrong from the eyes of men? If he had, at the time of his inauguration, but hinted at the possibility of such a proclamation, he would long since have been sleeping in an ignominious grave. And if at a later period, when he was appealing to the States for soldiers, he had hinted at the cause he has since entered upon, his call would have been answered in such a manner as would have long ago cut short his nefarious schemes. The unmanliness and cowardice of the act is disgraceful to Americans.—The able-bodied men of the South are almost to a man in the war— some willingly, others unwillingly. Their old men, mothers, wives and children, without any one to protect or defend them, are left at home; and it is these helpless non-combatants against whom Lincoln indirectly incites the negroes to direct their savage barbarities. Where is the man so lost to every principle of manhood as to excuse or indorse such barbarity.

Jonesboro Gazette, January 10, 1863.

H. FORD DOUGLAS AND THE MEANING OF FREEDOM

In July 1862, Chicago's H. Ford Douglas, before the war a biting critic of the Republican Party and forceful advocate for black emigration, enlisted in Company

G, Ninety-Fifth Illinois Infantry, resolved now to fight slavery with powder and steel. Passing as white—Douglas was the light-skinned son of a slave mother and her white owner—he saw action in Tennessee and Louisiana before being discharged and promoted to captain in the Eighth Louisiana Colored Infantry in June 1863, a regiment that he personally raised. By war's end, Douglas was one of nearly eighty black commissioned officers in the Union army. In this letter to Frederick Douglass, printed in Douglass' Monthly, H. Ford Douglas lauds the Emancipation Proclamation and the promise it holds out to black Americans.

Colliersville, Tennessee,
Jan. 8th 1863

My Dear Douglass:—My wife sent me this morning the Monthly for December containing your appeal to England to *"hands off "* in this fearful conflict for freedom. It was indeed gratifying to me who have always felt more than a friendly interest in you and yours to read your eloquent and manly words of admonition to the old Saxon mother States to give no moral or legal countenance to the claims of the impious Confederate States of America in their attempt to set up a Government established upon the idea of the perpetual bondage of the Negro. England has wisely withstood every temptation to do so—Abraham Lincoln has crossed the Rubicon and by one simple act of Justice to the slave links his memory with immortality.

The slaves are *free!* How can I write these precious words? And yet it is so unless twenty millions of people cradled in christianity and civilization for a thousand years commits the foulest perjury that ever blackened the pages of history. In anticipation of this result I enlisted six Months ago in order to be better prepared to play my part in the great drama of the Negroe's redemption. I wanted its drill, its practical details for mere theory does not make a good soldier. I have learned something of war for I have seen war in its brightest as well as its bloodiest phase and yet I have nothing to regret. For since the stern necessities of this struggle have laid bare the naked issue of freedom on one side and slavery on the other—freedom shall have in the future of this conflict if necessary my blood as it has had in the past my earnest and best words. It seems to me that you can have no good reason for withholding from the government your hearty cooperation. This war will educate Mr. Lincoln out of his idea of the deportation of the Negro quite as fast as it has some of his other pro slavery ideas with respect to employing them as soldiers.

Hitherto they have been socially and politically ignored by this government, but now by the fortunes of war they are cast morally and mentally helpless (so to speak) into the broad sunlight of our Republican civilization there, [sic] to be educated and lifted to a higher and nobler life. National duties and responsibilities are not to be colonized, they must be heroically met and religiously performed. This mighty waste of manhood resulting from the dehumanizing character of slave institutions of America is now to be given back to the world through the patient toil and self denial of this proud and haughty race. They must now pay back to the negro in Spiritual culture [and] in opportunities for self improvement what they have taken from him for two hundred years by the constant over-taxing of his physical nature. . . . Now is the time for you to finish the crowning work of your life. Go to work at once and raise a Regiment and offer your services to the government and I am confident they will be accepted. They say we will not fight. I want to see it tried on. You are the one to me of all others, to demonstrate this fact.

I belong to Company G, 95th Regiment Illinois volunteers—Captain Eliot N. Bush—a christian and a gentleman. You must pardon my miserable chirography. There is not in me one particle of mechanical genius, and it does seem to me that I can learn almost any thing but to write a decent hand. If you can by what you see marked on this paper decipher my meaning, I shall be content.

Very truly your friend,
H. Ford Douglas.

Douglass' Monthly (Rochester, NY), February 1863.

FIVE

~

Divided Houses

*T*HE YEAR 1863 was a whirlwind of breathtaking losses and stirring victories, of bitter division and violence on the home front, and yet more grievous casualties on blood-soaked fields of battle. The Union's new strategy of emancipation—and its adjunct, the enlistment of black troops—both elevated the stakes and purpose of the war and produced determined opposition. Spring saw Grant's campaign for Vicksburg stall, and Lee's uncanny victory at Chancellorsville. Next came another of Lee's bold gambits: a risky offensive into central Pennsylvania. The Union's controversial draft law sparked intense and violent resistance. That resistance, the work of Peace Democrats—or copperheads, as the Republicans derisively labeled them—continued even after July's dramatic reversal of military fortunes: Grant's victory at Vicksburg and Meade's crushing defeat of Lee's army at Gettysburg.

Against this backdrop Illinoisans divided as never before. Democrats had swept into office on hostility to Lincoln's wartime policies. Yet while Democrats were united in their opposition to Lincoln and his "black Republican" allies, they also faced serious problems. It was one thing to find fault with specific policies, quite another to offer a strategic alternative for winning the war. By 1863 two distinct Democratic factions emerged and harmonizing them proved difficult. War Democrats, harking back to Stephen Douglas's example, urged prosecution of the war and restoration of the Union, even as they opposed Republican means to that end. Peace Democrats called for armistice and negotiation with the Confederacy; more than a few seemed to openly hold pro-Confederate sympathies. Copperheadism attracted support across the Union, but Illinois's movement was arguably the largest and potentially most destabilizing of any state because it encompassed both a legitimate political arm capable of delivering votes and policies and a paramilitary element capable of visiting violence on loyal communities.

When the 1863 legislative session opened, Democrats wasted little time exercising their newfound political power. The general assembly sent Congressman William Richardson to fill Orville Browning's Senate seat. The Quincy Democrat was a fiery critic of emancipation and a voice for the state's antiwar faction. A house committee drafted a habeas corpus law intended to stop military authorities from arresting Illinois civilians—in effect, nullifying federal law. Though never enacted, this bill was a response to the military arrests of Congressman William J. Allen and other prominent Democrats carried out in the fall of 1862. But the most striking product of the 1863 general assembly was the so-called Peace Resolutions bill passed by the house in February. The resolutions indicted Republican wartime policies, called for an armistice with the South, and recommended a committee of six to help organize a peace convention in Louisville, Kentucky. Only a Republican filibuster in the senate thwarted passage of these explosive resolutions. The general assembly then moved forward with proposals that would give it and the Democratic state treasurer more power over wartime expenditures, a direct challenge to the authority of Governor Yates. Clearly Democrats were bidding fair to take control of Illinois's war.

In June, Yates counterpunched. The governor seized on a technicality—a disagreement between the house and senate over the date of adjournment—to prorogue (literally, to discontinue) the general assembly. This was an unprecedented assertion of executive power over the legislative branch, the first such example in the state's history. While the order itself involved technical constitutional issues of executive authority and legislative prerogative (ultimately Yates's order was upheld by the Illinois Supreme Court), Yates's battle with the Democratic assembly was fundamentally a political struggle over wartime policy.

The federal draft was another flashpoint of conflict between Republicans and Democrats when Congress enacted the Enrollment Act earlier that spring. In authorizing a draft, Congress was responding to sagging levels of volunteerism, compounded by the growing problem of desertion in the Union army. Both problems were symptoms of low morale, but in Illinois—which recorded more than thirteen thousand desertions throughout the war—desertion was, according to one historian, most numerous "in the months following emancipation, the arming of Negroes, and the military reverses of 1862."[1] The new federal law empowered U.S. provost marshals to canvass every congressional district in the Union and enroll all able-bodied males aged eighteen to forty-five, who would then be eligible for a lottery draft. Congress intended the Enrollment Act as a stimulus to further volunteering; each state was assigned a quota of enlistments for the year distributed equally among its congressional districts. Conscription would take place only after a district failed to meet its quota. Through a combination of patriotic appeals and financial bounties paid up front to enlistees, Illinois managed to exceed its quota through volunteers in 1863 and came close to doing so in 1864. Thus only about thirty-five hundred Illinoisans saw service during the Civil War via the draft, and then only in the final eight months of the conflict. Nevertheless the draft was among the most controversial policies of the entire war. Part of the problem was the law's provisions allowing a man to pay $300, either for a substitute or for a one-time commutation from compulsory service. This gave the draft a controversial class dimension, as few workingmen could afford these fees. But Illinois Democrats more often assailed the very idea of a draft as patently unconstitutional, another in a growing list of tyrannical federal policies designed to usurp personal liberty.

Reports of both passive and open resistance became increasingly common in Illinois. Northern Illinoisans seeking to avoid their local militia muster simply fled the state. By the fall of 1862 the problem was severe enough that Secretary of War Edwin Stanton ordered that a pass system be implemented to regulate out-of-state travel. Legitimate travelers protested the inconvenience, and the system was swiftly abandoned, but "skedaddling" slowed to a trickle. Antiwar Democrats in Illinois also proved willing to use local power to resist federal policy. In 1863 Clark County Circuit Court judge Charles H. Constable freed four Union army deserters and arrested the soldiers who had captured them. Constable reasoned that the arresting soldiers, who were based in Indiana, had no authority over deserters in Illinois and thus were guilty of kidnapping. Constable's audacity brought local civil authority into conflict with U.S. and military law. Over two hundred troops under the command of Colonel Henry B. Carrington, headquartered in Indianapolis, rushed to Marshall, the Clark County seat, to arrest Constable for violation of the Enrollment Act and its provisions against encouraging desertion. Constable was found not guilty in U.S. district court on technical and procedural grounds, but the case illustrated how antiwar Democrats in positions of local authority could frustrate federal policy.

By far the most threatening resistance occurred in central and southern Illinois after passage of the 1863 draft law. Draft officials in Olney shut down their work when a mob of five hundred marched on their office and commandeered the enrollment lists. A similar scene was reenacted in Fulton County, where only months before a local Democratic newspaper had warned ominously, "the first attempt to carry out [the Enrollment Act's] provisions will be the signal for an united uprising of a determined and desperate multitude of freemen who will court annihilation rather than submit for one moment to the tyrannies of the Lincoln Despotism!"[2] To protect enrollment officers in Marion, martial law was declared and the military sent in two companies of cavalry. Indeed, throughout 1863 came alarming reports from across central and southern Illinois of roving guerrilla bands, their numbers fortified by recent army deserters, swearing resistance to the draft and terrorizing Union officials. Assaults on persons and property were commonplace; in several instances U.S. officials and civilians were fatally shot. Summarizing the situation, the state's acting assistant provost marshal, Lieutenant Colonel James Oakes, concluded that "in the present attitude of the disaffected elements here I do not think it would be prudent or safe to begin the draft."[3] Some of this antidraft activity was associated with the Knights of the Golden Circle, an armed, secretive, pro-Southern fraternal organization with pockets of support across the lower Midwest and the border South. It is impossible to know precisely how extensive and well organized the KGC or related groups actually were in Illinois. But at the time few Illinoisans doubted their existence or their ability to sow mayhem on the home front.

The outbreak of armed resistance to federal policy generated more military arrests—two thousand between June and October alone—and more violations of civil liberties in Illinois. In June commander of the Western Department, General Ambrose Burnside, issued general order no. 84 shutting down the *Chicago Times* and *Jonesboro Gazette*, two of the state's most inflammatory antiadministration newspapers. The evening of Burnside's order a crowd of twenty thousand gathered in Chicago to denounce this latest example of military despotism. Troops were ordered to Chicago in anticipation of an armed riot there. The troops were stopped en route at Urbana, where word came that Lincoln had wisely rescinded Burnside's order (though the *Jonesboro Gazette* remained closed for nearly ten months). Later that month forty thousand administration opponents assembled in Springfield. The throng delighted in rousing antiadministration oratory from Senator Richardson and Congressman John Eden and endorsed a plan for a national peace convention. In response, proadministration forces sponsored ostensibly nonpartisan yet highly politicized Union League rallies. Indeed, the very term Union League implied that the opposition was, of course, against the Union. Probably the most important of the many Union League gatherings of 1863 occurred at Springfield on September 3. In preparing for the rally, James C. Conkling, president of the Springfield Union League, invited his old friend Lincoln to attend. Lincoln could not leave Washington, but he did send a letter for Conkling to read aloud at the rally. A crowd estimated at fifty thousand heard Lincoln's words on that day; soon countless more had read the "Conkling letter," reprinted in newspapers across the country and considered to be Lincoln's formal response to his copperhead critics. Buoyed by the historic victories at Vicksburg and Gettysburg, and by their president's eloquent defense of his policies, proadministration forces braced for still more battles and sacrifices.

THE PEACE RESOLUTIONS

In early 1863 the Illinois House of Representatives passed a controversial bill known as the Peace Resolutions. The resolutions can be read a number of ways. Certainly they catalogue the long list of grievances that motivated opponents of the Lincoln administration by the middle of the war. Yet they also reveal some of the difficulties that Democrats faced as an opposition party in wartime.

We . . . *declare*, that the act of the federal administration, in suspending the writ of *habeas corpus*, the arrest of citizens not subject to military law, without warrant or authority, transporting them to distant States, incarcerating them in political prisons, without charge or accusation, denying them the right of trial by jury, witnesses in their favor, or counsel for their defense—withholding from them all knowledge of their accusers, and the cause of their arrest—answering their petitions for redress by repeated injury and insult—prescribing, in many cases, as a condition of their release, test oaths, arbitrary and illegal; in the abridgment of freedom of speech, and of the press, by imprisoning the citizen for expressing his sentiments, by suppressing newspapers by military force, and establishing censorship over others, wholly incompatible with freedom of thought and expression of opinion—and the establishment of a system of espionage, by a secret police, to invade the privacy of unsuspecting citizens—declaring martial law over States not in rebellion, and when the courts are open and unobstructed for the punishment of crime; in declaring the slaves of loyal, as well as disloyal citizens, in certain States and parts of States, free; the attempted enforcement of compensated emancipation; the proposed taxation of the laboring white man to purchase the freedom and secure the elevation of the negro; the transportation of negroes into the State of Illinois in defiance of the repeatedly expressed will of the people; the arrest and imprisonment of the representatives of a free and sovereign State; the dismemberment of the State of Virginia, erecting within her boundaries a new State without the consent of her Legislature, are each and all, arbitrary and unconstitutional—a usurpation of the legislative functions, and a suspension of the judicial departments of the State and Federal Governments—subverting the Constitution—State and Federal—invading the reserved rights of the people and the sovereignty of the States, and, if sanctioned, destructive of the Union—establishing, upon the common ruins of the liberties of the people and the sovereignty of the States, a consolidated military despotism. And we hereby solemnly declare that no American citizen can, without the crime of infidelity to his country's constitution, and the allegiance which he bears to each, sanction such usurpations. Therefore,

Resolved by the House of Representatives, the Senate concurring therein, That the army was organized, confiding in the declaration of the President, in his inaugural address, to-wit: that he had no purpose, directly, or indirectly, to interfere with the institution of slavery in the States where it existed, and that he believed he had no lawful right to do so, and that he had no inclination to do so; and upon the declaration of the Federal Congress, to-wit: that this war is not waged in any spirit of oppression or subjugation, or any purpose of overthrowing any of the institutions of any of the States; and that, inasmuch as the whole policy of the Administration, since the organization of the army, has been at war with the declarations aforesaid, culminating in the emancipation proclamation, leaving the facts patent that the war has been diverted from its first avowed object, to that of subjugation and the abolition of slavery; a fraud, both legal and moral, has been perpetrated upon the brave sons of Illinois, who have so nobly gone forth to battle for the constitution and the laws. And while we protest against the continuance of this gross fraud upon our citizen soldiers, we thank them for that heroic conduct on the battle fields that sheds imperishable glory on the State of Illinois.

Resolved, That we believe the further prosecution of the present war cannot result in the restoration of the Union and the preservation of the Constitution as our fathers made it, unless the President's emancipation proclamation is withdrawn.

Resolved, That while we condemn and denounce the flagrant and monstrous usurpations of the Administration, and encroachments of Abolitionism, we equally condemn and denounce the ruinous heresy of secession as unwarranted by the Constitution, and destructive alike of the security and perpetuity of our Government, and the peace and liberty of the people; and fearing, as we do, that it is the intention of the present Congress and Administration, at no distant day, to acknowledge the independence of the Southern Confederacy, and thereby sever the Union; we hereby solemnly declare that we are unalterably opposed to any such severance of the Union, and that we never can consent that the great Northwest shall be separated from the Southern States comprising the Mississippi Valley. That river shall never water the soil of two nations, but, from its source to its confluence with the Gulf, shall belong to one great and united people.

Resolved, That peace, fraternal relations, and political fellowship should be restored among the States, that the best interests of all and the welfare of mankind require that this should be done in the most speedy and most effective manner; that it is to the people we must look for a restoration of the Union and the blessings of peace, and to these ends we should direct our earnest and honest efforts; and hence we are in favor of the assembling of a national convention of all the States to so adjust our national difficulties that the States may hereafter live together in harmony, each being secured in the rights guaranteed respectively to all by our fathers; and which convention we recommend shall convene at Louisville, Ky., or such other place as shall be determined upon by Congress or the several States, at the earliest practical period.

Resolved, further, therefore, That to attain the objects of the foregoing resolution, we hereby memorialize the Congress of the United States, the Administration at Washington, and the executives and legislatures of the several States to take such immediate action as shall secure an armistice, in which the rights and safety of the Government shall be fully protected for such length of time as may be necessary to enable the people to meet in convention as aforesaid. And we therefore, earnestly recommend to our fellow citizens every where, to observe and keep all their lawful and Constitutional obligations, to abstain from all violence, and to meet together and reason each with the other, upon the best mode to attain the great blessings of peace, unity and liberty:

And be it further Resolved, That to secure the co-operation of the States and the General Government, Stephen T. Logan, Samuel S. Marshall, H. K. S. Omelveny, William C. Goudy, Anthony Thornton and John D. Caton, are hereby appointed commissioners to confer immediately with Congress and the President of the United States, and with the legislature and executives of the several States, and urge the necessity of prompt action to secure said armistice, and the election of delegates to, and early assembling of said convention, and to arrange and agree with the General Government and the several States upon the time and place of holding said convention, and that they report their action in the premises, to the General Assembly of this State. . . .

Illinois State Journal (Springfield), February 5, 1863.

ILLINOIS SOLDIERS WRITE TO THEIR NEWSPAPERS

Soldiers in the field followed events back home through their state and town newspapers, which circulated, if only intermittently, in their encampments. Soldiers sometimes wrote back to their home newspaper, both to describe their experiences in the field and in response to events at home. Reading and corresponding with their local newspaper not only provided soldiers with welcome relief from the boredom and drudgery of camp life, it also served to reconnect their sacrifices to the social and political conflicts that divided Illinois communities. The next three documents show how these Illinois soldiers reacted to and sought to influence the emergence of the copperhead movement back home.

At a meeting of the officers of the Sixty-second Illinois Infantry convened for the purpose of enabling them to give some expression of their views relative to the condition of our country, and the continued prosecution of the war,

Col. JAS. M. TRUE was called to the Chair, and Adjutant E. R. WILEY, jr., appointed Secretary.

On motion of Lieut. Col. D.B. ROBINSON, Surgeon V. R. BRIDGES, Capt. JESSE CROOKS, Lieut. R. J. FORD and Lieut. GUY S. ALEXANDER, were appointed a committee to draft resolutions expressive of the sense of the meeting.

The committee retired, and after a short consultation, reported the following resolutions, which were unanimously adopted, and signed by the officers—every officer present with the regiment signing it. . . .

Resolved, That we hereby proclaim to the world our undying love for the Union of States, and at the same time our eternal and everlasting abhorrence for traitors, whether found in armed rebellion in the South, or in disloyal conventions and legislatures North.

Resolved, That we denounce the wickedness and baseness of those citizens of the North, who by disloyal speeches and otherwise, would impart confidence and hope to rebels in arms against this Government—who encourage Union soldiers to desert, and threaten armed resistance to their recovery; and who, by letters, speeches or acts, endeavor to promote disaffection in the army—the last hope of the nation: That we appeal to our fathers, our brothers and our friends at home to discountenance, oppose and put down those base and infamous wretches who, while breathing the free air of Illinois, sympathize with treason and denounce the Government which has given them peace and security with liberty from their childhood, now struggling almost in a death agony, and who from motives of ambition, or for their own personal aggrandizement or advantage, would lend their aid, however indirect, to reduce Illinois to the unhappy situation of these rebel southern states, the seat of blighting and desolating war.

Resolved, That we abjure all partisan issues, prejudices and strife; that we are for our Government and the flag [of] our fathers first, last and all the time, before and above all institutions, organizations and systems, and against all enemies and opposers whatsoever: That we will lend our support to the Government in the prosecution of this war till its power is known and felt throughout the whole world, and the Spangled Banner waves again over every foot of American soil.

Resolved, That we revere the parting admonition of the lamented [Stephen] DOUGLAS when he warned us that there could be but "patriots and traitors" in this struggle, and that whoever is not for his country is against it, and deserves the scorn and condemnation of all honest citizens and soldiers.

Resolved, That the Sixty-second Regiment, Illinois Infantry, will follow the flag that waved over the battles of our fathers, wherever it may go, whether it be in the sunny fields of the South, or against the miscreants, vile and perjured abettors of treason in the North, and for the honor of that banner we pledge our lives, our property and our sacred honor. . . .

On motion of Col James M. TRUE a copy was ordered to be furnished to the Mattoon *Gazette*, with a request to publish it also.

Mattoon *Independent Gazette*, February 14, 1863.

MEMPHIS, TENN., Feb. 7, 1863.

Editors Chicago Tribune:

In the perusal of your paper, lately, I *have been made to become very much embittered* against some of our Illinois men.

I wish all those politicians, who feel secesh enough to offer resolutions, in Illinois, that the soldiers be instructed, *not* to enforce the President's Emancipation Proclamation, were in the South, and in the secesh army, where they ought to be. I would like to be one of the first to draw the heart's blood of all such scandalous villains. I would just like to hear of the people of Illinois "cleaning out" (by the application of a hempen rope) all such persons who dare express their sympathies with Jeff. Davis. I tell you what it is, let these secesh sympathizers come down here and stay a year and a half, and if they had any sympathy for the Union cause they would not be belching forth resolutions protesting against the Emancipation Proclamation. . . . I think that a great injustice was done when the army was not allowed to vote in the different elections since the commencement of this war. Through this the secesh of the North are daily venturing to show themselves. But "the day of retribution am a-coming," and that day will be when this army is discharged, and the soldiers return to their respective homes, in the North. Then, *then* will be the time, that many of these black-hearted Northern secesh will have to atone for their miserable low-lived breathings against this unequalled and just Government. Mr. Editor, I shall rest in hope of hearing better news from the North than what I have been in the habit of hearing lately, in regard to secesh sympathizers. They can set it down that at least seven-eights of Gen. Grant's army feel as bitterly against them as myself. I can speak for one company, and I know that they would as leave fight them as secesh shot gun cavalry.

I remain yours, &c.,   G. H.,
                                                        Co. A, 2d Illinois Cavalry.

Chicago Tribune, February 23, 1863.

Extract from a private letter from a soldier, dated BUTLER'S CANAL, CAMP OPPOSITE VICKSBURG,

Jan. 28 [1863] . . .

I see by the papers there have been some pretty strong speeches made denouncing the management of this war. If the people of the North knew the exact condition of the army, they would feel more indignant than they now do, and perhaps be more energetic in their endeavors to take some measure toward putting a stop to the butchery that is now carried on, seemingly for the purpose of building up and filling the pockets of officers, army contractors, &c.

There are strange things occurring nowadays,—peace overtures being made; talk of dividing the North; discontent and demoralization of the army, mutinies, desertions, &c. I am afraid, if this nigger war is not settled soon, the boys will stack arms and go home.

As this is turned to be a nigger war, and not what we enlisted for, all think it will end soon in some way or other, and we be home by July 4th at longest; but, if the soldiers knew for certain that the war would continue, one third of the boys would be amongst the missing.

If any one up there has not yet got enough of freeing niggers, let him come here and learn the consequences of such an act. Many of them will not leave their masters at all, and, if you manage to coax one off, it will be but a few days before you will find him sighing to be back again. Besides, this country is calculated expressly for negroes. They are better cared for than the poor people of the North, and, if they were to have their freedom, I doubt their making good use of it. . . .

Last night our regiment, on dress parade, were called to vote on a series of resolutions that were drawn up by the field officers of the Illinois regiments in the 15th Army Corps, concerning the action of THE CHICAGO TIMES and all those that ask for an armistice, denouncing them as traitors. In favor [of] said resolutions one third of our men voted, and when asked if any were opposed to them, not a man moved. Our Colonel considered it a unanimous vote, and it will probably be so termed by the papers; but by officers and men it is considered to the contrary. The two thirds that did not vote for them must be against them. They are brave, true soldiers,—true to the Union, and true to the constitution as it was,—but tired of this abolition crusade. They are willing to endorse the peace resolutions of the North.

Printed anonymously in *Chicago Times*, March 9, 1863.

JOSEPH MEDILL WARNS OF RESISTANCE TO THE DRAFT

Writing to President Lincoln, Joseph Medill, Republican owner of the Chicago Tribune, *worries about the draft's political consequences in Illinois. In the second half of the letter, Medill urges the swift organization of black regiments and reveals his goals for Illinois's Union Leagues.*

Willard's Hotel [Washington, DC]
May 15, 1863

President Lincoln

Not having either time or inclination to hang round waiting rooms among a wolfish crowd seeking admission to your presence for office or contracts or personal favors, I prefer stating in writing the substance of what I would say verbally.

Your army is melting away rapidly by battle, disease and expiration of term of service, and there is great delay in putting the conscription act into effect. The hot weather is at hand, to be followed by the sickly season.

The act itself will not furnish you with soldiers if you construe the 13th sec. as obligatory on the Gov't to receive $300. commu[t]ation for personal service. You will get but few men under it, and they will consist of the poor, penniless, soulless, ragged loafer class who have neither credit, money, or stake in the perpetuity of the union. The attempt to enforce [the bill's commutation clause] will do your administration immense harm and cause it to [lose] all the state elections next fall. The copper-heads are gloating over the prospective harvest of votes they will reap against a bill that "puts the rich man's dirty dollars against a poor man's life."

A law ought to be construed in harmony with its obvious purpose. The conscript act is not a revenue measure, but a law to raise *men*. What is the Sec of War to do with twenty or thirty millions of dollars that may be paid over to his agents? They are under no bond nor is he. What is to be done with the money? The law makes no provision, except that it is received for the *"procuration of such substitute"*

I contend that the Sec of War is not bound to receive any conscripts money unless he has a substitute standing ready to receive it and to take the conscripts musket. If you put this construction on the law you have plain and safe sailing. You will get exactly as many men as you call for—either as conscripts or substitutes. The country will sustain that construction of the law. . . .

The country is impatient at the slow progress making in raising colored regiments. The blacks of our State are clamorous for the privilege of raising a regiment. So they are in Ind, so in Ohio. If you would give commissions in the West to white officers they would raise in the Western free states, in Missouri and West Tennessee ten to fifteen thousand able bodied, robust and brave colored soldiers. The opposition to colored soldiers has passed away. The Republicans are all loudly for them, and the Democrats have withdrawn their opposition. A hundred regiments of blacks can be raised between Chicago and New Orleans if you will resolve to have them. Transportation and rations ought to be provided for each colored volunteer as soon as he takes the Oath. If blacks are to be used at all why not let the Union cause have the full benefit of their powerful aid? The war is dragging too slowly. It is now in the *third* year. Twelve months hence we shall be in the midst of another presidential struggle. If the copperheads elect their ticket all the fruits of this bloody and costly war will go for naught; all will be undone and the plans and policy of the rebels will achieve perfect triumph. The value of time and concentration of our armies I fear are not sufficiently appreciated.

In order to rally the Union sentiment and prepare for the great Presidential struggle I have organized a Union League somewhat secret in its action but at the same time strictly patriotic. I wrote the *ritual,* and the forms and devised most of the signs, and set it going. I have worked hard and zealously on it for eight months. It is now spreading in every state. There are 4,000 members in this city, and there are 75,000 in Illinois. A national convention of my calling, meets in Cleveland on the 20th inst. With any sort of decent success on the part of the army the League will keep the people up to the support of the administration. My labors and services may not be appreciated by you now, but no matter; if the union is saved the rebellion crushed and the principles of liberty established I will be content, and die happy.

Very Truly Yours

J. Medill . . .

Joseph Medill to Abraham Lincoln, May 15, 1863, Abraham Lincoln Papers, Library of Congress, Washington, DC.

GOVERNOR YATES PROROGUES THE STATE LEGISLATURE

In June 1863, Governor Yates stunned Illinoisans by announcing that he was proroguing the General Assembly. Yates felt threatened by the legislature's moves to control military spending, viewed the Peace Resolutions as a shameful embarrassment to the state, and feared that if allowed to continue, Democratic lawmakers would further encourage opposition to the Union war effort, of primary concern at a moment when officials were hoping to meet the state's quota for volunteers without resort to a draft. The proroguing order itself was brief and cast in dry legal language, but its political effect sent shock waves across Illinois. In response, Democratic assemblymen signed a formal protest, excerpted here.

Upon this 10th day of June, A. D. 1863, the general assembly being in session and engaged in the discharge of their constitutional duties, an attempt by the governor of Illinois was made to dissolve this body; which attempt, illegal, unconstitutional and outrageous as it is, must inevitably result in the cessation of any further legislation at this time. . . .

By this action [Governor Yates] has deliberately and designedly defeated the passage of measures of great public importance, and demanded by the exigencies of the times.

He has defeated the appropriation of one hundred thousand dollars for the gallant sons of Illinois, who are bleeding and dying upon the battle-field and in the hospital, and whose terrible condition invites the sympathy of every human heart, and demands the earnest effort in their behalf of every citizen of the state on which they have shed imperishable glory. The bill for that purpose, already passed both houses, and pending simply upon a slight difference of opinion as to some of its details, in the lower house, which difference has now been happily removed, is defeated merely because the miserable partisanship of the chief executive, who usurps the unmerited title of the "soldier's friend," prevented him from consenting that a legislature having a majority of his political opponents should have the honor, as they would enjoy the privilege, of flying to the rescue of their gallant brethren. . . .

He has defeated the passage of the general appropriation bills already passed [in] the senate, and pending in the house, and ready for passage, which the senate had acted on without delay, and to which no obstruction was intended to be, would or could have been, interposed by the house.

He has defeated the printing of the report of the State Agricultural Society, an appropriation for which had passed house and was on its passage in the senate, and the distribution of the appropriation for agricultural purposes made by the general government, and as yet unapplied to the ends for which it was intended, to the great detriment of the vast agricultural interests of Illinois, for whose benefit these measures were intended.

He has defeated the appropriation for the State Normal University; the property will be sold under the existing judgments, and this noble institution be destroyed.

The memory of the great dead [Union soldiers] could not restrain him, and the appropriation for the erection of a monument to Douglas receives its death blow at his hands. . . .

He has done all this without the shadow of a legal pretext, and in defiance of a well-nigh universal public opinion.

Even partisanship affords no palliation for the pursuit of such a course, since no political measure has been pressed upon either branch of the assembly during the recent period of its session. Which is the more guilty, the individual who proposes, or the wretched agents who carry into effect an act so utterly indefensible, it is not for us to determine. It is sufficient that all the actors, aiders and abettors of this scheme to block the wheels of government, will receive the condemnation they deserve from an outraged people. . . .

Reprinted in *Illinois State Register* (Springfield), June 11, 1863.

ARMING THE RESISTANCE

Throughout 1863, Brigadier General Jacob Ammen, commander of the District of Illinois, received alarming reports of organized copperhead activity in the state. Reports written to him and his staff document the breadth and character of the copperhead movement in Illinois.

Springfield, Ill. April 24th, 1863

Brig. Gen. J. Ammen;

I have the honor to submit to you the following report—In pursuance of Special Order no. 2 from your hdqrs. I proceeded to Salem, Ill. I found Dr. Wm.

White a man of influence, and apparently of honor, though undoubtedly a *dangerous traitor.*

As per order I arrested him, not without some difficulty. As I saw it was creating considerable excitement among his townsmen, many of whom as I was reliably informed said he should not be taken from the place, and as he offered to go quietly, and peaceably if I would allow him a parole of the place till morning that he might provide for his family, and prepare to go, I gave him a parole till 9 ½ oclock next morning, (Apr. 23rd) which parole he has violated, and could not be found.

I think he is concealed in the town and accordingly left Sergt. Robert Tilkins with instructions to remain concealed while some loyal men are watching for him (White); to keep track of him if found, and report it to you, and to take him if he found a good opportunity, proceed at once to "Hdqrs. Dept. of Ohio," and return to Camp Butler—I ascertained that secret organizations known as K.G.C's [Knights of the Golden Circle] were numerous, and evidently organized for disloyal purposes—

Inflammatory speeches are made, incendiary periodicals, and publications are circulated, and threats of the destruction of the property, and the death of Loyal persons, are so rife as to excite in them apprehensions of alarm, and members of loyal citizens have been driven from their homes. Prominent men are scouring the country holding meetings of secret societies almost nightly, and often daily.

In numerous instances which can be proven they have counceled resistance to the enforcement of the laws, characterized the Govt. as "Damned and Doomed," as "No Govt," &c &c; and its acts as a "crusade to free the negro and enslave the white man,"—These utterances are exciting the people to overt acts of disloyalty, weakening the Govt. in that district, and are the results of the incessant labors of a few bad men to undermine the Govt.

Against several of them I think I have collected ample evidence to cause their arrest—among them J. W. and E. L. Messitt [Merritt], Editors of a paper called "The Advocate," three copies of which I enclose are prominent—The article headed "The conscription" in the No. dated March 19th is certainly full of disloyalty—One of them is a Lawyer, and says he will resist conscription, and also that he "would rather put down Abe Lincoln, than Jeff Davis" if he had the power—The K.G.C's meet for drill, armed, and people are turned back from the roads on which they are drilling by armed guards. . . .

James E. Moss
1st. Lt. 58th Ill. Vols.

Jacob Ammen Papers, Manuscripts, Abraham Lincoln Presidential Library, Springfield.

Head Quarters
Camp Manchester
Scott County—ILL
Nov- 28- 1863-

W.P. Ammen—
Capt. & A-A- Gen'l -
District of Ill.—

Captain:

In accordance with your instructions I have the honor to submit the following report. . . .

Friday morning [Captain William Fry, provost marshal, Tenth Military District of Illinois] receive[d] intelligence of a large band of lawless men and deserters and bushwhackers from Mo. having collected in the S. W. Corner of Cass County and were threatening to make a raid upon Jacksonville to burn the city, Masacre some of the Union men and to pillage. Thereupon he requested me to send a part of my force at White Hall to Jacksonville to protect his office and render assistance to the constituted authorities in repelling any attack. I immediately ordered Cap't Saunders of the 10th Minnesota Vol. to proceed there with 53 men with full instructions a copy of which I herewith transmit.

In conclusion Captain I will remark that from the best of evidence collected by Cap't Fry and myself after several days of carefree investigation I can assure you that 1st—There is a large organization of traitorous and desperate men extending through the central and southern portions of this state. 2nd—These men are quite well drilled by deserters and recruiting officers from the so called Southern Confederacy, but are porrly armed with rifles and shot guns and revolvers. They are also mounted or have horses many of which have been stolen. 3rd—The outbreak in Scott & Green Counties referred to above was premature and hence their trying to keep out of the way of U.S. troops.
4th They are expecting 20,000 Enfield rifles within one month and when received they design serious mischief
5th They have Company, Regimental and Brigade organizations with Captains—Colonels—and Generals.
6th Their leader lives in Chicago, Ill, once they have other Generals living in other parts of the state.
7th The ostensible object of this organization is to protect deserters from arrest and to forceably resist any draft, but I have good reason to believe that the real

object is to bring upon the Southern & Central portions of this state, the same system of Guerrilla warfare lately prevailing in Mo. Ky. and Tenn. And that the head leaders are in the confidence and pay of Jeff Davis.

I have captured 35 prisoners, 22 of whom were armed deserters 35 arms, 3 or 4 revolvers and several horses. Some of the arms were Springfield and Enfield Rifled Muskets but most of them were squirrel rifles and double barreled shot guns loaded with buck shot. All the prisoners have been sent to Camp Butler, Ill.

Do not be surprised, Capt. at these views from me,

You know that I am no alarmist. I assure you I am only giving you my candid opinion based upon a close investigation of the whole subject After carefully questioning separately all the men taken by me in arms, and others, who becoming frightened by the prompt and earnest efforts put forth by you to punish this lawlessness have abandoned the organization and have reluctantly made admissions which point to this state of facts. . . .

Geo. R. Clarke
St. Col. 113 Regt. Ill. Vol. Inf.
Comd'g. U.S. Forces at Manchester, Ill.

Jacob Ammen Papers, Manuscripts, Abraham Lincoln Presidential Library, Springfield.

DIVIDED NEIGHBORHOODS

In places where copperheadism was strong, Illinois Unionists faced verbal harassment, physical intimidation, and sometimes worse. Letters from ordinary Illinoisans offer further evidence on the copperhead movement in Illinois and suggest as well how the war's battle lines were drawn through the heart of Illinois's communities.

Anna, Union Co. Ill. Apr 23/63

Gen Ammen
Springfield, Ill

Dear Sir

As a loyal and law abiding citizen of Illinois I appeal to you for protection from the depredations of secession traitors as malignant and vile as any in the rebel army. I am a poor man a fruit grower and my rebel neighbors have destroyed my fruit trees (400 very fine ones) they throw down my fences and annoy me in various ways because as they say "my politics don't suit" I am a "d—d Lincolnite" and they say they intend to drive me out of the neighborhood. Some 10 valuable orchards have been destroyed, horses have been poisoned, fences thrown down and various other depredations have been perpetrated within the past 3 months in this county and good union men among our best and most intelligent citizens have in every instance been the sufferers. Now what are we to do? Must we tamely submit to those vile miscreants and allow them to destroy our property, to *insult* us daily as we meet them on the public roads? Union men like myself who live remote from a village and entirely surrounded by these traitors are *much* worse off than union men in towns.

Deserters are plenty here, very bold and also very annoying.

I should be glad to give a list of the vilest rebels in this locality and also give what testimony I can concerning their loyalty.

Such persecution as some of the loyal men of this county have suffered cannot be endured much longer. If we do not get *aid* of some kind we must leave our homes or attempt to retaliate.

Yours Respectfully
A. Babcock

Jacob Ammen Papers, Manuscripts, Abraham Lincoln Presidential Library, Springfield.

State of Illinois Shelby County Tower Hill May 23 [1863]

To General Ammen commanding at Springfield, Illinois I here enclose to you the names & Residents of two home Traitoresses one Elizabeth Millican & one Mary Ann Sphar both [are] Residents of Shelby County & are sisters & are living about five Miles south of Tower Hill Shelby County[.] the said persons did on the 21 day of May AD 1863 Make use of disloyal Language in a company & I assume the Priviledge of siting them to your notice & I will give you some of there conversation & also the names of those Present that heard the conversation[.] the above named Elizabeth Millican did say that she wished that if the Govenor sent Soldiers to help take the deserters the Soldiers would get there devlish black Brains but out & she said she wanted the south to whip & Jeff Davis to Rule over the north she said the war was not to save the union but it was to free the Nigroes & that old Abe Lincoln was as black as hell in Principle & that he had no men but Nigroes & then when interrogated she said that if A Democrat got sick in the Army he was not Doctored nor cared for but if a black Abolitionist got sick they was cared for & sent home & she said she did not believe that there was a drop of honest blood in the veins of any Abolitionist; when she said she wanted Jeff Davis to rule some of the women told her we would send her South & she said she dared them to send her south she said she had A home of her own & she would stay at it

& say what she pleased I told her that I would Report her[.] her sister Mary Ann Sphar used similar Language on the same day May the 21 AD 1863 & the said Mary Ann Sphar said to some of the women that if I Reported them that I would soon be under the sod if I had friends enough to bury me or whoever would report them . . . now general I beg of you not to think because this comes from A woman that it is not worth notice[.] it is more than I can bare to here sutch as to have all my sons in the Army defending there countrys cause[.] now general if it is not your duty to Attend to traitors in Illinois you know whose it is & you will Please bee so good as to send it to the proper ones to have it attended to

This from a truly loyal woman yours &c
Hannah Throne

Jacob Ammen Papers, Manuscripts, Abraham Lincoln Presidential Library, Springfield.

MARY LOGAN DEFENDS A CONTRABAND

Mary Logan, wife of Democratic Party leader General John A. Logan, spent the war living in southern Illinois, where her husband had built a loyal political following. Here she engaged in relief work for wounded soldiers, helped supply a hospital at Cairo, and regularly traveled to Marion and Carbondale both to socialize with friends and to gauge local opinion, always with a keen eye on her husband's political reputation. Indeed Mary acted as one of John's closest political advisers before, during, and after the war, and influenced his later conversion to Republican stalwart. Long an opponent of slavery, Mary watched carefully the unfolding drama of emancipation and the turbulence it generated in southern Illinois. Here she describes her battle with local white prejudice.

The [contrabands] providentially supplied the places of the men who were in the army. In my own case I blessed the day when they came to southern Illinois, because before that I had been, with the assistance of my companion and friend, Miss Mary E. Tuthill, obliged to play the part of man and maid of all work, feeding, currying, and caring for the animals in the barn-yard, harnessing and driving the horses, washing the buggies and carriages, and performing every species of manual labor necessary to be done, at the same time trying to help others more dependent and timid. Besides this we had to protect ourselves from annoying persecutions inflicted by the senseless sympathizers with the rebellion who were too cowardly to go South and cast their lot with the people for whom they professed so much sympathy.

One day Miss Tuthill and I were driving we passed a colored man who sat under a tree beside the road wondering where he should go for a home, food, and clothing. Our "copperhead" rulers of the community had forbidden negroes to stop in that part of the country. I was unable to secure the services of a man servant, and was about as desperate as poor "Albert" as he sat there, an exile and a wanderer. I stopped the horse I was driving and asked the poor fellow what he was doing there and where he was going. He timidly replied: "I ain't doin' nuffin,' Miss, and God knows I doesn't know whar to go. Bless de Lord, I would be glad to get sumfin' to do, an' be 'lowed to stay sumwhar."

I told him that I wished to hire a man to work for me, and if he would come with me I would build him a little house in my yard; that if he would work and obey me, taking care of my cattle, horses, and garden, I would pay him fifteen dollars a month and give him his board. . . .

Not long after it was noised about that "John Logan's wife has hired a nigger to work for her, and he is on the place to stay." They resolved that he should not do so, and that "if she did not send him away, they would go there, and send him off in a jiffy, and if she interfered to protect him, they would thrash her too."

A member of the secret organization known as the Knights of the Golden Circle, who kept up their warfare and made trouble for every Unionist, had been raised with me, and while he was intensely disloyal to his country he was the soul of honor and loyalty to his friends. He knew I would try to protect the colored man when they should attack him, and he could not bear the thought of any harm coming to me. So he came to me, begging that I send the "darky" away, warning me there would be trouble if I persisted in keeping him, because they were "not going to let the country be filled up with niggers." I thought of the matter long and seriously. It seemed so outrageous that men in a free land would undertake, by mob violence, to decide who should and who should not live in a country that I was inclined to test the question and see whether or not these men, avowed enemies of the nation, should dictate to loyal people what they should or should not do. . . .

So I told my friend James Durham that, while I appreciated beyond expression his friendship and warning, I must be frank enough to tell him I intended to keep the man and protect him to the best of my ability. . . . [I also told him] that if Durham would trust me still further by telling me who was going to take part in the dastardly deed of maltreating an inoffensive creature who had never even seen them I would under no circumstances betray him, but that I would make them afraid to come on my premises or to harm the negro. After some hesitancy he told me the names of the men who proposed for the society. . . .

I waited patiently that day for one of the men, whom I knew must pass my house going into and out of the town. As soon as I spied him coming down the road on his way to town I walked out to my front gate and called him, asking him if he would not come in a moment as I desired to see him on a matter of business. He was much embarrassed, but came in. I at once told him that I had been informed by a member of the "Circle" all about their proposed attack upon the colored man in my employ; that I was sorry to hear he was one of the most active parties in the matter; that I had a vivid recollection of having accommodated him in many ways by loaning him my horses, farming-utensils, wagons, etc.; that I should be sorry to cause his arrest and imprisonment, but I had made up my mind to single him out as the one person whom I should hold responsible for the welfare of the colored man. I told him if the colored man was molested in any way I should cause his arrest, and I thought I could prove that he had made threats of violence, not only to the man, but to me personally if I tried to protect Albert; that Miss Tuthill, the colored man, and myself were splendid shots; that we practiced daily the use of firearms; that we had a sort of arsenal for our protection; and that the slightest intrusion on the premises would be greeted with a volley from the house and from the darky's quarters near by. The frequent change of color in his face betrayed his guilt in the matter, but of course he protested innocence of any knowledge of anything of the kind and avowed his willingness to protect the "nigger" for me. . . .

My friend reported to me afterward that at the next meeting of the "Circle" the fellow told them it would never do to trouble that "nigger" at John Logan's house, because he had found out that Mrs. Logan had heard about what they had talked of doing; that all their names were now in the hands of officers; that if anything was to happen to the "nigger" he was certain they would all be arrested and soldiers would be stationed there to protect Logan's family; therefore, they had better let the "nigger" alone. They did, and we kept the man long after General Logan's return home after the war, till Albert desired to go South to hunt up his family. . . .

Mrs. John A. Logan, *Reminiscences of a Soldier's Wife: An Autobiography* (New York: C. Scriber's Sons, 1913; Carbondale: Southern Illinois University Press, 1997), 147–51.

OF PROMISES MADE AND PROMISES KEPT—THE CONKLING LETTER

In August 1863, Springfield's James C. Conkling invited Lincoln to speak at a large Union League rally in support of the administration's policies. The president could not leave Washington, but he carefully crafted a lengthy letter for Conkling to read to the mass meeting. Historians consider the so-called Conkling letter the embattled president's formal response to his Democratic critics. Here Lincoln brilliantly exploits weaknesses in the peace movement's positions and simultaneously clarifies and ennobles the Union's cause.

Executive Mansion,
Washington, August 26, 1863.

Hon. James C. Conkling

My Dear Sir.
Your letter inviting me to attend a mass-meeting of unconditional Union-men, to be held at the Capitol of Illinois, on the 3d day of September, has been received.

It would be very agreeable to me, to thus meet my old friends, at my own home; but I can not, just now, be absent from here, so long as a visit there, would require.

The meeting is to be of all those who maintain unconditional devotion to the Union; and I am sure my old political friends will thank me for tendering, as I do, the nation's gratitude to those other noble men, whom no partizan malice, or partizan hope, can make false to the nation's life.

There are those who are dissatisfied with me. To such I would say: You desire peace; and you blame me that we do not have it. But how can we attain it? There are but three conceivable ways. First, to suppress the rebellion by force of arms. This I am trying to do. Are you for it? If you are, so far we are agreed. If you are not for it, a second way is to give up the Union. I am against this. Are you for it? If you are, you should say so plainly. If you are not for *force*, nor yet for *dissolution*, there only remains some imaginable *compromise*. I do not believe any compromise, embracing the maintenance of the Union, is now possible. All I learn, leads to a directly opposite belief. The strength of the rebellion, is its military—its army. That army dominates all the country, and all the people, within its range. . . . A compromise, to be effective, must be made either with those who control the rebel army, or with the people first liberated from the domination of that army, by the success of our own army. Now allow me to assure you, that no word or intimation, from that rebel army, or from any of the men controlling it, in relation to any peace compromise, has ever come to my knowledge or belief. All charges and insinuations to the contrary, are deceptive and groundless. And I promise you, that if any such proposition shall hereafter come, it shall not be rejected, and kept a secret from you. I freely acknowledge myself the servant of the people, according to the bond of service—the United States Constitution; and that, as such, I am responsible to them.

But to be plain, you are dissatisfied with me about the negro. Quite likely there is a difference of opinion between you and myself upon that subject. I certainly wish that all men could be free, while I suppose you do not. Yet I have neither adopted, nor proposed any measure, which is not consistent with even your view, provided you are for the Union. I suggested compensated emancipation; to which you replied you wished not to be taxed to buy negroes. But I had not asked you to be taxed to buy negroes, except in such a way, as to save you from greater taxation to save the Union exclusively by other means.

You dislike the emancipation proclamation; and, perhaps, would have it retracted. You say it is unconstitutional—I think differently. I think the constitution invests its Commander-in-chief, with the law of war, in time of war. The most that can be said, if so much, is, that slaves are property. Is there—has there ever been—any question that by the law of war, property, both of enemies and friends, may be taken when needed? And is it not needed whenever taking it, helps us, or hurts the enemy? . . .

But the proclamation, as law, either is valid, or is not valid. If it is not valid, it needs no retraction. If it is valid, it can not be retracted, any more than the dead can be brought to life. Some of you profess to think its retraction would operate favorably for the Union. Why better *after* the retraction, than *before* the issue? There was more than a year and a half of trial to suppress the rebellion before the proclamation issued, the last one hundred days of which passed under an explicit notice that it was coming, unless averted by those in revolt, returning to their allegiance. The war has certainly progressed as favorably for us, since the issue of the proclamation as before. I know, as fully as one can know the opinion of others, that some of the commanders of our armies in the field who have given us our most important successes believe the emancipation policy and the use of the colored troops constitute the heaviest blow yet dealt to the Rebellion, and that at least one of these important successes could not have been achieved when it was but for the aid of black soldiers. Among the commanders holding these views are some of who have never had any affinity with what is called abolitionism or with the Republican party policies but who held them purely as military opinions. I submit these opinions as being entitled to some weight against the objections often urged that emancipation and arming the blacks are unwise as military measures and were not adopted as such in good faith.

You say you will not fight to free negroes. Some of them seem willing to fight for you; but, no matter. Fight you, then, exclusively to save the Union. I issued the proclamation on purpose to aid you in saving the Union. Whenever you shall have conquered all resistance to the Union, if I shall urge you to continue fighting, it will be apt time, then, for you to declare you will not fight to free negroes.

I thought that in your struggle for the Union, to whatever extent the negroes should cease helping the enemy, to that extent it weakened the enemy in his resistance to you. Do you think differently? I thought that whatever negroes can be got to do as soldiers, leaves just so much less for white soldiers to do, in saving the Union. Does it appear otherwise to you? But negroes, like other people, act upon motives. Why should they do any thing for us, if we will do nothing for them? If they stake their lives for us, they must be prompted by the strongest motive—even the promise of freedom. And the promise being made, must be kept. . . .

Peace does not appear so distant as it did. I hope it will come soon, and come to stay; and so come as to be worth the keeping in all future time. It will then have been proved that, among free men, there can be no successful appeal from the ballot to the bullet; and that they who take such appeal are sure to lose their case, and pay the cost. And then, there will be some black men who can remember that, with silent tongue, and clenched teeth, and steady eye, and well-poised bayonet, they have helped mankind on to this great consummation; while, I fear, there will be some white ones, unable to forget that, with malignant heart, and deceitful speech, they strove to hinder it.

Still, let us not be over-sanguine of a speedy final triumph. Let us be quite sober. Let us diligently apply the means, never doubting that a just God, in his own good time, will give us the rightful result.

Yours very truly
A. Lincoln.

Abraham Lincoln, *Abraham Lincoln: His Speeches and Writings*, ed. Roy P. Basler (Cleveland: World Publishing, 1946), 720–24.

SIX

The Soldiers' War

*M*ORE THAN 259,000 Illinoisans—about 15 percent of the state's population—served in the Civil War, and of those, nearly 35,000 lost their lives. Approximately 10,000 died in battle or later as a result of wounds; the many diseases that
swept through filthy encampments and unsanitary hospitals claimed the rest. Tens
of thousands more survived with permanent wounds or missing limbs, and no
veteran escaped the war's emotional and psychological effects. "You can form no
conception of what a battlefield looks like," wrote one Illinois soldier after wit-
nessing the dead and wounded at Fort Donelson. "No pen and ink description can
give you anything like a true idea of it."[1] The haunting experience of a fratricidal
war wrought an indelible imprint, both physical and emotional, on individual enlistees and on friends and loved ones back home. The nation's bloodiest war left
no one untouched.

Illinois soldiers ascribed a variety of purposes to the war and therefore to their
sacrifices. To be sure, all hoped to crush rebellion and restore constitutional government. For the state's recent immigrants, fighting for the Union made concrete
their sense of belonging in their new country. "Would I still be worthy of living in
this land, enjoying this freedom," Friedrich Martens of the Sixth Illinois Infantry
asked his family back in Germany, "if I were not also willing to fight for this freedom, and if need be, to die for it?"[2] As Union goals shifted over time, moreover, so
too did the perspective of many soldiers. Many fought bravely for the Union but
were dubious of emancipation. Such opposition could threaten morale, and in extreme cases led to desertion or mutiny among some soldiers. Nearly 20 percent of
the 109th Illinois Infantry, a regiment composed almost exclusively of men from
Union County, deserted in the wake of the Emancipation Proclamation. Following
a series of military arrests, investigations, and hearings, the 109th was exonerated
of charges of disloyalty. But in February 1863 eight of its officers were found guilty
and discharged. One of these was Adjutant James Evans, who returned to Union
County and reassumed his editorship of the notorious copperhead newspaper the
Jonesboro Gazette. In April 1863 the 128th Illinois Infantry, a regiment from mostly
Williamson and Grundy Counties, was simply disbanded after 70 percent of its
soldiers and officers abandoned their posts in protest of emancipation. However,

other Illinois soldiers embraced antislavery goals from the outset, and many more over time came to accept and indeed venerate emancipation. In the end, despite the great variety of political and cultural outlooks held by Illinois soldiers, all who fought did so with a deep emotional commitment to the men in their regiment, and to the communities from which those regiments came.

Illinois regiments naturally reflected the diversity of the state and its people. Nineteenth-century gender ideology emphasized courage, honor, and duty among men, which partly explains why only a small fraction of Illinois soldiers experienced the "shame" of being drafted into service. Regiments nearly always consisted of volunteers from the same area of the state, and the companies that comprised those regiments frequently came from the same county or even town or neighborhood. As a result, those who stayed home identified strongly with their town's unit and saw its successes and failures as a reflection of local initiative. The 100th Illinois Infantry was dubbed the Will County Regiment after authorities there raised $60,000 in bounties to raise a local regiment; Fulton County residents undertook similar efforts to raise the 103rd. "It is for the interest of every man to join a home company, even if he does not get half the bounty he could in some other localities," explained a typical editorial exhorting men to volunteer, "because he is then with his old friends and neighbors, who will take more interest in his welfare than any newly made acquaintances possibly can do."[3] In addition to local ties, enlistees could also share ethnic or occupational bonds. The Thirty-Third mostly comprised college students enrolled at the Illinois State Normal School, near Bloomington. The Forty-Fifth, dubbed the Lead Mine Regiment, attracted mostly miners from Galena and its environs. The Twenty-Third, organized by the Chicago Irish attorney James Mulligan and known as the Irish Brigade, attracted Irish immigrants from Chicago as well as Wayne, Grundy, and LaSalle Counties. The Eighty-Second was Hecker's Regiment, named for the Lebanon farmer Colonel Friedrich Hecker, a proud and fiery leader of the 1848 revolutionary uprisings in Baden, Germany. One of Illinois's three German regiments, the Eighty-Second also included immigrants from Switzerland, Scandinavia, France, and Bohemia. In August 1862, as the Eighty-Second was forming, leaders of Chicago's Jewish enclave met and pledged their "sincere attachment to this land of our choice," resolving to raise $10,000 for the purpose of organizing a company.[4] This became the Eighty-Second's Company C, made up of Jewish Chicagoans from Germany and Poland. Close knit and familiar, the typical Illinois regiment faced the hardships of service with a high level of camaraderie to be expected when friends and neighbors, relatives and colleagues, came together in shared sacrifice.

But that camaraderie was also at times fragile. The ebb and flow of the war's progress could take its toll on unit cohesion and morale. Then too, those who initially volunteered out of a combination of patriotism, adventure, and personal advancement increasingly came to understand the hard realities of war: prolonged separation from loved ones, spartan living conditions, dreadful meals, endless marches, long periods of inactivity and boredom punctuated by sudden battles and the suffering and death of comrades. To cope, Illinois soldiers—like soldiers everywhere—chose a variety of outlets and diversions. Some turned to religion. Others escaped through drink, gambling, and the brothels that opened for business wherever the armies camped. Many passed the time by foraging for food and creature comforts among Confederate civilians, an activity that became more frequent and purposeful over time. But one constant in the soldier's life were the letters, both written and received. Illinois boasted a literacy rate of 95 percent, and correspondence with friends and loved ones back home formed a vital, ongoing component of the soldier's war. As one Illinois soldier described the excitement of writing to his wife, "My Dear I am lost for words, being so delighted to have an opportunity to write you once more. You would think the camp was a large School every man with a piece of paper on his knee writing to his friends."[5]

In the first months of the war relatively few Illinois soldiers saw action, mostly in minor battles or skirmishes in Missouri. Beginning in early 1862, however, Illinois soldiers took center stage in the western theater. The state supplied 177 generals to the Union army, including Benjamin Grierson, John Logan, John McClernand, Benjamin Prentiss, and W. H. L. Wallace, all of whom won praise as capable field commanders. But one general distinguished himself above all others. When the war came few would have predicted greatness for an obscure thirty-nine-year-old living in Galena and clerking at his father's tannery. Born in Ohio, Ulysses S. Grant enrolled in West Point as a teenager, graduating in the bottom half of his class. He showed promise during the Mexican War, but squandered it while posted in California and Washington Territory when he turned to drink to fight off the boredom of post life and the melancholy of being separated from his family. He resigned from the military in 1854. He then failed at several civilian endeavors—farming, retailing, and real estate. The Civil War gave Grant another chance. He volunteered and soon was training and supplying regiments as an assistant quartermaster general. Among a relative few with extensive military experience at the start of the war, Grant rose quickly up the chain of command in Illinois, first as colonel of the Twenty-First Illinois, then as brigadier general in charge of federal forces based at Cairo. From here Grant, under command of General Henry Halleck, drew up plans for an offensive into the heart of the western Confederacy, supported by Union gunboats on the Cumberland and Tennessee Rivers. In February 1862, Grant led Union forces to victory at Forts Henry and Donelson, where he earned the nickname Unconditional Surrender Grant. Next Nashville, Tennessee, fell to Grant. Meanwhile another Illinois general, John Pope, moved forces down the Mississippi River, securing still more territory for the Union. Grant's offensive met its stiffest challenge near Pittsburg Landing, Tennessee, when Albert Sidney Johnston's army attacked in April 1862.

The famous battle of Shiloh that ensued was the largest and bloodiest encounter of the war up to that point, and the most important Union victory of the war's first year. No state sent more regiments into battle at Shiloh than Illinois (28 of 65 Union regiments engaged), and no state suffered more casualties (nearly 4,500). The murderous loss of life at Shiloh shocked and sobered Illinoisans and indeed the nation, but it also proved that Grant was a fighter, in contrast to more cautious commanders—such as George McClellan—back east. Indeed, with the victory at Shiloh Grant had seized the initiative in the West, and he never relinquished it.

In 1863 Grant set his sights on Vicksburg, the last Confederate stronghold on the Mississippi River. By mid-May his Army of the Tennessee, which included some twenty thousand Illinoisans, approximately 30 percent of Grant's forces, surrounded the city. Vicksburg's surrender, on July 4, came just one day after Lee's defeat at Gettysburg; the two nearly simultaneous victories proved to be the war's great turning point. Grant had cut the Confederacy in two, while Lee's legendary Army of Northern Virginia was never the same after Gettysburg. Grant's aggressive campaigning won him overall command of Union forces in the western theater, which now started moving eastward toward the seat of rebellion. In November, Illinois units again played a prominent role in Grant's offensive at Missionary Ridge and Chattanooga, Tennessee. Lincoln, convinced that he had at last found the general who could end the war, now made Grant lieutenant general of all Union forces, a position previously held by only one other, George Washington.

In 1864 Grant, along with his friend and trusted lieutenant General William Tecumseh Sherman, unleashed the full might of the Union military. But it came at enormous cost. In Virginia, Grant ran up unprecedented casualties in his pursuit of Lee's diminished yet still determined army, again raising frustration on the home front. Meanwhile, Sherman's forces, which included nearly eighty battle-hardened infantry, cavalry, and artillery units from Illinois, maneuvered to destroy Joseph Johnston's army, dug in outside Atlanta. In the war's last great breakthrough, Sherman took Atlanta in September, set it ablaze, and then marched eastward to the sea, along the way liberating thousands of slaves and visiting destruction on the Confederate countryside. Total war had arrived.

"YOUR SON IS A SOLDIER IN AMERICA"

At age nineteen Friedrich Martens migrated from Delve, in northern Germany, and settled in Joliet in 1857. There Martens apparently struggled to find reliable work. He took odd jobs as a painter, bartender, and teacher before moving to Peoria in 1860. Despite being a Democrat, Martens enthusiastically answered Lincoln's initial call for troops, joining Company E, Sixth Illinois Infantry—a company that brought together many of the area's German population. After his three-month term ended, Martens reenlisted in the Seventeenth Missouri Infantry, another unit with large numbers of Illinois and Missouri Germans, seeing action at Pea Ridge, Arkansas, and the siege of Vicksburg. In letters to his parents back in Germany, Martens conveys his reasons for becoming a soldier.

[letterhead] Second Brigade, Sixth Division, Seventh Regiment, ILLINOIS VOLUNTEER MILITIA / Camp Defiance,

Cairo, Ill., June 15, 1861

My dear ones,

. . . . As you probably already know, a civil war has broken out in this free country. I don't have the space or the time to explain all about the cause, only this much: the states that are rebelling are slave states, and they want slavery to be expanded, but the northern states are against this, and so it's civil war! I also followed the drums when the first call to arms went out through the land. All volunteers, 250,000 men have taken up arms against the rebels, and if the government had wanted a million men they would have been there.

I've been in the field for 9 weeks now, life is very bad. Haven't been out of my clothes for 9 weeks, a little bit of straw for a bed, bread and meat for food, and on top of it the great heat doesn't make it any more pleasant. But it's a sacred cause, and so we don't feel the hardship. . . .

Peoria, August 24, 1861.

My dear ones,

. . . . Your son is a soldier! *Yes*, parents, your son is a soldier in America.—and the fact that this letter is being written in Peoria is because I took a week of leave to take care of some business. As you have probably already read in the newspapers, a revolution has broken out in this beautiful free country, and it is of such dimensions that all our forces must be roused to secure freedom, to crush the revolution.

We now have 400,000 men in the field, and our enemy has almost as many. But I must tell you briefly about the main cause of this horrible war; as you know, in our southern states, slavery exists in all its atrociousness, so in order to crush and stamp this out, last fall the northern men elected a president from the party with an antislavery policy, and then they passed some laws that were not to the advantage of the slaveholders, and the revolution began. Now, father, I'd like to know what you'd think of a son who stayed at home when the enemy was at the door, making war on freedom, suppressing the freedom we paid so dearly for. Would I still be worthy of living in this land, enjoying this freedom, if I were not also willing to fight for this freedom, and if need be, to die for it? Oh, I know my freedom-loving father, I know he will say I am right, for now he finally has a true reason to be proud of his son! And dear father, if it please the dear Lord to let me die on the *field of honor*, then you must also have enough strength to comfort my dear mother, and you will tell her and anyone else that your son couldn't have died a better death!

I also want to tell you that in the North no one is forced to become a soldier, instead the entire enormous army consists of volunteers, more evidence that the cause we're fighting for must be sacred! I signed up the first day, 4 months ago, and am now a *sergeant* [in the Seventeenth Missouri Infantry]. I've been in two battles where much blood was shed, but not every bullet hits its mark.—

. . . Teach my nephew to hate tyrants, abhor oppressors and teach him to love and venerate freedom, true freedom, for our Germany must someday be free as well, and who knows whether he may need to play his part to make it free. Oh, truly God liveth, and God does not want slaves but free men. God does not appoint a government to oppress the people, but to rule them wisely! Once again, my best wishes to all from your son / Fr. Martens

From *Germans in the Civil War: The Letters They Wrote Home*, 317–19, edited by Walter D. Komphoefner and Wolfgang Helbich. Copyright © 2006 by the University of North Carolina Press. Used by permission of the publisher.

COLONEL ULYSSES S. GRANT DESCRIBES
HIS FIRST MARCH INTO BATTLE

In his memoir, Colonel Ulysses S. Grant describes his regiment's first march into battle in Missouri in July 1861 and reveals some of the character traits that would make him the Union's most celebrated commander.

I took my regiment [Twenty-First Illinois] to Palmyra and remained there for a few days, until relieved by the 19th Illinois Infantry. From Palmyra I proceeded to Salt River [in Missouri], the railroad bridge over which had been destroyed by the enemy. Colonel John M. Palmer at that time commanded the 13th Illinois, which was acting as a guard to workmen who were engaged in rebuilding this bridge. Palmer was my senior and commanded the two regiments as long as we remained together. The bridge was finished in about two weeks, and I received orders to move against Colonel Thomas Harris, who was said to be encamped at the little town of Florida, some twenty-five miles south. . . .

... While preparations for the move were going on I felt quite comfortable; but when we got on the road and found every house deserted I was anything but easy. In the twenty-five miles we had to march we did not see a person, old or young, male or female, except two horsemen who were on a road that crossed ours. As soon as they saw us they decamped as fast as their horses could carry them. I kept my men in the ranks and forbade their entering any of the deserted houses or taking anything from them. We halted at night on the road and proceeded the next morning at an early hour. Harris had been encamped in a creek bottom for the sake of being near water. The hills on either side of the creek extend to a considerable height, possibly more than a hundred feet. As we approached the brow of the hill from which it was expected we could see Harris' camp, and possibly find his men ready formed to meet us, my heart kept getting higher and higher until it felt to me as though it was in my throat. I would have given anything then to have been back in Illinois, but I had not the moral courage to halt and consider what to do; I kept right on. When we reached a point from which the valley below was in full view I halted. The place where Harris had been encamped a few days before was still there and the marks of a recent encampment were plainly visible, but the troops were gone. My heart resumed its place. It occurred to me at once that Harris had been as much afraid of me as I had been of him. This was a view of the question I had never taken before; but it was one I never forgot afterwards. From that event to the close of the war, I never experienced trepidation upon confronting an enemy, though I always felt more or less anxiety. I never forgot that he had as much reason to fear my forces as I had his. The lesson was valuable.

Ulysses S. Grant, *Personal Memoirs of U. S. Grant*, 2 vols. (New York: Charles Webster and Company, 1886), 1:248–50.

"NOW WE BEGAN TO REALIZE THE HORRORS OF WAR"

In April 1862, Confederate general Albert Sydney Johnston's 40,000-man army attacked Grant's 42,000-man army (reinforced on the second day of battle by General Don Carlos Buell's force of 20,000) camped at Pittsburg Landing on the Tennessee River. The battle of Shiloh produced over 23,500 dead and wounded, and was a major strategic victory for Union forces in the western theater. One of those who survived was Private James Milner, Battery A, First Illinois Light Artillery, also known as the Chicago Light Artillery. Milner's account of Shiloh, written to his father, is excerpted here.

Pittsburg, Tenn., April 12, 1862.

Dear Father:—I thank God that I am still preserved, and am still permitted to communicate with my friends at home with my own right hand. We have at last had our wish for a hard battle gratified, and never again do I expect to hear the same wish from the lips of our men. We are just as ready now to do our duty as we ever were, but to desire another hard battle, with the same chances of loss to our company, is quite a different thing. . . . You will learn the story of the battle in the papers, so I will only inform you in regard to what I saw, heard and felt during those two terrible days.

The Sabbath dawned upon us clear and warm. At the watering call I took a team of extra horses, of which I have charge, and after letting them drink in the brook, led them into a meadow to let them feed on the new grass. While there I heard what sounded like skirmish firing and thought it best to hurry towards camp. Before I arrived there, however, there was no mistaking the sound, and the boom of artillery was heard with the crack of musketry. I found the postillions throwing the harness on their horses, the cannoneers filling the ammunition chests, packing knapsacks, and getting in order for a move. After we had taken our positions, numbers of wounded passed our camp, and the cowards, just as they did at Donelson, were hurrying by reporting their regiments "*all* cut to pieces." Our men ridiculed them and shamed some of them into going back to the front. But soon Parsons Rumsey, a Chicago boy on Gen. W. H. L. Wallace's staff, brought orders for us to move to the front. With the 9th and 12th Illinois, we went to our position on the left. Donelson had taught us what we were to expect, and we approached the scene of action. A few shells burst around us as we neared the line, causing us involuntarily to start a little, and then to laugh at each other for it. . . .

Now we began to realize the horrors of war. The infantry poured a storm of balls against them, and as we saw the detested gray coats on the hill, across the ravine, we poured in a well directed fire of shell. As I dropt on the ground, I could see the shell bursting among them, the smoke from our own guns preventing me from seeing our own shots, but I knew Tom would do well. In this action we suffered. Ed. Russell, a young man whom you have often seen behind the counter of Smith's bank, as gentlemanly a young man as we had in the battery, had his bowels torn out by a solid shot. He lived but half an hour. His last words were, as he lay on his face, "I die like a man." And good man Farnham, a Christian man, my tentmate for six months, while I remained in squad one, was shot through above the heart while serving the same part that I was. Flannigan, a merry hearted Irishman, and the intimate friend of Ed. Russell, was shot through the mouth—also No. 4 on his gun. Several were wounded here, but stood manfully to their posts. Our horses were shot here, and some had to be replaced. When I could I kept my eyes on the enemy, and saw them bringing a battery to bear on the flank of our infantry; and soon a deadly fire raked the lines to the right of us. Our lines broke and run, right across our front. We yelled at them to keep away from our fire, but they didn't hear. I ran forward

and waved my hat, but to no purpose, and I went back to my post and fired
through them. No laying down now; we fired and loaded so fast that it was one
continued roar. The infantry would not be rallied; they were panic-stricken, and
we limbered up and were ordered to retire on a walk, for fear of increasing the
panic. . . . In about a quarter of a mile we again made a stand, and unlimbered.
I learned here that our No. 6 was shot (through the bowels) and I had to take
his place—giving my tools to the gunner. But one shell was left in the limber
[part of a gun carriage containing ammunition]. I gave it to No. 5, and looking
around discovered the Infantry still retreating, the enemy following us close.
We limbered up by order of Lieut. Moore and walked our horses still. This was
our last stand. I now knew we were beaten and in full retreat. I stopped, and,
with the aid of some infantry, helped one of our guns out of a mud-hole, and
walked on till we came to a road jammed with wagons; I felt then that I had
never witnessed so painful a sight as a disorganized army. Here I found Billy
Williams, our No. 6, riding in a baggage-wagon. He said to me in a pitiable
tone, "Jimmy, won't you come and take care of me, I am shot through?" I had
to refuse. This to me was truly painful. I helped him down and put him into an
ambulance, and helped [Jerry] Paddock in too. I got up into the ambulance and
examined Paddock's wound, found that he was shot through the liver, and that
there was no blood coming from the wound, made up my mind he was bleeding
internally, he was very frail, and I thought he must die. I put his handkerchief
over the wound and went back to my gun. I have learned Jerry was dead, and my
heart was filled with hatred and revenge against the enemy. When we reached
the landing, as I talked about the death of the boys, I could not restrain the tears,
and felt that I could then hazard my life in any position to mow down their ranks
with canister. After this I had a feeling of the utmost indifference as to my fate.
I could be taken prisoner, make a desperate resistance, or whatever the order, I
should comply. Not surrender, the thought of that never came into my head. . . .

It now began to rain and we were subjected to the discomforts of a wet night
in the open air. The troops on the line lay on their arms, and once in about
ten minutes a flash lighted up the sky, followed by the boom of a heavy gun;
again a flash would be seen in front of our lines, followed by the sharp report
of a bursting shell. A weary night dragged by slowly. With the light of day the
battle was renewed. We had recovered nearly all the ground lost the day before.
The fire opened fierce from the start, and we did not wait long for orders to
the front. Our position was near the centre, and we commenced shelling with
the four guns we were still able to man. . . . Again our lines began to waver
and Gen. Sherman galloped across the field and ordered us to the front. We
mounted the chests and galloped forward at a swinging pace, and went into
battery at the front. The lines falling back to us again we had difficulty in

keeping the infantry from in front of the guns, [the men] not now running as they were the day before, but falling back steadily and shooting from behind the trees. I had to pull over the heads of some of them, and as the smoke cleared away looked to see if any had fallen, for we were firing cannister now. They appeared to be standing yet and stuck to their positions. We fired canister for some time running our pieces forward by hand until they fell back to a new position. The lines moved up to the front and again there was a doubtful action. Gen. Sherman again rode up and ordered us to go to the new front. "Come on," said he, "I'll lead you;" and he did. We limbered up, mounted our seats, two postillions leaped in their saddles, and we galloped forward through a fierce storm of shell and bullets. "Well up to the front," said Lt. [Peter] Wood, and we took position in advance of the infantry and poured in a rapid fire of shell. General Sherman who (as Gen. Wallace says is perfectly crazy on the subject of artillery) told a Louisiana officer in the presence of one of our men it was the grandest thing he ever saw done by artillery, and our caisson postillions, who were ordered to remain behind, said it looked like a charge. . . .

We are now in our camp and are comfortably situated again. I have gone into these tedious details to show you exactly what war is. I have since rode over nearly the whole battlefield, but will spare you the horrid and disgusting details of the thousands of suffering, wounded, and mangled corpses I saw. Suffice it that the enemy's loss far exceeded ours. I had many narrow escapes, but survive without the slightest injury. . . .

Yours, &c.,

James W. Milner

James W. Milner to Robert Milner, April 12, 1862, reprinted in *Chicago Tribune*, April 18, 1862.

GENERAL POPE ORDERS HARD MEASURES

Initially most Northerners hoped to win the war without destroying Southern property or hurting Southern civilians. But in the summer of 1862 Union leadership, both civilian and military, began to reassess what it would take to defeat the Confederacy. That evolution is apparent in the brief command of Kaskaskia's John Pope. Aggressive and self-confident, Pope performed well during Grant's spring 1862 offensive, taking New Madrid, Missouri, and Island No. 10, on the Mississippi River. These victories, coupled with his connections—he was related to Lincoln by marriage—won Pope a promotion to major general in command of the Union's newly constituted Army of Virginia. But in August 1862, Lee routed Pope at Second Bull Run. In the aftermath Pope was reassigned to duty in Minnesota, where he would spend the remainder of the war, while the Army of Virginia was permanently merged into the Army of the Potomac. Yet historians agree that Pope's brief command in Virginia (less than two months) was highly significant, for he was among the first commanders of a major Union army to initiate, as a matter of official policy, hard war measures on the South. Pope's draconian general orders, excerpted below, outraged Southerners, but many in the Union army and on the home front applauded them.

GENERAL ORDERS, HEADQUARTERS ARMY OF VIRGINIA,
Washington, July 18, 1862.
Numbers 5.

Hereafter, as far as practicable, the troops of this command will subsist upon the country in which their operations are carried on. In all cases supplies for this purpose will be taken by the officers to whose department they properly belong under the orders of the commanding officer of the troops for whose use they are intended. Vouchers will be given to the owners, stating on their face that they will be payable at the conclusion of the war, upon sufficient testimony being furnished that such owners have been loyal citizens of the United States since the date of the vouchers. . . . By command of Major-General Pope:

GEO. D. RUGGLES,
Colonel, Assistant Adjutant-General, and Chief of Staff.

Numbers 7.
Washington, July 10[?], 1862.

The people of the valley of the Shenandoah and throughout the region of operations of this army living along the lines of railroad and telegraph and along the routes of travel in rear of the United States forces are notified that they will be held responsible for any injury done to the track, line, or road, or for any attacks upon trains or straggling soldiers by bands of guerillas in their neighborhood. No privileges and immunities of warfare apply to lawless bands of individuals not forming part of the organized forces of the enemy nor wearing the garb of soldiers . . . Evil-disposed persons in rear of our armies who do not themselves engage directly in these lawless acts encourage them by refusing to interfere or to give any information by which such acts can be prevented or the perpetrators punished. . . .

It is therefore ordered that wherever a railroad, wagon road, or telegraph is injured by parties of guerillas the citizens living within 5 miles of the spot shall be turned out in mass to repair the damage, and shall, beside, pay to the United States in money or in property, to be levied by military force, the full amount of the pay and subsistence of the whole force necessary to coerce the performance of the work during the time occupied in completing it.

If a soldier or legitimate follower of the army be fired upon from any house the house shall be razed to the ground, and the inhabitants sent prisoners to the headquarters of this army. . . .

Any persons detached in such outrages, either during the act or at any time afterward, shall be shot, without awaiting civil process. . . .

Numbers 11.

Washington, July 23, 1862.

Commanders of army corps, divisions, brigades, and detached commands will proceed immediately to arrest all disloyal male citizens within their lines or within their reach in rear of their respective station.

Such as are willing to take the oath of allegiance to the United States and will furnish sufficient security for its observance shall be permitted to remain at their homes and pursue in good faith their accustomed avocations. Those who refuse shall be conducted South beyond the extreme pickets of this army, and be notified that if found again anywhere within [our] lines or at any point in rear they will be considered spies, and subjected to the extreme rigor of military law.

If any person, having taken the oath of allegiance as above specified, be found to have violated it, he shall be shot, and his property seized and applied to the public use. . . .

United States, War Department, *The War of the Rebellion: Official Records of the Union and Confederate Armies*, ser. I, vol. 12, part 2 (Washington, DC: Government Printing Office, 1899), pp. 50–52.

No. 13.

Washington, July 25, 1862.

Hereafter no guards will be placed over private houses or private property of any description whatever. Commanding officers are responsible for the conduct of the troops under their command, and the Articles of War and Regulations of the Army provide ample means for restraining them to the full extent required for discipline and efficiency.

Soldiers were called into the field to do battle against the enemy, and it is not expected that their force and energy shall be wasted in protecting private property of those most hostile to the Government. . . .

By command of Major-General Pope:

GEO. D. RUGGLES,
Colonel and Chief of Staff.

United States, War Department, *The War of the Rebellion: Official Records of the Union and Confederate Armies*, ser. 1, vol. 12, part 3 (Washington DC: Government Printing Office, 1899), 509.

"THE TROOPS ARE BECOMING VERY MUCH DISHEARTENED"

By the fall of 1862, casualties had mounted, the Union's strategy had changed, and the enthusiasm that had marked the war's beginning wore thin among many Illinois soldiers. The first two letters below, from Vandalia's William H. Ross and Princeville's Levi A. Ross (no relation), reveal attitudes that many held by the middle of the war. The final letter is from Jonesboro's James Evans. In it Evans explains the arrest of his regiment, the 109th Illinois Infantry, and offers a critical appraisal of the Union army's morale.

Memphis Tenn Oct 6th 1862

Father

I have not received a letter from you for some time. I wrote to you a bout a month a go but have received no answer as yet. I would like very much to heare from you again I had a very heard spell of sickness in September but now I am able for duty. We are still at Memphis and I do not think we will leave here this winter we can not muster over three hundred for duty in our Regt, now we have lost a good many men by sickness since we have been in this City

Levi wrote to me that he had some idea of volunteering I hope Father that you will not let him do so for I do not think he could stand it[,] for it . . . is the hardest life that every a man led to be a soldier[;] ther is nothing in civil life to be compared to it. It does very well when we are in camp. . . . But then let us git on a march, and git out of Rations and have to march from twenty [to] twentyfive miles with little or nothing to eat—and night when you stop you find that you socks is wet with the blood that run from you feet then it will do for a solider to think of home. it is hard to tell when you start on a hundred mile march what men will go throug I have seene the s[t]outest and Bigest men fall by the side of the rode So I want you to tell Levi when I come to think over the hard times I have seen I do not think he could stand it. but if I knew when I was at home what I do now I would have no idea that I could have stood what I have but I have went through well[.] the Regt. has neve[r] made a march but what I have been along But if you do let Levi go send him to this Regt. where I can watch over him, and then I know he will be under good Officers, and that is one great Point. . . .

I have no more to write answer soon give my love to all.

Your Son
Wm. H Ross [corporal, Fortieth Illinois Infantry]

William H. Ross Papers, Archives and Manuscripts, Chicago History Museum.

Nashville Tenn. Feb. 3rd 1863

A K Ross
Dear Father

By request of our Col, I sat up with the Quarters Master Sergeant, who is very sick. For the reason that I was up last night, acting as nurse and "butcher," I am excused from other duties today. I will cheerfully improve the opportunity in writing to "Pa" and "Ma."

The first thing that occurs to my mind is my bleeding country. What else should more interest the soldier and the patriot?—Every true soldier of his common country earnestly desires and prays for the end of this bloody strife, and deadly, terrible carnage. But the soldier, as well as the people North, are divided in their views and opinions on this important subject,—The troops are becoming very much disheartened in consequence of recent disasters in the field and the bad management of the War Department. When we enthusiastically rushed into the ranks at our Country's call, we all Expected to witness the last dying struggles of Treason and Rebellion Ere this. We expected to see the old stars and stripes triumphantly waving over all of Dixie, and return in peace to our homes and friends. But in these expectations we have been disappointed. Over 200,000 of our noble soldiers sleep in the silent grave. Almost countless millions of treasure has been expended in the unsuccessful effort of the Government to put down this Rebellion. But after all this great sacrifice of valuable life and money, we are no nearer the goal of peace and the sunshine of happiness in a united Country, than we were at the first booming of Sumter's guns. You can judge how we feel here in the 86th when I tell you that only 8 men in Co. K. approve the policy and proclamation of Mr. Lincoln. Many are deserting 23 men from one Company in this brigade have deserted. I think it was inexpedient. *Yet* I am in favor of anything that will tend to cripple the enemy and crush this vile Rebellion. The unfortunate division of the North is the worst feature of the times. The army of traitors at the north is truly formidable. They ought to hang higher than Haman; many of the boys are in favor of a compromise, some are of the opinion that the Southern Confederacy will soon be recognized by the U.S. Alas! for our beloved Republic!! Father I am trying to be a true, faithful soldier of our common country. I am still ready and willing to sacrifice everything for my country's sake. Regret this unhappy state of affairs, sorry that the soldier's have lost their patriotism and are discontented.

I have a severe cold which makes me cough continually. Over half of our splendid army are either dead or sick in hospitals. God save us.

L. A. Ross [corporal, Eighty-Sixth Illinois Infantry]

Levi Adolphus Ross Papers, Manuscripts, Abraham Lincoln Presidential Library, Springfield.

Levi Ross. *Courtesy Abraham Lincoln Presidential Library, Springfield, Illinois*

FROM THE HUNDRED AND NINTH.

Camp of the 109th Reg't Ills. Vols., Fort Pickering, Memphis, Jan. 31, 1863.
To the Editor of the Jonesboro Gazette.

My last was directed to you from LaGrange, 50 miles interior, just as we were boarding the train for this place. . . . After considerable delay in transporting baggage, we got underway and by two o'clock had our tents pitched and pots on the fire cooking our remnants of bacon and beans, which constitute the staple articles of army diet.

We were here for the second or third time informed that the charges alleged against us, which prompted our arrest, had been shown to be entirely groundless, and that the commanding officer had the fullest confidence in our loyalty and superior fighting qualities! Of course we were glad for shoulder straps to announce that we were loyal although sentiments of an opposite character had never been entertained by any of the regiment. Certainly our men were not convinced of their own devotion to their country simply because that conclusion had had been arrived at by a subsidized Conclave, whose ambition never rose above a free nigger. . . . Our arrest was prompted by malice, for certainly if any regiment in the field can show a proud record of prompt obedience to orders and a faithful discharge of all the duties imposed upon them, that regiment is the One Hundred and Ninth Illinois. We all rested in the proud satisfaction of having done nothing but what we could refer to with pleasure, and the whole matter of arrest, tedious investigation, and final result, were treated as they should have been, with the most perfect contempt by the great mass of the regiment. . . .

I suppose the Western army is "in good condition and eager for the conflict." Telegraphic dispatches announce it, and news paper correspondents assert it. Therefore I presume it is so, thought it requires a person of much keener observation than I can boast to discern it. The mass of the soldiers have had no pay for six or eight months; their clothing is none the better or more comfortable for five or six months wear; their families are needing the necessities of life at home, while high officials are squandering the public money on fanatical experiments; nearly all denounce the President's proclamation as a violation of plighted faith, and an insult to the soldiers of the army; and thousands openly declare that they are sick of the war and intend going home in the spring. Niggers on horseback or in the cars, and soldiers afoot, went on without much complaint for a short time, but the "shiny pints" are all worn off now, and the soldiers begin to feel a desire for an exchange of position with Sambo, who is plainly the favorite individual in this war. The niggers are collected in large numbers at different military points, provided with warm comfortable tents or other quarters, furnished with an abundance of provisions, have nothing whatever to do, and are transported from place to place on the railroads, to the utter exclusion of everything except officers' cotton. . . . Is it any wonder that the army is becoming dissatisfied? They have no victories to cheer them up. They are told that we have gained a "splendid victory in Virginia," or somewhere else, but the army has fallen back for some reason best not to be made public; that "we are going to drive the rebels out of Mississippi," and meanwhile the army is falling back and the rebels occupying the different points as we evacuate. I believe knowing ones call an army in this condition "demoralized." Whatever it is called, one thing I am sure of it is a very bad fix for an army to be in. I do not look for the brilliant results achieved at Belmont [Missouri], Donelson, and Shiloh from soldiers so thoroughly dissatisfied. A different policy must be pursued. "Free nigger" is not a popular saying here with the army. The soldiers will think of the forty or fifty cents a day for which they will be compelled to labor when brought in competition with negroes at the close of the war. Curious, ain't it? But then men are curious things. . . .

                    J.E. [James Evans, adjutant, 109th Illinois Infantry]

Reprinted in *Jonesboro Gazette*, February 7, 1863.

"I THINK THERE IS REASON TO HOPE FOR BETTER TIMES"

In the following letters to his father, private James Watson of Middletown (now Mahomet) describes scenes he witnessed during and after the battle of Stones River, outside Murfreesboro, Tennessee, while serving in Company I, Twenty-Fifth Illinois Infantry. A fitting capstone to the string of large and bloody battles of 1862, Stones River lasted five days and produced over twenty-four thousand casualties. Watson's letters home convey both the horrors of battle and his hope that the war would soon come to an end.

                              Murfreesborough, Tenn. Jan. 27th 1863

Dear Father,—. . .

We had been for three days under fire, but nothing very severe till the 30th of Dec. Wednesday when part of [Brigadier General Richard W.] Johnson's division on our left was driven back by overwhelming numbers, and left us exposed to a terrible fire of artillery and infantry. (This was early in the morning of the 30th the day Col. Williams was killed. We lay the night before in fence corners near a corn field; it was very cold, too.)

The day before this we had marched ten miles and laid in a cotton field with the rain coming down on us all night without any fire to warm by. Some had their blankets, others none myself included: we pulled up the cotton bushes and laid them in the furrows for a bed, and the water run under us all night: in the morning we made some fires and warmed ourselves. On Thursday about daylight skirmishing began again. They did not fire but a few rounds when the rebels advanced in force from- a piece of woods in our front, across a cotton field. We waited until they got near enough, and then gave them a sudden volley which staggered them and they had to stop, but tried it again; as we were behind a fence, we had a little the advantage of them and hold them off for several charges that they made: there was about the hardest fighting of the battle for three or four hours. We were driven from the fence three times, and twice took it again but being overpowered three to one we had to retreat and fought the best we could, every man for himself, under a heavy fire of grape and shells. . . . The next day we were in reserve but kept in readiness for anything, but were not called on. On the 2nd of Jan. in the evening the rebels drove our left flank [Major General Thomas L.] Crittendon's and [Major General Lovell H.] Rouseau's divisions and we went to their aid, with [Brigadier General James S.] Negley division. We had to wade the river three different times, as it was so crooked there, before we got to them; it was only knee deep, but pretty cold, at last we got out of it and charged with a yell, and drove them back with great loss. We were in a perfect hailstorm of shot and shell, but were partly sheltered by the rivers banks and hollows. Negley division took a battery close to us that had been doing a good deal of mischief and also a rebel flag. It then being dark, there was no more fighting that night only picket firing; our division went to carrying rails and soon had a good line of defense in case of an attack. We laid behind it on cornstalks in the rain and mud all night, but were not molested. After daylight we made fires and warmed ourselves. It rained all day, but there was not much fighting, till in the evening they made a charge on our right, but were soon driven back; that was their last charge. . . . It is almost beyond the power of human mind to describe the horrible spectacles witnessed on a battle field. A man feels when engaged in fighting almost indifferent to the suffering around him, as well as the danger, and pitches in with all his might, and dont think about getting hurt hardly in the excitement of it no matter how timid or fearful he may be just before it, at least that is the way I always feel as near as I can describe it, and suppose others feel the same or nearly so. I will now close, and enclose fifty cts. for which please send me some stamps, Yours,—

James G. Watson

Murfreesborough, March 24th 1863

Dear Father,—. . .

We often go three days on one days rations out foraging and make up the deficiency off of hen roosts and pig pens and so forth. It's against orders but a soldier dont pay much attention to orders when he is after grub and its handy to get. I think there is reason to hope for better times soon as people are beginning to find out that the rebels wont have a peace on any but their own terms, and that no sensible man will grant that loves his country; so the only way left is to whip them so bad that they will have to submit to *our* terms; and I am glad that some of the democrats are beginning to find out that they will have to support the government if they want it saved.

I see by the southern papers that there is a great deal of discontent in the south resulting from the high prices of provisions, and the governments pressing all the best men into the service, and paying for things in their worthless scrip. While our green backs are almost as good a[s] gold theirs are only worth 30 cts. on the dollar. Straws show which way the wind blows. It [the war] certainly does look more encouraging now than it has for some time. Confidence is being restored, and people see that it only needs united effort to dry this war up this summer, and if the people at home will only give the soldiers and the President their united support we will do it. Let the civil authorities attend to the traitors at home, and we will do our share in the field. I will close. Yours,—

James G. Watson

"An account of the Campaigns of the 25th Illinois Volunteers. Written in a Series of Letters to His Parents by James G. Watson," typescript, Champaign County Historical Society, Department of Archives and Manuscripts, Urbana Free Library, Urbana.

GEORGE CARRINGTON WITNESSES THE FALL OF VICKSBURG

In April 1863 Grant took two corps of the Army of the Tennessee and marched south of Vicksburg, crossing the Mississippi River from the west, near Bruinsburg. Cutting himself off from his supply line, Grant moved north, winning one engagement after another: Port Gibson, Raymond, Jackson, Champion's Hill. By the end of May, Grant's army surrounded General John Pemberton's Confederate forces, dug in along a series of heavily fortified positions on the hills and bluffs just east of Vicksburg. Pemberton's army, ragged and outnumbered, fought desperately to hold Vicksburg, repelling a frontal assault on their breastworks on May 22. Grant then laid siege to the city, forcing its surrender on July 4. Grant's Vicksburg campaign added to his growing fame as the Union's premier field commander and resulted in one of the most important strategic victories of the entire war. Among the witnesses was Lacon's George Carrington, lieutenant in the Eleventh Illinois Infantry, whose diary is excerpted here.

May 22d, We have found a sheltered position in a ravine where we bivouac, Cool and fine this morning, Batteries being planted, Rifle pits dug as near as posible. Getting ready for an assault upon the enemys works. To charge at 2 P.M., Formed our ranks marched out through the ravines and hollows. Finally took position on the slope of a hill barely cover from the rebel fire, We formed in column of Companies right in front closed en mass. As it happened our Co was at the foot of the hill. The intention was to forward and deploy into line on the brow of the hill then advance, Lying here waiting for other Regt's to get in position and for the word to [move] forward. . . . While here chewing canes that were growing at our feet, to keep our minds from what we knew was coming, a wood pecker lit on an old dead snag sounding a tattoo with his bill then flew away with a "churp," (Happy woodpecker,) . . . After a long wait the word came to "Forward." Every man raised to his feet and all moved forward the front Companies advanced to the crest of the hill and were fairly swept off their feet by the most deadly, concentrated, cross and enfilading fire, we were ever under spread death and destruction in our ranks, seeing the ground ahead was covered with slashed trees and brush that no man could get through on a charge, besides a ravine to cross before climbing the opposite slope crowned by the rebel breast works, and this ravine and all entervening space was slashed full of brush and tree tops cut and lopped in every direction, almost utterly impossible for a man to crawl through, No line could be maintained under such conditions. It was over 100 yards from the brow of the hill behind whose slope we lay, to the reb' entrenchments, Their rifle pits and breast works well constructed not a man visible unless he rashly showed him-self in his eagerness to fire at the advancing "Yankees" The whole Regt' wilted and immediately fell back under cover, After losing quite a number of men, Col [Garrett L.] Nevius fell at the head of the Regt' leading them on, a musket ball struck him about the center of the forehead from which the blood and brain was flowing. . . . While near the crest of the hill in this position we were exposed to an artillery fire from Fort Hill. Here we lost 30 men in about five minutes. . . . Our artillery plumping in shot and shell from every hill top, the sharp crack of rifles and muskets, the drift of the wounded to the rear, fighting all around. . . .

June 8th, Hot as usual, not much firing, It does not seem possible that 20,000 rebels are as close to us as they are. We talk with them from the rifle pits nearly every night back and forth, joking, and some times "cussing," ["]asking about grub" &c. Trade canteens, Ours are of tin covered with blanket wool, keeps the water cool longer, while theirs are made of red cedar.

June 10th, Very wet after the rain last night. At work from 6A M until 11 A M Throwing up breast work for cannon within 200 yards of the Rebel rifle pits, fair range. I would dig up a shovel full of the yellow clay throw it up in front then jump up and wave the shovel at the rebs, then "juke." How the bullets would sing over our head while we were down behind the bank.

McAlisters four gun battery on the point of hill above our quarters are 24 pounders. we would take empty peach cans that just fit these guns, fill them with bullets, pieces of iron, taps or bolts, and carry these up to the artillery men to fire over to the rebels. The cans would be torn to pieses and scatter the contents far and wide. . . .

June 28th, Hot this morning, We are around Vicksburg like a picket fence. It is "Hello Yank." And how are you "Jonnie," "Jonnie Rebs," While talking last night some one asked "How do you like your new General," "What General?" "Why Gen'l Starvation," Then they all laughed. "Hello Yank!" Well what is it? "When you'ns coming in," "Soon's we get hungry for mule beef," ha ha, We hear they are down to mule beef now, short rations, Our men got hold of some blue beans, "Refugee beans," they call them, they are fine eating however. . . .

July 3d, Heavy firing on the left last night. Lively cannonade this morning. 10 AM. A flag of truce. They are going to surrender, Hooray! Firing ceased, Heads pop up all along the lines on both sides. Some one fired a musket, "Down every body," "Hunt your holes." No more firing and gradually the heads come up again, Sitting on top of the trenches looking at each other, thousands of men, At 4 PM. Genl Grant and Genl Pemberton met near an oak tree that grew in an open space on the outer slope of Ft Hill. To agree on terms of surrender. . . .

July 4th, So quiet last night could hardly sleep, No firing this morning. The white flag flies on the rebel works, 10 AM. Pemberton has surrendered, Prisoners to be parolled, About 30,000 men! . . . Silently they marched out and silently they marched back, We stood looking on, Genl Logans Division, [Brigadier General Thomas] Ransom's Brigade (being attached to Logans Division during the siege), Formed to march in. Lieut [Samuel B.] Dean placed me at the left of the first platoon, However we marched in column of fours our usual formation, As we passed down the Jackson road through the dust and heat the rebels sat on each side looking on, They were taking it easy now while we had to march in the dust and take posession. We marched down to the Court House and at 2 15 P M, Stacked arms. The Stars and stripes were soon flying from the dome of the Court House, We had now an opportunity to look around, I saw mule meat on the block in the rebel commissary, Its true they ate it no other meat to be had, we cut off supplies sure enough, It seems they had rice and beans with 4 ounces of flour per day to the man,. After chatting with the Rebs, occasionally handing out a hard tack as some of them looked hungry, We fell in and marched out to

the North east angle of their works stacked arms, cooked some "grub." I had a
can of cove oysters in my haversack, with hard tack I made a meal, (And so we
celebrated *our* 4th of July.)

George D. Carrington Diary, Archives and Manuscripts, Chicago Historical Museum.

"EQUALITY WE ARE FIGHTING FOR"

*Sometime in 1863, John Abbott, from Bloomington, left Illinois and traveled to
Massachusetts. He was among the thousands of black men from across the country
who eagerly responded to Massachusetts governor John Andrew's call for volunteers
for an all-black Union regiment. The surge of volunteers resulted in the formation
of the famed Fifty-Fourth and Fifty-Fifth Massachusetts Colored Infantry. Private
Abbott was mustered into Company F of the Fifty-Fifth on June 15, 1863, and served
until the close of the war, seeing action in North Carolina, South Carolina, and
Florida. One of thirteen black soldiers from McLean County to serve in the Fifty-
Fifth Massachusetts, Abbott writes of his determination to defeat both secessionism
and the "mean partiality" against troops of color in the Union army.*

Folly Island, S.C., Nov. 10, '63.

Most worthy and esteemed friends:—You will please excuse this humble effort to
let you know something about what we are doing away down here in Dixie.

In the first place, we are all very well, and doing well, but the main thing is yet
pending, and that is what we came here for. So far as we have had opportunity,
we have been true to the [a] man; and those in command of us say that they
don't want better soldiers.

We have done all the work that was to do here in regard to taking Charleston,
including the taking of Fort Wagner and Fort Gregg. The gallant 55th has the
praise of being the best regiment that has ever been in this department, and yet
they don't feel disposed to give us what is the most essential to us as a people and
a race—and that is, equality with the white man.

In the capacity that I am in, I have more time and opportunity to see and
compare things together: and I can see more distinctions shown than any one
else would imagine, having the honor of being brigade wagon master. A great
portion of this mean partiality comes under my particular notice; but if I
continue in this strain you will all think that I am dissatisfied; and I would not
like to have you think that, because I am very well satisfied, with the exception
of what I have told you. . . .

Our motto is, that every man is born free and equal, and that equality we
are fighting for, and we expect to fight, with the help of the Almighty, until we
get it. We have worked night and day for months to try to accomplish this great

end, and they give us credit for all we have done, and why won't they give us this that we most desire? I am afraid that they think that if we excel them as soldiers, that we might possibly excel them in other things: therefore, we might contend in various things. In the first place, we left our home and friends with the expectation that we were going to do something for the elevation of our race, and therefore we kept ourselves in good cheer, hoping that we might have an opportunity to free some of the bondmen: and if that which we came for is to be denied us, we can't well tell what we are fighting for: but if they fulfill their contract, we will fight on and take Charleston like men: and if we are men in this capacity, why not let us be men in any other? Because I am told that this is the most noble way a man can show his manhood. I am even now under the immediate sound of the cannon which are hurling death and destruction at the enemy, and it makes my heart leap with joy when I think that I helped plant those same cannon, and stand ready to sustain them if they should be overpowered by the enemy. . . .

We hope that you will all write to us, at least as many as can, so that we may have something to revive us when we think of home. Yours truly,

JOHN ABBOTT.

Bloomington Pantagraph, December 2, 1863.

THE TWENTY-NINTH U.S. COLORED INFANTRY

About eighteen hundred black soldiers are credited as having enlisted from Illinois, though some of those were from other states. It is also the case that, because Illinois lagged behind other states in organizing a black regiment, many blacks, like Bloomington's John Abbott, left Illinois to enlist in regiments elsewhere. The only black regiment mustered entirely in Illinois—the Twenty-Ninth U.S. Colored—was organized in Chicago in 1864, under command of Colonel John A. Bross, and saw its most noteworthy service in the sieges of Petersburg and Richmond, Virginia. The following sources provide further insight into the experience of Illinois's black soldiers and how those soldiers figured prominently in the ongoing debate over race and freedom in Illinois.

BLACK SOLDIERS.

. . . Those who saw the Africans on the street the other day wearing their military uniform, were much surprised to see how like *soldiers* they looked; and that the color, instead of being a drawback, was rather a set-off. And many a convert to the idea of black soldiers was made in a few moments, by a single look. They may be better or worse for actual service than white men. That will depend on many things;

as whether they have sufficient intelligence to learn drill; docility in obeying orders; enthusiasm for a military life; courage to stand fire; strength and endurance to bear the hardships and face the exposures of the field and the camp. . . .

The only question which underlies the case, is—Will the black make a soldier? Before it was tried, all men had doubts. Even those who wished him well, feared that between his low condition before being made a slave, and his bad tuition in slavery, he would fail; that though some of the more intelligent, and especially such as had an infusion of white blood in their veins, might succeed, the great mass of them would only do for camp laborers and attendants.

It was therefore a kind of new revelation to many—not to say to most—that the African would fight; would fight in rank as infantry, and stand to it like a hero. Milliken's Bend [Mississippi], Port Hudson [Louisiana] and Fort Wagner [South Carolina] told a new story to all the world. A new day dawned upon Africa when those heroic blacks went down in those terrific fights. More was done then for the race in those three days, than three centuries before had accomplished. The black is a man beyond peradventure! And that solved the whole question of black enlistments which had been so long hanging fire. And now, even copperheads begin to give in, especially as it will save their own precious carcasses. . . .

Chicago Tribune, January 9, 1864.

[First Sergeant William McCoslin, of Bloomington, writes of his experiences in the Twenty-Ninth USCI.]
. . . On the 30th of May our regiment was ordered to take transportation from Alexandria for White House Landing, Va.; . . . After disembarking from the boat, we went into camp. For several days, during our stay here, our men were engaged in throwing up redoubts and rifle pits. Then, about the 7th of May, we were ordered to escort a large train of supplies to the front. This was our first march, and a sorry one it was. It was a forced march, and many of the men had to throw away nearly all their baggage, so as to keep up. We expected to get a rest here for a day or two, but were disappointed. We had to start almost immediately en route for Petersburg. Here, at Old Church Tavern, we joined our corps, and were assigned to the 4th Division, 2d Brigade, 9th Army Corps. Our brigade being the rear guard of the corps, we had a great deal of hard marching; and being in a very important position, we all felt the responsibility that was resting on us as rear guard. We proceeded along finely till we arrived at Dawson Bridge, near the Chickahominy, where we rested one day, and a Godsend it was to us. So, the next evening we started, but went only a short distance, and stopped till morning, crossing the Chickahominy. We expected to be attacked. The crossing was accomplished without any difficulty,—our regiment being the last to cross the river. We learned since that a brigade of rebels were watching us at the time we crossed, but they did not

molest us. We continued on our march until we came to Charles City Point, on the James River, which being a fortified place, we stopped over night; but next day, learning that a large force of rebels intended to attack us, we crossed the river on a pontoon-bridge. . . .

Although the men were very tired, they were anxious to give fight to their enemies; but, on arriving at the front, the programme being changed, we were ordered to rest until further orders, which was a godsend to us. We had two days' rest, and then were ordered to the front, to take a position in the rifle-pits. Here we expected to see the rebels face to face, but in this we were disappointed.

At daybreak the next morning we were relieved and marched to the rear to rest. We are and have been building forts and rifle-pits, which we consider healthier than going into the fight; but, when ordered, we are ready and willing to fight. . . .

Another thing that I wish to speak about is this, that the county agreed to pay a bounty to all colored men that would enlist in Bloomington. Many of us did enlist, and are now in the army, battling for the Union and our rights. Our families at home are suffering for the necessaries of life, and still we cannot get the bounty promised us. We think it very hard, but it may be for the best. We have not received any pay from the Government yet, and the bounty that ought to come from the county would be of immense service to our families during our absence. If we cannot get it, please let us know, so that we may not expect it. Under the circumstances, it is very hard to be promised such a bounty, and then not get it, particularly by the citizens of our own city, and I hope that the loyal citizens of Bloomington will stand by us, and see that we are properly represented as soldiers, and that an effort will be made by the people to have our promised bounty paid us.

> Yours, truly,
> WILLIAM MCCOSLIN,
> 1st Serg't Co. A, 29th U.S.C.T.

Philadelphia Christian Recorder, August 27, 1864.

JAMES AUSTIN CONNOLLY'S MARCH TO THE SEA

In March 1862, Charleston's James Austin Connolly (after the war a U.S. congressman and a U.S. district attorney) stowed away on a steamer to see the battlefield after the fall of Fort Donelson. Within months he was raising a regiment, the 123rd Illinois Infantry, of which he was elected major. Connolly's unit saw action throughout the war: Perryville, Chickamauga, Missionary Ridge, Atlanta, and Sherman's march through Georgia and the Carolinas. Following are excerpts from the diary he kept during November and December 1864 and a letter he wrote to Illinois congressman Henry Pelham Bromwell regarding Brevet Major General Jefferson Columbus Davis's treatment of fugitive slaves.

Wednesday, Novr. 16th [1864]

The eventful day has come; we turn our backs upon Atlanta, and our faces seaward. How many prayers for our success went up from our Northern homes this morning. We must succeed. Not a man in this army doubts it. We'll march straight through and shake the rebellious old State from center to circumference. . . .

Saturday, Nov. 19th

. . . There are no wealthy planters in the immediate vicinity of the "Ulcofauhatchee" along our line of march. The farms are all in hundred acre lots, but their owners call them "Plantations"; the citizens look at our troops as they pass, with the utmost astonishment; they have no idea where we are going, and the negroes stare at us with open eyes and mouths, but generally, before the whole column has passed they pack up their bundles and march along, going, they know not whither, but apparently satisfied they are going somewhere toward freedom; but these wretched creatures, or a majority of them, don't know what freedom is. Ask them where they are going as they trudge along with their bundles on their heads, and the almost invariable reply is: "Don't know Massa; gwine along wid you all." Our men are foraging on the country with the greatest liberality. Foraging parties start out in the morning; they go where they please, seize wagons, mules, horses, and harness; make the negroes of the plantation hitch up, load the wagons with sweet potatoes, flour, meal, hogs, sheep, chickens, turkeys, barrels of molasses, and in fact everything good to eat, and sometimes considerable that's good to drink. Our men are living as well as they could at home and are in excellent health. Rain falling all the forenoon, roads heavy and marching difficult. Passed through Sand Town today about 2 o'clock. It is a little weather beaten village of about 250 or 300 inhabitants. The citizens were not much expecting us, but they heard of our approach day before yesterday and have spent the time since in carrying off and hiding in the swamp their valuables, but the negroes told the soldiers of these hiding places and most of these hidden valuables found their way into our camp tonight. Went into camp at dark. We have neither seen nor heard of any armed rebels yet, and we march along with as much unconcern as if we were marching through Ohio. . . .

Saturday, Nov. 26th

. . . The rebel papers we get hold of from Augusta also call on all the citizens to turn out and fall timber across the roads—destroy their forage and provisions, and do everything possible to harass us and retard our march. Let them do it if they dare. We'll burn every house, barn, church, and everything else we come to; we'll leave their families houseless and without food; their towns will *all* be destroyed, and nothing but the most complete desolation will be found in our track. This army will not be trifled with by citizens. If citizens raise their hands against us to retard our march or play the guerilla against us, neither youth nor age, nor sex will be respected. Everything must be destroyed. This is the feeling that has settled down over the army in its bivouac tonight. We have gone so far now in our triumphal march that we will not be balked. It is a question of life or death with us, and all considerations of mercy and humanity must bow before the inexorable demands of self preservation. We are nearing the coast, threatening both Augusta and Savannah. The rebels are quite certain we are first going to Augusta, but we are not, and that erroneous opinion may relieve us of a large amount of the opposition we would otherwise encounter. . . .

Wednesday, Dec. 21th

With the first streak of dawn our pickets—the fingers of our army—felt their way amongst the tangled vines, and gloomy swamps on the left of our line until they found themselves within full view of the deserted works of the enemy. Almost with electric speed the word ran around the entire lines of our army: "Savannah is evacuated," and in less time than it takes to tell it, the heaviest sleepers in the army, as well as the lightest, were out, some dressed, and some *en deshabille* [partly or carelessly dressed], shouting and hurrahing from the bottom of their lungs. This was indeed a joyful morning. Savannah is ours. Our long campaign is ended. If the world predicted our failure, the world must acknowledge itself mistaken. I am glad I was permitted to have a part in this campaign. . . .

James A. Connolly, "Major Connolly's Diary," *Transactions of the Illinois State Historical Society* (Springfield) 35 (1928): 401, 403–4, 411–12, 438.

Before Savannah Ga Decr 18, 1864

Hon. H. P. H. Bromwell

Sir

On the 12th of November the army of General Sherman, viz 14th, 15th, 17th & 20th Corps, abandoned its Communication with the North, and started on its march through the State of Georgia. From General Sherman's published orders it was understood by the officers of his army that we were to subsist on the Country, and that the negroes along our line of march would be permitted to join us, or rather would not be turned back to slavery if they chose to march to the coast along the same roads we should travel. We have made the march—have reached the coast—have destroyed all important Rail road lines in the State of Georgia, and have lived as well as any army ever lived. About five to eight thousand Slaves—men, women and children—have followed us through our long march, and are now here with us. The men, from day to day as they came to us, were placed in pioneer corps, and removed obstructions, built bridges, repaired roads &c &c along our line of march, while their wives and children trudged along through the woods and fields by the roadside, picking up their subsistence as they went along. Indeed it is the universal opinion amongst the most intelligent officers of this army that the fugitive negroes have assisted rather than retarded us in our march. . . .

[Our] Division had been marching all night, and about 4 o'clock on the morning of [December 9] I crossed Ebeneezer Creek in Effingham County Ga, in advance of the Division, for the purpose of finding a place for the troops to bivouac on the South side of the stream.

This creek at the point of crossing is about 30 yards wide, very deep, and spreading out into a dismal cypress swamp which Extends along its northern bank for several miles. The bridge at the crossing of the creek, is accessible only by a narrow Causeway over this swamp; the causeway being about one mile in length. On approaching the bridge, in company with an aide-de-camp of General Davis, I saw camp fires at the roots of the cypress trees in this swamp, and found two Soldiers standing with fixed bayonets at the north end of the bridge, General Davis' Provost Marshal (Major Lee) being seated near by. On inquiring of the aide-de-camp what this meant; he told me with an air of triumph that: "By God the General had set the d—d she niggers and young ones off in the swamp—he dont intend to be bothered with them any more, and he has put Major Lee there to see that not a d—d one of them gets across the bridge—he put about 500 off there to-night." . . .

By 9 o'clock on the morning of the 9th inst this Division and the brigade of Cavalry were all over the creek, the bridge was destroyed and the rebels came up on the other side; they immediately discovered the negroes that General Davis had turned off into the Swamp and commenced firing on them. Some of the women and children were shot, as I have Since learned from those who escaped; others sprang into the Stream and attempted to swim over to us rather than fall into rebel hands, but were drowned, while others succeeded in getting across on logs and rafts, being protected in their perilous passage, by our skirmishers, who, with muskets in their hands manfully fought for those "d—d niggers" whom our Corps Commander, Genl. Davis, had left to starve or drown in the swamps of Ebenezer Creek. Personal grievances have not caused me to make these statements. General Davis has always treated me kindly; but his heart is not right; he would Save the "peculiar institution" *if he could;* he would treat with the greatest deference any wealthy rebel, and apologize for the treason of the rebel Jeff Davis, and he complains because, according to his ideas, the President has converted the army into a machine for the abolition of Slavery. His views have been discussed and condemned around all the Camp-fires of this Corps, and his treatment of fugitive negroes bitterly denounced, and I cannot feel that I am doing my whole duty as an officer, unless I make these things known to some one whose civil position will enable him to procure an investigation of the many grounds of complaint against Genl. Davis. . . .

Many other officers, besides myself, have sent these facts to the North, and many members of Congress will hear of them as you do, through private sources.

I am Very Respectfully
Your Obdt Servant
James A Connolly Major 123^d Ills Vols &
Inspector 3 Div 14 A. C.

James A. Connolly to H. P. H. Bromwell, December 18, 1864, Henry Pelham Holmes Bromwell Letters, Illinois History and Lincoln Collections, University of Illinois Library, Urbana.

SEVEN

Hearts and Minds in the Days of Total War

$\mathscr{B}$Y THE WAR'S midpoint all aspects of Illinois life had adjusted to the reality of a long and bloody ordeal. The state's economy increasingly reflected the changes—and opportunities—generated by war. Secession augured potential problems for Illinois farmers, who before the war were linked to Southern markets via the Mississippi and Ohio River basins. The outbreak of war disrupted this Southern trade and produced a commercial downturn in 1861 and 1862 that decimated the state's banking industry and pinched many Illinois farmers. By 1863, however, with demand for foodstuffs and supplies soaring, Illinois agriculture rebounded. As more and more men marched off to battle, rural women assumed new economic roles, managing the day-to-day operations of the family farm. Farmers with the means to do so also responded to the labor shortage by purchasing labor-saving devices such as the McCormick reaper, increasing productivity in the countryside and stimulating the farm machine industry in Chicago, Moline, and other Illinois towns. Illinois farms, especially larger ones, eventually realized handsome profits from the provision of cereals and livestock to the western armies, but wartime prosperity came at the cost of greater reliance on railroads and powerful grain elevators, which after the war reoriented Illinois's farmers to markets north- and eastward.

Illinois railroads saw their profits rise on the shipment of foodstuffs and military supplies, adding further momentum to the state's growing iron and coal industries. During the war Chicago, at the center of the West's rail system, secured its place as the largest market for processing beef, pork, grain, and lumber, eclipsing Cincinnati, St. Louis, and other contenders. The western armies relied on Chicago's workforce for everything from harnesses and wagons to boots and shoes, from wool uniforms to salt pork and other packed meats. Little wonder that Chicagoans cheered the Union army's Quartermaster Department as the primary "stimulus to trade and manufacture in our midst."[1]

Not everyone benefited equally from the wartime expansion. Inflation—in part a function of the 1862 Legal Tender Act, which flooded the Union with paper "greenbacks"—outpaced wages during the war years. Facing rising rents and prices for goods, coal miners, locomotive engineers, iron molders, printers, stevedores, and carpenters all staged strikes, while skilled workers in several Illinois cities established trade unions. The most active of these movements was based in Chicago, where one-half of the state's rapidly expanding class of industrial workers resided. Here workers formed a citywide trades assembly to concentrate labor's emerging political and economic clout. High on labor's list of demands was repeal of the so-called LaSalle Black Laws, enacted in 1863 in response to a wave of strikes in Illinois coal towns. These statutes made it a criminal offense to advocate or engage in strikes or related activity, such as picketing. Coal operators hoped the legislation would destroy the state's largest union at the time, the Miners' Union Association (precursor to the American Miners' Association), which had formed in Belleville in 1861 and spread to many other Illinois coal towns. But the LaSalle Black Laws—so called to underscore the workers' feelings of second-class status— limited the freedoms and organizing capacity of all workers. As such their repeal remained a paramount object of the Illinois labor movement for decades to come.

Meanwhile women's activism on the home front continued to evolve. In late 1862 the U.S. Sanitary Commission was restructured in an effort to enhance efficiency and coordination of relief. The reorganization imposed greater centralization on the commission's regional branches, which up to this point had worked fairly autonomously. Jane Hoge and Mary Livermore, directors of the Chicago Sanitary Commission, joined in the reorganization (reflected in their office's name change to the Northwest Branch of the USSC, in early 1863). By 1863 their Chicago offices—including a large warehouselike depot on Madison Street—was receiving bulk donations of goods from across the Northwest and coordinating their distribution throughout the western theater of war. The organizational and business talents of Hoge, Livermore, and many others were displayed in the hugely successful Northwest Sanitary Fair, held in Chicago in October 1863. The Northwest Branch followed this success with the 1864 Illinois State Sanitary Fair, held at Decatur, and a second Northwest Fair at Chicago in May 1865.

Still, the vast majority of Illinois women were not paid nurses or USSC staff; their contributions to Illinois's war remained grounded in community- or church-based networks, even as their activism channeled money and supplies to big relief projects like the sanitary fairs. Some women even questioned the utility of a large and complex relief organization. The Ottawa nurse Sarah Gregg, who served at Mound City in 1863, complained of the "red tape" involved in acquiring hospital supplies from the Northwest Branch, at one point choosing to go "on a begging expedition" in Mound City for needed supplies rather than deal with USSC staff in Chicago. Other women simply preferred their local soldier's home or charity to the Sanitary Commission. "I am decidedly in favor of appropriating our means to the 'Soldiers Home at Centralia,'" wrote one Richview woman, "in preference to sending stores to the Sanitary Commission, for I believe more actual, real good, can be done to sick weary despairing soldiers in our midst who naturally look for quiet womanly offices of kindness."[2] Still others associated with a rival relief agency, the United States Christian Commission, with local branches across Illinois, questioned the propriety of paid female nurses and relief workers, seeing paid work as an affront to traditional values of Christian charity and womanly self-sacrifice.

As Illinoisans adjusted to the new social and economic landscape created by war, tensions between loyal Unionists and Peace Democrats continued to escalate. By mid-1864 volunteering in most Illinois districts had plummeted to new lows, and authorities began preparations for a draft, which went into effect later that fall. Illinois now buzzed with reports of bloody clashes between Unionists and Peace Democrats; of bands of armed guerrillas plundering central and southern Illinois; of secret plots to set Chicago ablaze and to free Confederate prisoners at Camp Douglas; and of other wildly fantastic conspiracies to lead Illinois out of the Union. Some of these reports were exaggerated for political purposes, but there can be no doubt that during these difficult months Illinois was a hotbed of civil strife. Montgomery County witnessed repeated violence when a gang of thieves led by an obscure leader named Thomas Clingman, reputedly a Confederate sympathizer from Missouri, terrorized Unionists in the surrounding area. Loyal Unionists, often aided by soldiers taking advantage of furloughs offered them in return for their reenlistment, engaged in acts of intimidation and reprisal against "disloyal" copperheads. In Paris furloughed soldiers and loyal citizens attempted to destroy the offices of a local Democratic newspaper. Local Democrats resisted, and the ensuing clash left one dead and two wounded. A similar scene took place in Cairo, where soldiers and civilians succeeded in destroying the printing press of the *Chester Picket Guard*, a vitriolic antiadministration sheet. By far the most lethal encounter occurred in Charleston, where soldiers from the Fifty-Fourth Illinois Infantry engaged in a deadly firefight with local citizens. The Charleston Copperhead Riot left nine dead and twelve wounded, making it the second deadliest episode of its kind during the war, surpassed only by the 1863 New York City draft riots, which claimed over one hundred lives.

Fueling the violence was a growing sense that the Union war effort was faltering badly. Grant's plan to defeat the Confederacy with a coordinated offensive involving five separate Union armies produced staggeringly high casualties and, at first, little in the way of results. In the face of home-front violence and a stalled military situation, Democrats organized a series of peace meetings that culminated in August with two huge rallies in Peoria and Springfield. These rallies readied peace advocates for the Democratic National Convention, held in Chicago in late August. Here the party nominated former Union general George B. McClellan for president. Little Mac was a War Democrat, but in a sign of how influential the copperheads had become, the convention tabbed Ohio Peace Democrat George

Pendleton for vice president, and produced a peace platform written by the infamous Ohio copperhead Clement Vallandigham.

For their part many Republicans despaired at the stalled Union war effort. Some in the party were disenchanted with Lincoln's lenient reconstruction policies toward the occupied South and hoped to replace him with someone more radical, such as treasury secretary Salmon P. Chase. In May a convention of mostly former abolitionists nominated John C. Frémont for president, a movement that briefly appealed to Illinois's crucial bloc of German voters. In the end, however, most Republicans understood that refusing to renominate Lincoln would constitute an admission of failure. In June the party met in Baltimore and renominated their embattled president. But few held out hope of victory that fall. By August, Lincoln and most Republicans were resigned to the likelihood of a Democratic victory in 1864.

But Admiral David Farragut's fleet took Mobile Bay, Alabama, in August. September saw William Tecumseh Sherman's army finally capture Atlanta, and the following month Philip Sheridan led Union forces to victory in Virginia's Shenandoah Valley. The string of victories undermined the rationale for a McClellan presidency, built as it was on the now discredited notion that the Union effort was a failure. Northern morale soared and Lincoln cruised to easy reelection. Predictions that Union soldiers might abandon Lincoln in favor of McClellan, who remained popular among veterans of the Army of the Potomac, proved unfounded. Four out of five Union soldiers voted for Lincoln. Illinois soldiers, who were denied absentee ballots by the Democratic legislature, received furloughs and reassignments from the War Department so they could vote back home. Their presence and support for Lincoln quieted the opposition. Riding Lincoln's coattails, Republicans regained control of the general assembly, elected eleven of fourteen congressmen, and sent Decatur's Richard J. Oglesby into the governor's office. Former governor Yates was rewarded for his service with William Richardson's U.S. Senate seat. With defeat of the Confederacy now only a matter of time, the Republicans' controversial war policies at last appeared vindicated.

DEAR HUSBAND

In the antebellum era married men and women labored in complementary ways to ensure the financial security of their family farms. Prevailing gender ideology dictated that both husband and wife were to be useful, but each, to a significant extent, in his or her own sphere. Wives certainly contributed to the farm's economic output, tending gardens, making soap, spinning wool, or churning butter for home use or surplus trade, and much more. But whatever economic contribution a wife made was subordinate to her husband's, who initiated and managed the farm's economic activity. The husband established formal commercial relationships with the wider world and superintended the allocation of labor power on the farm; ideally the wife's central role was fulfilled in her domestic responsibilities and, especially, in the moral and religious upbringing of children. *Illinois law buttressed the husband's transactional authority: under the common-law doctrine of coverture, a woman's property belonged to her husband upon marriage (Illinois did not begin liberalizing married women's property rights until the 1860s and 1870s). The Civil War, by removing so many men to the frontlines of battle, in a sense constituted a challenge to these long-standing sex roles. In the following letters, Permelia Gordon of Hamilton, Emily Wiley of Makanda, and Sophronia Chipman of Yellowhead write to their husbands in the Union army and suggest how Illinois farm women assumed new responsibilities during the war years, even as they kept one eye on the war's progress.*

Hamilton Dec 23 [1862]

My dear husband [Samuel Gordon, 118th Illinois Infantry],

I received your letter of Dec. 13 last evening I was so glad to hear from you again for it had been so long scince I had heard from you that I was afraid you was sick. About two week ago the children all took a severe cold. . . . as Ella is going to school you may ju[d]ge I have had a hard time of it Mr Bell killed the hogs last Friday I have got a few sausages made the lard dried out the meat salted and I am very tired but not sick Father and Mother staid with me last Saturday night Mr Bell was very busy and he wanted me to get Father to salt the meat which I did I have nearley as much lard as we had last fall Mr Bell keepes me plenty of wood and fodder for the cows Lefler paid six dollars on his note last Thursday Daniel is very anssous [anxious] to hear from you about Mr. Browns offer he had an oppertunity to sell that ten acre lot of yours last week if he had had the authourity Land is rising in value this winter Mr Gregg was here last evening and wanted to know where that fifteen acars lay that you turned out on the press [advertised for sale] he said he thought that if it was once soled it could not be got back again for twice the sum it was bid off for I do not know what he intendeed to secure it in some way so that you can get it back again if you wish to he went to see Mr Humphry when he left here I have not seen him to day so I do not know [what] will be done about it There is a great deal of sickness this winter Mr Barcley has been very sick again Mr Philbrick has lost his boy with the Diphtherie his little girl is very sick with the same disease I have been trying to coock some to day I made nutcakes while I was frying them I thought of you eating hard bread and bacon how I wish I could send you a bushel of them I whish I had urged you to s[t]ay at home insted of consenting to your going I did

not know how hard it was to do without you I know you are doing your duty but
when I think of the dangers you are exposed to I can hardly endure it I want you
to write often and tell me all the perticulares of you[r] camp life are you goine
int[o] winter quarters if so cant you get a furlough to come home May God keep
you from all danger is the prayer of your

wife Permelia Gordon

Samuel Gordon Papers, Abraham Lincoln Presidential Library, Springfield.

Makanda Ills
Apr 5th 1863

My Dear Husband [Benjamin L. Wiley, Fifth Illinois Cavalry]
. . . Have received the last of our tax receipts have paid in all with Sitters $70.
77 have paid all as far as I know Paid on those lands you gave me the numbers
in Jackson & Washing also on lots in Anna and some in South Pass did not pay
on those two in Jonesboro where our garden was for Mr Hileman told me that
Mr Briggs had bought them of Smith and had a deed to them Smith told me
last yr that he held the lots under condition that you was to have them back
if you wanted them[.] was that so[?] Hileman told me that he sold them for
considerable less than he gave. Here is a nice apple wish you had it I will eat it for
you if that will do any good It is gone I got a few more clover seed all I could get.
Hattfield made it do. The boys and children have just found a turkeys nest with
four eggs in it they have gone to take them out hope may raise some this year
Our lumber is not sawed yet Tilly went over when she was at station the other
day [George Rendleman?] told her he would saw it soon His family had been
sick think it was George Rendleman Tilly has to do a good deal of the running
around this yr for I dont feel able to walk much and am afraid to ride with out
I am obliged to worked in garden one day and can hardly get up some times
when I sit down with my back and hip think [I] must have strained my hip this
winter yr ago when was doing up our butchering for it hurt me a good deal then
and now when I have to be on my feet Tilly went down to Mr George Vancil
yesturday to get me some bean seed and try and hear if we could where [we]
could get any sweet potatoes to bed out Mr Vancil died about a week ago had a
bad cold and was complaining about a week was not confined to his bed got up
about an hour before he died and went and got him a drink there was a woman
in that neighbourhood died yesterday morning the same way he was buried at
Jonesboro Mrs Wallace went to the funeral she heard that some of them down
there was making preperations to defend the deserters. Think there is only
between 2 and 3 hundred of the 109[th Illinois Infantry] left the rest is either dead

or deserted. . . . I have five cts will have to write to Daniel again and see if he can let me have any more or get some from Mangold or Grear. Grear promised to send me some last Monday but did not I wrote him Friday to send it up Sat but he did not Emily was here yesturday after hers gave her five cts to get her a paper she said she had not saw a paper since she left here I owe her 10,00 am going to try and do without a girl for a while it cost so much Had I better try and get Bob Miller or rent part if I can how much can Hattfield tend by himself or what had I better do One of Mr Jake Haglers horses died a few weeks ago and the other one was about to die the other day he wants to buy one so I heard had I better try and sell him one if so which one and at what price. Mr Upton wants to sell his old cow Mrs Hagler says she is a very good one and gives rich milk price twelve dollars what think you of that

I believe that is all I have to write this morning Oh I heard that all the letters wer opened at Cairo has any of yours been The babies kiss me at night for you and Benj crawled up this morning hugged & kiss me then lay down got up again and said give me one for Pa so you see you are not forgotten by the little ones

With my love to you and best wishes for your safety
remain as ever yours truly
Emily Wiley

Benjamin Wiley Papers, Special Collections Research Center, Southern Illinois University, Carbondale.

Yellow Head
July 3rd 1864

Dear Husband [Albert Chipman, Seventy-Sixth Illinois Infantry]
I seat myself to answer your kind letter of the 21st which came to hand with two others on Saturday, which found us in as good health as you could ask for. . . . O Albert I am very sorry that you have been exposed to the small pox, for it is a terrible disease especially for one of your age but I will not fret but trust to the Overruling Power that commands us all hoping that all will be well We have all been carried safely through the measles, which is thought to be next to the small pox we all have good health again, (Thank God Elder Campbell preached at our school house this fore noon. I went to hear him I liked the discourse very much his text were these words, "and there shall be no more night" there from the 25th verse 21st chapter of Revelations[3] I do not think there were any there but what liked him well and especially us he was a Soldier and neighbor he starts back on Tuesday Morning We have had some bad luck again we have lost our yearling colt We have had them pastured in Mr Shed's pasture for some time, the colt run

against the sharp point of a rail that stuck out from where it was nailed on, it run into her side nearly a foot she did not live but a short time

July 4th

... Ansel has bargainedd away his farm to Mr Wallace but not the crops not this part either. I do not know what the railroad Co say, about giving more time to us to pay in but will find out in a few days and write again, in the mean time you can make up your mind as to what is best for us to do, sell or not, there does not seem to be any thing to pay up the interest with this Summer unless I sell the other colt which will bring a good price, 75 or 80 dollars, had I better do it or not

I have ordered one copy of the Gazette to you at the regt. and do not take any at home A. B. has one and it will do for both of us All of the boys of this school have gone to Manteno to day to spend the 4th it is a very pleasant day a good cool breeze just enough for comfort Ansels folks are all well, he is having his chamber finished the mason is there now they have got to get it all finished and painted before they leave it so Mrs garlon says. She has sore eyes for her comfort in warm weather. Philander's folks have gone to Uncle Truman's to dinner and I am at home of course and Mrs Tranor is here picking currants on shares, I have a fine lot, the best that I ever had. I tried to make some wine this summer but could not get sugar it is so high 25 cts per pound and butter the same. I will give you an account of the money that I have paid out since the first of June. I will write it on a separate piece of paper so that you can keep it if you like I also send you some accounts of that awful defeat in Mississippi [battle of Brice's Crossroads] in which the 113th were so badly dealt with It is all the effects of drunkenness in the commanding General [Samuel D. Sturgis] I think it is worse than the fort Pillow affair I suppose that Grant is pretty close to Richmond by this time I hope so I am very anxious to hear that he is Victorious over that Worst of all Places on earth.

... Well I send you My best love and good wishes good bye fore now

Sophronia Chipman

Albert Chipman Papers, typescript, Abraham Lincoln Presidential Library, Springfield.

ANOTHER CIVIL WAR

In December 1862 coal miners in Grundy County struck the Morris Coal Mining Company for higher wages, greater control over mining operations, and union recognition. Across Illinois other coal miners followed with strikes of their own. Illinois coal companies refused to yield to the workers' demands and hired strikebreakers, prompting violent clashes, especially at LaSalle. The following documents illustrate this largely forgotten history of labor conflict on the Illinois home front.

COAL MINING IN ILLINOIS.

Important Action of Coal Operators.

At a Convention of the coal operators of Illinois, convened in Chicago on the 18th of February, 1863, Col. E. D. Taylor was appointed Chairman, and Major J. Kirkland, Secretary.

Major Kirkland, Mr. Mason, and Mr. Galloway, were appointed a committee on resolutions. The committee reported the following preamble and resolutions which were unanimously adopted:

WHEREAS, The coal miners of Illinois, or a portion of them, have, within the past year, conspired to control each other and their employers as to wages, as to the management of mines, as to the individuals to be employed or discharged, and as to the amount of coal to be produced daily; and

WHEREAS, The effect of the secret Society formed by the miners [i.e., the Miners' Union Association], has been to enhance, exorbitantly, the price of coal all over the State, while lessening the quantity produced in proportion to the demand, and

WHEREAS, The history of other mining communities, and the experience of our own, have proved that such a course, if encouraged by submission on the part of the operators of coal mines, leads to the injury of the public, the ruin of coal operators, and the impoverishment of the coal miners themselves: therefore.

Resolved. That the coal operators of Illinois here represented, will not, after the first day of April next, acknowledge or deal with any association of miners whatsoever, but will hire and discharge individuals, as the exigencies of the business and the conduct of those individuals may compel them to do, paying their employees such wages as the market for coal may authorize, making such arrangements for the internal management of their mines as they may consider best adapted to the work, and leaving to each of those employees the right to quit their service whenever it may be his interest or his desire to do so. . . .

[Signed by the presidents of twenty-four Illinois coal companies.]

Chicago Tribune, February 20, 1863.

Mr. Editor—SIR:

I once more crave a small portion of your valuable journal, for the insertion of this letter which I intend for the edification of all the Miners of Illinois, Missouri,

Pennsylvania, Ohio, Virginia, Kentucky, and all other places, where this journal
can be sent by mail; and also wherever the Miners' Union Association exists,
which is one of the most powerful organizations of Working Men in the States
of America. This Association is composed of not only talent, but also of capital,
that will at some future period of the history of this, our glorious country of
adoption, astonish those that look upon a Coal Miner as if he was one of the
most degraded of human beings upon the face of the earth. But, as I have just
remarked, there is talent there, that will yet, I have not the least doubt, be heard
in our Legislative halls, advocating the rights of the working man; instead of the
nabobs of wealth advocating the oppression of the working man. This thing has
been done long enough, and I would say here that those that are in power must
beware how they use that power, for we have a mighty weapon, which is simply
the Ballot Box, the most powerful weapon the citizens of this country are armed
with, even sharper than a two edged sword. We are becoming more strong and
powerful every day. There are a great many Miners on a strike throughout Illinois;
some for price some for other causes, but we are not getting discouraged yet, for
we are confident that victory is on our side; for it is a settled point of argument
that labor must, in my opinion, rule capital, for without labor, what would capital
be worth to the capitalist? Without labor, where would all our inventions be?
Without labor where would all our mineral wealth be? Without labor where
would our fireside instruction and amusement be? . . . Without labor where
would our Railroads and our Steamboats be? Without labor our Canals would be
undug—our Rivers nothing but fish ponds; our mineral wealth would be buried
in the bowels of the earth. . . . Where would our millions of tons of iron ore, our
lead, our copper, and last, but not least, our millions of tons of coal just here in
the wealthy and flourishing State of Illinois? Is it brought into our market without
labor? No. Labor is, and ever will be, the ruling power of a nation like the one
we live in. It may be the case in a country under Monarchial Government, but
in this Republican country where "equal rights" is our motto—why should the
laboring men be governed by capitalists? It must not be tolerated by any freeman,
because if it is tolerated, it would belie the principles of the founders of this great
Republican nation. I would ask of any man, can he doubt the principles advocated
by such men as the signers of the Declaration of Independence? I think any man
who would for a moment doubt that such men as they were intended that this
country was to be governed by capitalists, is not a friend to neither himself, his
fellow man, or his country. Labor and capital should go hand in hand, and not as it
is at the present time with the Coal Operators and the Miners of Illinois. . . .

Union Miner

A COAL STRIKE AT KEWANEE.

Fifty Amazons on the Rampage.

The coal region near Kewanee, in this State, was the scene of tumult and riot a few days ago. Some forty to fifty of the wives and other female members of the families of the miners who have been for some time on a strike, appeared on the field, armed with sticks, stones, lumps of coal and other impromptu weapons, and with an equal or greater number of their male friends deployed in the woods and bushes as skirmishers, marched on the banks where work was still going on, with wild shouts, screams, threats, and corresponding gesticulations. They demanded that all work should stop till all employers allowed the prices demanded, and the whole body of miners were furnished with full employment. Teamsters hauling coal were stopped, and threatened with severe punishment if they did not stop hauling at once, and they "hauled off." They visited in succession the "Mill Bank" of Weiseker & Co., and those of Binks & Bradbury, John Patrick & Co., Wm. Martin, Wm. Bates, and Beadle & Steele, warning and threatening the principals, and calling on the men to "come out." Mr. Bates they pelted with coal; assaulted and nearly tore the shirts from the backs of two or three other; amused themselves by turning over coal cars, breaking up dump fixtures, etc.

By the time the viragos got to Beadle & Steele's bank they were excited to a furious pitch of passion, appearing more like wild creatures than civilized women. On Mr Beadle mildly refusing to accede to their demands, they pitched upon him tumultuously, struck him with sticks and clubs, threw stone or coal at him, pulled his hair, and finally attempted to ride him on a rail. At this last indignity he demurred, and by a little exertion saved himself from it, though he came out of the melee with a severe contusion near the left eye. Meantime the *brave* male reserves were hovering near by, encouraging the women with shouts and exclamations, and seeming to direct the whole disgraceful proceedings.

Chicago Tribune, September 1, 1863.

MINER'S RIOT IN LASALLE.

The Coal-Miners in LaSalle have lately been on a strike, and for several months no work has been done in the Kentucky shaft.

The proprietors, unwilling to submit to the exorbitant demands of the miners, discharged the whole gang, and sent to Belgium for a new set of workmen.—The Belgium colony arrived last week, when a riot ensued, kicked up by the discharged Irish gang, which culminated in their burning the shaft, and destroying the property of the Company. A force of military was sent by Gov. Yates from Springfield, to quell the disturbance, and it is rumored that several deaths have occurred.

Bureau County Patriot, September 29, 1863.

CITY IMPROVEMENTS

No city in the state, or arguably the nation, benefited more from the wartime stimulus than Chicago, whose population grew from 109,000 in 1860 to nearly 299,000 by 1870. In this 1863 article the Chicago Tribune *celebrates the "wonderful growth of the city."*

SCARCITY OF BUSINESS HOUSES AND RESIDENCES.

Notwithstanding our country is in the midst of war, and thousands of our citizens have been summoned from their homes and places of business to the battle field; although there is scarcely a block in our whole city, nor a mercantile house or manufacturing establishment but has a representative in the army—and although the city, county, and State taxes have never been as heavy as at present, yet there has probably never been a year in the history of this city, when so many buildings have been erected, as during the present season—excepting, perhaps, 1856. . . .

The first impressions of a stranger are that everything is new—that all he sees has been commenced nearly at the same time, and that no part of the city is yet finished. On every street and every avenue, he sees new buildings going up—immense stone, brick and iron business blocks, marble palaces, and new residences everywhere; the grading of streets, building of sewers, and laying water and gas pipes, are all in progress at the same time. Warehouses, stores and residences are moved into and occupied, in many instances before the buildings are completed, side-walks laid before them—and some even before the roofs are on.

The unmistakable evidences of active, thriving trade, are everywhere manifest—not at any particular point, but everywhere throughout the city, where the enterprise of man can gain a foothold. Manufacturers are crowded with work—have orders ahead for weeks, and can not get hands nor increase facilities to keep pace with the increasing demand. Our wholesale merchants are doing a heavier business than ever before—receiving orders for dry goods, hardware, groceries, clothing, &c., &c., from new customers daily—and from points that have heretofore made their purchases in other cities. This trade, in every department increases not only as the country increases in cultivation and settlement, but many old established merchants in the West have found it to their advantage to purchase goods of all kinds here, in preference to sending East for them. Several of our heaviest houses are doing three-fold more business than during any previous year.

Mechanics, too, of every trade, are busy as bees. One can scarcely get a job or work of any kind done promptly, and the numerous signs posted up, "Carpenters Wanted," "Tinners Wanted," "Moulders Wanted," indicate that hands are scarce in those departments throughout the city. Carpenters and masons are worked to their utmost, and get well paid for their labor. . . .

The reader who has not seen Chicago as it is, may well wonder what use will be made of all these new buildings—who are to occupy them. The facts are that the demand to-day largely exceeds the supply of all classes, and we venture the assertion that there is not one in a hundred of the new buildings but are engaged before they are completed; nor is there any prospect of adequate relief or satisfaction, to the scores and hundreds who still wait for places of business and tenements. Rents seem, and really are enormous. . . .

Chicago Tribune, October 8, 1863.

THE NORTHWEST SANITARY FAIR

In 1863, Mary Livermore and Jane Hoge, directors of the Sanitary Commission's Northwest Branch, conceived of a plan to hold a huge fair in Chicago. Opening on October 27, 1863, the Northwest Sanitary Fair attracted tens of thousands of visitors and raised nearly $90,000. Its success prompted other cities to mount sanitary fairs of their own. In her war memoir, Mary Livermore recounts the efforts that went into organizing the fair.

. . . The expenses of the Northwestern Sanitary Commission had been very heavy through the summer of 1863, and every means of raising money had seemed to be exhausted. At last, Mrs. Hoge and myself proposed a great Northwestern Fair. We had been to the front of the army ourselves, and had beheld the practical working of the Sanitary Commission, with which we were associated. We knew its activity, its methods, its ubiquity, its harmony with military rules and customs, and we knew that it could be relied on with certainty when other means of relief failed. . . .

Accordingly, we consulted the gentlemen of the Commission, who languidly approved our plan, but laughed incredulously at our proposition to raise twenty-five thousand dollars for its treasury. By private correspondence, we were made certain of the support and co-operation of our affiliated Aid Societies, and our next step was to issue a printed circular, embodying a call for a woman's convention, to be held in Chicago on the 1st of September, 1863. Every Aid Society, every Union League, and every Lodge of Good Templars in the Northwest, were invited to be present, by representatives. Some ten thousand of these circulars were scattered through the Northwest. A copy was sent to the editor of every Northwestern paper, with the request that it might appear in his columns—a request generally granted—and clergymen were very generally invited by letter to interest their parishioners in the project.

Pursuant to this call, a convention of women delegates from the Northwestern states was held in Chicago on the 1st and 2d of September, at Bryan Hall. The convention was harmonious and enthusiastic. The fair was formally resolved on. The time and place for holding it were fixed. The delegates came instructed to pledge their respective towns for donations of every variety, and help to the utmost. The women delegates were remarkably efficient and earnest; for each society had sent its most energetic and executive members. This convention placed the success of the fair beyond a doubt, and Mrs. Hoge and myself saw clearly that it would surpass in interest and pecuniary profit all other fairs ever held in the country. . . .

This first Sanitary fair, it must be remembered, was an experiment, and was pre-eminently an enterprise of women, receiving no assistance from men in its early beginnings. The city of Chicago regarded it with indifference, and the gentlemen members of the Commission barely tolerated it. The first did not understand it, and the latter were doubtful of its success. The great fairs that followed this were the work of men as well as of women, from their very incipiency—but this fair was the work of women. . . .

Preparations now went on in good earnest. . . . Twenty thousand copies of the second circular, specifying what articles were needed, when, where, and how they should be sent, were distributed over the Northwest. The aid of the press was in-voked, and it was granted in a most hearty and generous fashion. An extensive cor-respondence was carried on with governors, congressmen, members of state legisla-tures, military men, postmasters, clergymen, and teachers. The letters addressed to the women of the Northwest, explanatory, hortatory, laudatory, and earnest, were numbered by the thousands. Some idea may be formed of the amount of machin-ery requisite to the creation of this first Northwestern fair—the pioneer of the great Sanitary fairs which afterwards followed, "the first-born among many brethren"—from the fact that on one occasion alone there were sent from the rooms of the Sanitary Commission, *seventeen bushels of mail matter,* all of it relating to the fair. . . .

During the last week of preparation, the men atoned for their early lack of inter-est, and their tardiness in giving, by a continued avalanche of gifts. . . . Such a furor of benevolence had never before been known. Men, women, and children, corpora-tions and business firms, religious societies, political organizations,—all vied with one another enthusiastically as to who should contribute the most to the great fair. . . .

An inaugural procession on the opening day of the fair was proposed, and the proposal crystallized into a glorious fact. The whole city was now interested. The opening day of the fair arrived. The courts adjourned; the post-office was closed; the public schools received a vacation; the banks were unopened; the Board of Trade remitted its sessions. Business of all kinds, whether in offices, courts, stores, shops, or manufactories, was suspended. All the varied machinery of the great city stood still for one day, that it might fitly honor the wounded soldiers' fair. Could a more eloquent tribute be paid our brave men, pining in far-off hospitals, who had jeopardized life and limb in the nation's cause? . . .

Mary A. Livermore, *My Story of the War* (Hartford: A. D. Worthington and Company, 1889), 409–13, 416–17.

THE CHARLESTON COPPERHEAD RIOT

In the spring of 1864 political and social tensions boiled over into deadly violence in Charleston's courthouse square. On March 28, armed antiwar Democrats from Coles and Edgar Counties clashed with members of Companies C and G of the Fifty-Fourth Illinois Infantry, on furlough from the fighting down south. As in the famous New York City draft riots, law enforcement officials failed to gain a single conviction in the wake of the Charleston riot. The accounts reprinted here, though from contrasting perspectives, convey details of the riot and supply context for understanding why violence erupted on that day.

Charleston, Monday, 9 P.M.—This afternoon a dreadful affair took place in our town. . . . Early in the morning, squads of Copperheads came in town, from various directions, and, as the sequel will show, armed and determined upon summary vengeance upon our soldiers. During the day the premonitions of the coming trouble were too evident.—Some of the soldiers, about to return to their regiments, were somewhat excited by liquor, and consequently rather boisterous, but not belligerent—were more disposed for fun than fight. About four o'clock, a soldier, OLIVER SALLEE, stepped up to NELSON WELLS, who has been regarded as the leader of the Copperheads in this county, and placing his hand good-naturedly against him, playfully asked him if there were any Copperheads in town? WELLS replied, "Yes, God d—n you, I am one!" and drawing his revolver shot at SALLEE, but missed him. In an instant SALLEE was shot from another direction, and fell, but raising himself up, he fired at WELLS, the ball taking effect in his vitals. He (W,) went as far as Chambers & McCrory's store, and passing in, fell dead. The Copperheads were gathered behind [County] Judge [Gideon] Edwards' office, loading their fire arms, and then would step out and fire from the corner at the soldiers indiscriminately, with guns and revolvers. Of course, having come fully prepared they had vastly the advantage over the soldiers, who were not expecting such an attack, and were, for most part, unarmed. Those who were armed would hardly know at whom to fire until they were fired upon. The Copperheads were seen to hurry to their wagons, hitched at the Square and gather therefrom several guns, which were concealed under the straw. They were freely used and with terrible effect. . . .

Unarmed as our boys were, Col. [Greenville M.] Mitchell soon rallied all he could, citizens and soldiers, and improvising such arms as could be had, gathered at the southwest corner of the Square, as the Copperheads retreated down the street running east therefrom. Dispatches were sent to Mattoon for soldiers, and three hundred were soon on the way. The Copperheads halted somewhere near Mrs. Dickson's and remained for sometime, then turned and went off. Beyond J. H. O'Hair's residence they gathered together, consulted for a time, and then moved off in a northeasterly direction, cutting the telegraph wire as they went—unfortunately before a dispatch could be sent to Dr. York's family, at Paris, giving notice of his assassination. . . .

How many there were of the Copperheads, we do not know, nor can we estimate the number, save by the size of the squads that retreated in several directions.—We think there may have been from 100 to 150, and all mounted. Who their leaders were, we do not know, precisely. J. H. O'Hair, Sheriff of this county, was seen to fire three times at the soldiers.—JOHN FRAZIER, while sitting on his horse was seen to deliberately fire five times at them, and then leave. Others of less prominence were equally war-like. . . .

Charleston Plain Dealer, extra ed., March 29, 1864.

Thursday Noon, March 31.

Up to the present time no material change in the aspect of affairs is visible. The Copperheads are said to be gathering from several Counties, and moving up to some place of concentration, probably in the north east portion of this county. Already several hundred are gathered at Donaker's Point, under command of "Colonel" J. H. O'Hair. Whether this concentration is for the purpose of offensive or defensive movements, we cannot tell—probably the latter, however. Up to this time invasion in force has been threatened, and ample preparations have also been made to receive them. . . . Last night several hundred soldiers, from Indianapolis, passed through here for Mattoon, where serious disturbance was threatened, and who, with others, will be ready for operations anywhere.

Prisoners are constantly being brought in, embracing some of the principal participants. On Tuesday thirty-two of the prisoners were sent away for safe keeping and trial, and more will follow. . . .

. . . It is no more than just to say that the leading Copperheads engaged in this work of death MUST KEEP AWAY FROM CHARLESTON, IF THEY WOULD BE SAFE.

The people here are much excited; no business is being done, and all are preparing for safety and peace. The cooperation of citizens and soldiers will forever put an end to such Copperhead outrages here; but of the MODUS OPERANDI thereof, we are not prepared to speak.—But an honorable peace will soon be CONQUERED. Men, who have, apparently been unmoved in these Copperhead outrages, are now decided—many FOR us; some AGAINST us. . . .

Charleston Plain Dealer, extra ed., March 31, 1864.

THE CHARLESTON TROUBLES.

Everybody who knows anything about Mr. Shoaff, of the Decatur *Magnet*, knows him to be a thoroughly upright, impartial and truthful man. Mr. Shoaff has himself served in the army, and is now publishing an independent paper; and his word is good evidence upon any subject on which he speaks positively. Mr. Shoaff was at Charleston on the day of the late riot, and in the course of an article upon the affair, gives the following account of the origin of the affray:

"We left Charleston on the 2 o'clock train last Monday, and the difficulty was then brewing which resulted in the terrible disaster. We were not informed as to the cause of the disaffection between the soldiers and citizens, but was an eye witness to many indignities inflicted on citizens by soldiers. The streets were full of drunken soldiers all the morning, and in several cases farmers were taken out of their wagons, when they were compelled to take an oath, manufactured for the occasion. The following is the substance of an oath we heard administered to farmers by drunken soldiers, on two different occasions: 'You solemnly swear that you will support the administration, and Abraham Lincoln, all proclamations now issued, and all that may hereafter be issued, so help you God.'" . . .

No honest and intelligent man, who knows anything about the conduct of soldiers towards citizens when they take it into their heads to get on the rampage, can doubt that this disturbance was brought on by the insolent and insufferable conduct of the soldiers themselves. Previous to the Charleston affair, they had indulged in the same line of abuse and outrage, but had been so strong as to [terrify] citizens into submission. They had killed two unoffending citizens, and no notice whatever was taken of the crime, and no attempt made by their officers to punish the murderers. At Charleston, when the same game of unbearable browbeating and intimidation was attempted, they found they had "caught a tartar." In no case will soldiers be molested by citizens if they behave themselves as soldiers ought to do. And the only reason that soldiers attempt such outrages on peaceable citizens, is the fact that they are instigated to do so by abolitionists. We have heard, recently, of several instances in which individuals were pointed out to soldiers as "copperheads," with a broad hint that they needed "attending to." Hereafter, when democrats are assaulted by soldiers, our advice is that after disposing of their assailants, they ascertain, if possible, who it was that incited the attack, and retaliate upon that man sharply, in kind.

Any state of affairs is preferable to these constantly repeated instances of individual violence. Ultimately, republicans are responsible for all of them, and until they are taught that they cannot instigate riots with impunity, we cannot expect that they will cease. It is the real authors of these outrages that deserve, and must receive, punishment, and it may as well be known that democrats are determined that their rights shall be asserted, and any attempt to infringe upon them severely punished. But there will be no trouble whatever unless they shall be first molested.

Illinois State Register (Springfield), April 2, 1864.

"EVERY THING SEEMS TO BE GOING AGAINST US"

Humphrey H. Hood, surgeon in the 117th Illinois Infantry, in this letter to his brother Benjamin, summarizes the discouraging effects of the failed Union military campaigns of the spring of 1864.

Fort Pickering Tenn.

May 3^d 1864

Mr B. S. Hood

My Dear Bro.

Though having written to you quite lately, I feel very much in the humor of writing again. I do so as a releif from most unpleasant feelings.

I think that at no time since the beginning of the war have I felt so thoroughly depressed by the *prospect* as *now*. In this, the opening of the *fourth* year of the war, every thing seems to be going against us. It seemed to be conceded on all hands, that this year was to be the *decisive* year. So *far as the year has gone the decision is against us.* What great results Grant may have in store for us, we can only *guess* and hope for. With me hope is becoming very feeble, though three months ago it was full of life and vigor. How magnificent the promise at the time the Sherman Expedition left here on the last of January and how poor the fulfillment. [Major General William Sooy] Smith's Ten Thousand Cavalry was to sweep through Mississippi with irresistible force, and forming a junction with Sherman they were to march to victory whithersoever they listed. We heard even *then* rumors of Rebel threats—that Smith would not be allowed to accomplish his part of the programme. We regard[ed] them as the idle wind. Still Smith lingered at Memphis; affording them ample time to concentrate on his front—and when he *did march* the result was that he was hurried back to Memphis on the double quick, bringing a few hundred Negroes and a few hundred Mules as *trophies:* but *leaving* a *few hundred* of his *brave soldiers killed* or in the hands of the enemy. This was disaster number one; the result of which was the failure of Shermans expedition, who could only boast of having, with twice ten thousand men marched to *Meridian* and then—marched back again. Then came the terrible Slaughter of our troops in Florida and the disastrous result of Col [Ulrich] Dalghren's [Dahlgren's] expedition in the neighborhood of Richmond. And then we lost the fine Iron Clad Housatonic in front of Charleston. And then [General Nathan Bedford] Forrest made a Successful raid in West Tenn. & Kentucky.—going *where* he *pleased* and doing *what* he pleased; adding largely to the Rebel army in recruits and Stores, and Captureing or destroying thousands of our men & Millions of dollars of our property. And now he has *gone*, laden with Spoil—meeting disaster nowhere except at Paducha. But all this time we consoled ourselves with *what was* to be done on the Potomac and at Chatanooga when our armies there were ready to move, and what Gen's [Nathaniel P.] Banks and Smith were doing in the Red River Country. But this consolation has, in part failed us. Like a clap of thunder in a clear sky, came the news of the great defeat in Louisiana—and now comes the further intelligence that Banks is not merely defeated but his Expedition broken up. . . .

But more dispiriting than all these is the bitter war now making upon the Administration, by Union men of undoubted loyalty. This war is certainly going to result disastrously to the Union cause during the whole of the campaign in the field. How it will encourage the *Copperheads*, to encourage the rebels to maintain, by all means in their power, the war until an easy victory over a divided enemy puts the government in their power. . . .

Yours Truly H. H. Hood

Benjamin Hood Papers, Abraham Lincoln Presidential Library, Springfield.

REELECTING LINCOLN

Letters from Illinoisans at home and in the field suggest the excitement and anticipation that attended the 1864 presidential campaign. In the first letter, Sergeant Tighlman Howard Jones (Fifty-Ninth Illinois Infantry), of Hazel Dell, describes his political views and those of his regiment. Next, Ellen Plattenburg writes her son Phillip Dodson—whom she affectionately called Dod—of the campaign's progress in her hometown of Canton.

Dear Father Brother & Sister . . .

Oct 17th 10 miles South West of
Tunnel Hill Ga

. . . The most unbounded enthusiasm exists for *Father Abraham* among the Armies of the *Cumberland Tennessee* & *Ohio*. The following is the returns of an election held in the 59th Ills V. for Pres. and Gov.

Lincoln 234	McClellan 37
Oglesby 239	Robinson 27
Lincoln maj. 197	Oglesby maj. 212

and it is the truth when I say that our Regt gives MC—a larger vote than 9/10th of the rest of States Troops. There is a reason for it but I will not tell it at present.

We are on the eve of an important main event. All convalescents and extra
baggage are to go to Chattanoga and the 4th Corps marches in the morning the
opinion is prevalent that we are going to make a raid into Alabama do not know
any thing certain.

The boys are in good health and willing to—give the Johnnies a ruf [time] if
they can catch them. . . .

Your son . . .

T. Howard Jones

Tighlman Howard Jones Letters, typescripts, Manuscripts, Illinois History and Lincoln Collections, University
of Illinois Library, Urbana.

Canton Oct 31st 1864

My dear Dod [Phillip Dodson],

I rec'd yours almost a week ago but having written to you a few days before
thought I would not reply till after the Valandigham meeting which was to
come off the next day (Wednesday). Well it came They raised all the forces
they could, they had delegations from neighboring towns who came with their
Mac [McClellan] flags & banners making quite a display and Vall came; all
came that could come The good folks, some of us prayed for rain and it came
just as the procession were forming to go to the grove and notwithstanding
the raining. . . . I went with the crowd, that I might be able to tell you that I
had seen the Rhinocrous [Vallandigham] and heard him speak, he did speak
as a traitor only can speak though I know he did not dare to say all that was
in his heart I never heard so much treason in my life as I heard on that day I
could have wished that you would have seen that part of the crowd of which
his friends were composed I don't know whether I should say it was a *motly*
crew, they were pretty much the same, the ugliest big mouthed glare eyed
ignorant looking bushwhacking set of scamps that I ever saw At night we had
Col [Charles E.] Lippincott of the 33rd Rg[mt] Ills Vols to speak for us at the
wigwam Aunt Anna & I went through rain to hear him and were well repaid
Val is working hard for his party but it will be to no purpose and I believe he is
only aiding the cause he means to oppose. As the procession passed our house
I stood at the gate and whenever there was a hurrah for Mac I shouted back
hurrah for Jeff Davis;—Thursday all was quiet as it once was on the Potomac
Friday afternoon we had a discussion at the wigwam between [Hugh] Fullerton
& Hon L[ewis W.] Ross opposing Candidates for Congress Fullerton spoke first
He commenced by ripping up two of the planks of the Chicago platform with
which he fired up in nice style He then charged Ross & [the Democratic] party
for having assisted in getting up the war and that they were prolonging the war

etc and dared him or any peace sneak or cop[perhead] to deny it When he gots through the lofty Knight arose to address the audience but what a contrast, he did not reply save to one charge which was (and that he had boasted of before) that he had never voted a man or a dollar for the war After he sat down Fullerton arose and said his opp had not replied to his charges Three times three rousing cheers were given for Lincoln groans for Jeff [Davis] and 3 weak cheers for Mac. At night Alonzo Swan spoke for us at the wigwam, he does first rate A crowd were out to hear him he denounced Val in the strongest terms and made Ross out as no better and emphatically as he tore up Ross's speech pronounced him a liar, he deserved it too, the sneaking Copperhead every bit of it but their cause is suffering and if they were not so blinded with their own poison they would see it[.] Wash Wills called to see us, he too is for little Mac Last night our M[ethodist] E[piscopal] Preacher Mr Cunning preached to a crowded house on the state of our Country his text "Let every soul be subject unto the higher powers" Some thought it the very best speech that we have had he said that the election of Mac would be the greatest calamity that had ever befallen us but am sorry I was not there I kept house to let others go and missed hearing it. All came home jubilant as though the die had been cast for Lincoln

Tomorrow night there is to be a meeting in the wigwam another on Thursday night another Saturday night and *the last one* Monday night. I guess the convention of liar Dems who are to meet in NY on tomorrow will be apt to play smash with the peace sneaks generally

All are in usual health

God bless and preserve My dear boy Hoping to hear from you soon

I am

Your aff Mother

Ellen D. Plattenburg [Mrs. Perry] Letters, Manuscripts, Abraham Lincoln Presidential Library, Springfield.

THE CHICAGO TRADES ASSEMBLY ANNOUNCES ITS POLITICAL GOALS

In 1864, following a series of strikes, workers in Chicago organized the Chicago Trades Assembly to address a growing list of grievances and to expand labor's political and economic clout. Through the pages of its newly established newspaper, the Workingman's Advocate, *the trades assembly announces its political agenda.*

GENTLEMEN: At a special meeting of "The Trade's Assembly," held on Tuesday evening last, a committee was appointed and instructed to prepare and propound to the Candidates for the Legislature, questions touching some of the State Laws, now in force, that seriously affect the social welfare and pecuniary advancement of some of the Trades represented in our body. The particular branches affected by the present system of farming out the convict labor of the State Penitentiary are the Coopers, Stone Cutters, Carriage and Wagon Makers and Cordwainers [shoemakers], and being in full sympathy with these our brother workmen, we all feel a deep interest in the matter. One of the laws that operate more disastrously than the rest against us is the "LaSalle Black Law." This law has been so tortured by the pettyfoggers of the local courts of Justice (?) that a mechanic is now liable to fine and imprisonment should he attempt to enter any workshop to apprise his fellow craftsmen of any change or impending difficulty in the labor market. Another law that needs careful, just manipulation is the "Mechanics' Lien Law," also a provision preferring the laborer and mechanic, before ALL others in cases of failure or assignment of incorporated bodies or private individuals. Also, some prompt and vigorous action to secure the for [sic] benefit of the children of Mechanics, the foundation of Polytecnical Schools or Institutions of practical instruction in the Mechanic Arts and the higher branches of education; and lastly, to consider some measure looking to the introduction of the eight hour system of daily labor.

Having thus plainly and briefly touched upon *some* points affecting our welfare; we beg leave to propound to you a few plain interrogatories, and request your unequivocal answers to them through the medium of our organ, THE WORKINGMAN'S ADVOCATE:

1st. Will you use your utmost endeavor to have the present system of farming out the convict labor of the State Penitentiary *totally and forever abolished?*

2d. Will you endeavor to procure the repeal of the *"LaSalle Black Laws?"*

3d. Will you endeavor to use all your powers to procure a rightful portion of the Public Lands for the purpose of founding Institutions of Education, by the U.S. Congress, so that our children may be benefitted by it?

4th. Will you labor earnestly to amend the "Lien Law" so that all workingmen may, before all others, become preferred creditors in case of failure or assignment of corporate bodies or individuals?

5th. Will you agree to introduce and advocate the passage of a bill to *shorten the hours of labor?* . . .

Chicago Workingman's Advocate, November 5, 1864.

EIGHT

~

In the Shadows of War

$\mathcal{T}$HE END OF war confronted Illinoisans with a changed world. The federal government's role in society had unmistakably grown, while the war had touched off a broad economic boom that pushed all sectors of the state's economy to the doorstep of the modern industrial order. The war's many casualties left Illinoisans in mourning and facing an uncertain future. The Union remained intact, that much was clear. But what lay ahead? As Illinoisans celebrated Union victory their joy turned to sorrow at the news of Lincoln's assassination in April 1865. Lincoln's remains traveled by funeral train back to Illinois. Two weeks later thousands gathered in Springfield to pay homage to their fallen president, now lying in state in the hall of the House of Representatives, where Lincoln had once delivered his House Divided speech. One witness was Charles Jacobs, a free black from Decatur. "[T]he people mourn the loss of a great and good man," wrote Jacobs, "but none mourn more sincerely than our race, who have lost their Moses."[1] Lincoln's immense legacy—savior of the Union, emancipator of the slaves—would live on in American memory for generations, preserved by men like Charles Jacobs, inheritors of the new landscape left behind by four years of war.

Despite the loss of Lincoln it did indeed seem as if the long-awaited jubilee had arrived. In February 1865, Illinois's legislature, now dominated by Republicans, made Illinois the first state to ratify the Thirteenth Amendment, abolishing slavery in the United States. Days later, the legislature repealed the odious 1853 Black Exclusion Law. For years Illinois's free black community had agitated for repeal of this prescriptive law, to no avail. By the fall of 1864 the dynamic had changed. Chicago's John Jones delivered a series of speeches aimed at pressuring Republicans to repeal the black laws. Jones's activism was part of a broader campaign launched by the Illinois State Repeal Association, which Jones had helped found in 1856. As 1865 dawned, outgoing governor Yates as well as his successor, Richard Oglesby, publicly endorsed repeal, and now Republicans had the unchallenged power in the general assembly to act. By repealing the 1853 Black Exclusion Law, Illinois Republicans signaled that Reconstruction would involve Illinois as much as the defeated South. But left unanswered was the issue of equality. Would blacks now vote in Illinois? Would they work and live on equal terms with whites? And what of the former slaves in the defeated South? Would freedom be meaningful for them?

Lincoln's successor, Andrew Johnson, was the first to provide a blueprint for the defeated South. His plan called for Southern states to accept the Thirteenth Amendment and for individual Southerners to renounce secession and sign oaths of loyalty to the Union. Their rights under federal law would then be restored and the Southern states could be readmitted to the Union. Though the South accepted the end of slavery, in 1865 and 1866 Southern state legislatures enacted a spate of discriminatory laws that sharply circumscribed the economic freedoms and civil rights of the former slaves. These "Black Codes" indicated that the vast majority of Southern whites viewed Reconstruction as a time to rebuild the economic and political foundations of white supremacy across the South.

The wholesale violation of the freedpeople's rights convinced congressional Republicans that a stronger federal policy was necessary. In January 1866, Illinois senator Lyman Trumbull introduced two bills that reflected mainstream Republican goals for the South. The first bill reauthorized the Freedmen's Bureau, created at the end of the war to provide assistance to the former slaves in their transition to freedom. Next, Trumbull offered the landmark Civil Rights bill, which for the first time defined the fundamental rights of citizenship and extended those rights to all persons born in the United States regardless of race. As citizens, the former slaves—as well as blacks in the North—were, according to Trumbull's bill, entitled to equal protection under the law. They could exercise legal rights to make and enforce contracts, testify and bring suit in court, and hold and transmit real and personal property. States were prohibited from passing laws that abridged these basic rights of U.S. citizenship. But President Johnson, convinced that both bills constituted an unprecedented expansion of federal power on behalf of black people, vetoed the legislation. In response Congress passed a modified version of the Freedmen's Bureau bill and moved to put the federal guarantees contained in the Civil Rights bill directly into the Constitution as part of the Fourteenth Amendment, passed later in 1866. The Fourteenth Amendment also stripped voting rights from former Confederate office holders, unless two-thirds of Congress said otherwise. Johnson, now bent on obstructing Republican goals in the South, urged Southerners to oppose the Fourteenth Amendment, commencing a bitter two-year battle with Congress that culminated in his impeachment. Meanwhile Congress passed the Military Reconstruction Act in 1867, which carved the former Confederacy into five military districts. Federal troops would occupy these districts until the Southern states ratified the Fourteenth Amendment and drafted new state constitutions granting the right to vote to black males. In a little over one year the Republican Congress had moved forthrightly to guarantee civil and political rights to the former slaves.

With some justice Southerners asked why Congress was requiring former Confederate states to give voting rights to blacks when most Northern states, including Illinois, did not. Indeed, though Republican dominance in Illinois peaked in these years, the GOP failed repeatedly to enact black suffrage. African Americans led by Jones and his colleague Richard De Baptiste continued to press Illinois Republicans to recognize racial equality at law, including the right to vote. Many Republican leaders, including governors Oglesby (1865–69) and John M. Palmer (1869–73) and congressmen John Wentworth and John Logan, publicly endorsed black voting rights. But many others remained opposed. Orville Browning frankly stated that the right to vote "was made by the Anglo-Saxon race . . . *for* them" alone. Illinois Democrats recognized that black suffrage was a wedge issue that divided the Republicans in the postwar years. Hoping to rebuild their party's prewar eminence, Democrats vowed to "restore political power exclusively to the Caucasian race" by steadfastly opposing voting rights for blacks.[2] The racially charged issue was finally resolved in 1870 with the ratification of the Fifteenth Amendment, which barred state governments from withholding the right to vote based on race. (The Illinois General Assembly, controlled by Republicans, ratified the amendment in 1869.)

The Fifteenth Amendment proved to be both the high-water mark of congressional Reconstruction and its turning point. Many Republicans supported the amendment precisely because it prefigured the end of further government assistance to blacks. With the vote in hand, the black man must now "run the race of life, dependent, like all others, upon his own energy, ability, and worth," announced a leading Republican newspaper.[3] Indeed, despite the revolution in race relations suggested by the Reconstruction amendments, real progress for Illinois's blacks in the ensuing years remained painfully slow. Illinois lawmakers finally opened the state's public school system to blacks in 1872 but left the question of integration up to local authorities. Accordingly many districts maintained separate schools for the races well into the twentieth century. Public accommodations remained segregated in Illinois until 1885, when Republicans in the general assembly, under pressure from the state's black voters, finally outlawed such practices. And for generations to come blacks experienced systematic job and residential discrimination in Illinois. Meanwhile in the South, organizations such as the Ku Klux Klan violently suppressed black political activism and, in tandem with the Democratic Party, "redeemed" the South in the name of white supremacy. While there were many white Illinoisans who deplored these developments, their ranks were outnumbered by those who opposed an open-ended government commitment to ending racial inequality.

As Illinoisans turned away from the South and the problem of the color line, the war's other legacies at home came into focus. During the war women had assumed new economic responsibilities and public roles. For most Illinois women peace was a welcome opportunity to reunite with their husbands and resume a more or less traditional "female" domestic life. Yet the war had bred a new assertiveness and self-confidence, and some women entered the postwar years determined to build upon the gains they had made during wartime. The war hastened the opening of higher education and some professions to women. After the war Mary Bickerdyke moved to California, studied law, and became an attorney. The Cairo nurse Mary Jane Safford studied medicine in New York, Vienna, and Breslau, Germany, before relocating to Chicago in the 1870s to open a private practice. Chicago's Mary Livermore became Illinois's leading suffragist. She lectured on women's issues, edited the prosuffrage newspaper the *Agitator*, and helped found the Illinois Woman's Suffrage Association in 1869.

Political corruption was another issue that emerged after the war to reshape Illinois. By the late 1860s a consensus emerged in favor of structural reforms that could limit the power of the legislature to grant special legislation, in theory limiting the influence of corporate lobbyists at the state capital. The reformers also hoped to reduce state spending, which had grown enormously during and after the war years. These goals lay at the heart of the state constitutional convention that opened in December 1869. The convention produced a new constitution, ratified by voters in 1870, that expanded the executive's veto power, set limits on the legislature's ability to raise the state's debt, curbed the legislature's power to enact special legislation, and authorized the general assembly to regulate railroads and grain warehouses, two of the state's most powerful economic interests. A proposal to grant women the right to vote in Illinois, however, elicited little support at the convention.

The embrace of regulation in the 1870 constitution reflected the influence of a broad-based and politically independent antimonopoly movement in Illinois. Following the Civil War farmers and merchants, now more dependent than ever on railroads and grain processors, united under the banner of antimonopoly in an attempt to pressure the Illinois legislature to regulate freight and storage rates. The movement succeeded in 1871 when the general assembly passed legislation establishing state railroad and warehouse commissions empowered to enforce maximum freight and storage rates and prevent rate discrimination between long- and short-haul transport. These Granger laws (so-called because some farmers had banded together into the Patrons of Husbandry, or the Grange, as part of the broader antimonopoly agitation) were the first of their kind in American history. In 1873, following a state supreme court decision striking down key provisions of the 1871 legislation, Illinois farmers organized a massive convention at Springfield that succeeded in compelling lawmakers to enact even tougher regulations on railroads. In 1877 the U.S. Supreme Court upheld these regulations in the landmark case, *Munn v. Illinois*.

Another prominent feature of the postwar years was increasingly strident labor conflict in Illinois's principal industrial cities and towns. The state's labor movement, born in wartime, grew larger and more restive, reflecting the growing importance of the state's industrial sector. Indeed, the total value of Illinois's industrial output grew by nearly 400 percent in the 1860s, and with that increase came an equally significant expansion of the state's industrial workforce. Some of that expansion owed to the migration of rural Illinoisans to cities in search of industrial work both during and after the war. Still, the rapid growth of Illinois's industries—and its urban populations—was built primarily on immigration from western and northern Europe. Illinois's exploding ethnic diversity made it difficult to organize workers into cohesive unions. But facing long hours of toil, unsafe working conditions, and condescending employers intent on controlling every aspect of production, some workers looked to unions as a means of improving their lives. Labor's clout showed in 1867 when lawmakers enacted the state's first eight-hour-day law. Yet the law contained a crucial ambiguity: Its terms allowed employers to sign contracts with their employees stipulating longer hours. With this loophole in hand employers easily evaded the law, a fact that greatly angered workers and increased their militancy. Strikes, rare before the war, now became common amid Illinois's rapid postwar industrialization. Ironically, Republicans— champions of the rights of former slaves—often were labor's sharpest critics following the Civil War. Chicago's Allan Pinkerton, a former antislavery man who had worked with abolitionists on the Underground Railroad, denounced labor unions as communist conspiracies and contemptuously labeled the men who joined them "vicious and unruly."[4]

The postwar conflicts between labor and capital, between farmers and railroads, underscored how the war had fundamentally transformed the state's social and economic character. Illinois emerged from the war as the pivotal link in the chain of people and commerce that bound together an entire continent. No longer an American frontier, Illinois was now the nation's gateway to the trans-Mississippi West. Its commercial agriculture and food-processing sectors enjoyed unrivaled railroad, canal, and river connections to the markets of the East, West, and South. Its bustling cities and fertile prairies continued to attract migrants from all corners of America and Europe, drawn by the cornucopia of opportunity that Illinois presented. Then in 1871, Chicago, Illinois's economic engine, confronted its greatest challenge. On the night of October 8 a fire began in a barn at the DeKoven Street address of Catherine and Patrick O'Leary. Fed by high winds and the mostly wooden structures and sidewalks that made up Chicago's built environment, the fire grew in size and intensity as it moved east into the central business district, and then northward, leaping the Chicago River and burning through the city's North Division. For twenty-seven hours the Great Fire burned out of control, consuming block after block in a hellish firestorm. Before a heavy rain put it out the fire had leveled nearly four square miles; eighteen thousand buildings lay in ashes; one third of the city's 300,000 residents were made homeless; and at least three hundred people lost their lives. "It is not possible for those who saw the city burn . . . to describe the scene so as to make it appear real to others," said one witness, struggling to put into words what he saw. "Indeed, they cannot make it real for themselves."[5]

More astonishing than the Great Fire itself was the rapid reconstruction of Chicago following the calamity. Here was yet another legacy of the Civil War era. If the Great Fire was a product of the unregulated and frenzied expansion of Chicago during the 1850s and 1860s, so too was the city's phoenixlike rise. Chicago's lax building codes were tailor made for a booming urban population in need of cheap housing and places of employment, but those codes enabled construction practices and settlement patterns that sowed disaster. So common were fires in these years that Chicagoans joked that the city witnessed one every Monday and Thursday. During those terrifying hours in October 1871 such complacency probably proved fatal for some, and certainly did little to assist the city's chronically undermanned fire department, rendered helpless in the face of a historic conflagration that fed upon gale-force winds and densely packed wooden sprawl. But Chicago's rapid growth during the previous two decades also explains the ease with which Chicagoans rebuilt their city. Despite the devastation major portions of the great metropolis remained intact. Machine shops, factories, lumberyards, food-processing facilities, and canal and river docks in the West and South Divisions were poised for the work of rebuilding. The personal and business connections between Chicago's barons of the Board of Trade, by now the center of the nation's commodities market, and Wall Street's powerful financiers meant that there would be no shortage of private capital to invest in the rebuilding effort. The turnaround began immediately and has been a source of civic pride ever since. Within a week of the Great Fire the city's railroad and lake traffic returned to normal—and continued to increase thereafter. Within a year visible evidence of the Great Fire could scarcely be found in the city; and within a decade Chicago was home to half a million people. The remarkable reconstruction and growth of Chicago following its most challenging crisis cemented its place as the nation's great interior metropolis, symbol of the promise and progress that was still Illinois.

Illinoisans emerged from the upheavals of war to face new challenges and conflicts. The reconstruction of Chicago following the Great Fire; the campaigns for racial equality and women's suffrage; the adoption of a new state constitution; the economic and political struggles of farmers and merchants against the growing power of railroads and grain processors; the clashes between labor and

capital—all revealed the postwar story of how Illinoisans reimagined their state
and their place in it following the Civil War. Meanwhile Illinoisans continued to
commemorate the dead and venerate the living. Both formally—through the
work of veterans organizations such as the Grand Army of the Republic, founded
in Decatur in 1866—and informally—through the efforts of ordinary people awed
by tragedy and triumph—the memory of war would move forward, its meaning
always contested, malleable, unfinished.

REPEALING THE BLACK LAWS

*In 1862, Illinoisans had gone to the polls and endorsed racial discrimination by
a huge majority. All the more striking, in February 1865 the general assembly
repealed the state's Black Exclusion Law. The culmination of months of work by
John Jones and the State Repeal Association, the successful effort demonstrated the
newfound influence of the state's African American population. Commentaries
such as the following reveal both the scope and the limits of change in Illinois's
racial politics.*

Petitions continue to pour into the General Assembly from all parts of the
State for the repeal of the infamous Black Laws, and all the other laws upon
our statute books placing disabilities upon the black race in this State. These
petitions are signed by large numbers of the very leading men of the State,
very many of whom, four years ago, voted against their being stricken from the
statute books of Illinois. These Black Laws will be repealed. There is no mistake
about it. . . .

It may not be generally known that Gen. John A. Logan was the author of the
Black Laws [of 1853] . . . and further that Hon. Andrew J. Kuykendall, the Union
representative elect to Congress from lower [Little] Egypt presented them in the
Senate, while he and Hon. S. W. Moulton, representative elect from the State at
Large, voted for them—all three at that time being leaders of the Democratic
party. Such is the fact as shown by the journals of the House. Gen. Logan is now
at the head of his army corps near Savannah, Ga. When word shall go to that
gallant and true hearted General on the wings of lightning that this work of his
hands, performed under the influence of a forgotten prejudice and a false sentiment, his noble heart will beat with emotions of gratitude, that this wrong has
been forever wiped from the statute books of his native State. Col. Kuykendall and
Mr. Moulton are now here; watching with interest the undoing of a work which
they had a hand in accomplishing under the same influences which controlled
Gen. Logan; and no men in our State will experience more heartfelt joy when the
work is done.

Chicago Tribune, January 15, 1865.

THE "BLACK LAWS" REPEALED.

Yesterday morning the house of representatives, by a vote of forty-nine yeas to thirty nays, passed the senate bill repealing all laws prohibiting the immigration of negroes into this state . . . and allowing negroes and mulattoes to testify in all our courts against white men.

This action of the present republican general assembly is certainly remarkable, and a most glaring piece of effrontery. In 1862 . . . the people of Illinois, by the emphatic and unmistakable expression of over *one hundred and seventy five thousand votes majority*, declared against what a republican legislature did yesterday. We well remember that during the late presidential canvass, members of the abolition party denied loud and long any intention or desire on the part of their organization to interfere with the present *status* of the negro in Illinois, and thought the democracy did them great injustice by even implying any such motives to them. Well, the laws are repealed, and we patiently wait to see if the white people of Illinois will indorse such infamous and unnecessary legislation.

Illinois State Register (Springfield), February 5, 1865.

COLORED JUBILEE AT METROPOLITAN HALL

Under the auspices of the Chicago Repeal Association, a jubilee over the repeal of the Black Laws, was last evening held by our colored citizens at Metropolitan Hall. The room was well filled—a small number of whites being present. The audience was enthusiastic, and their hearts seemed to overflow with gratitude for their success in securing the consummation they assembled to celebrate.

The exercises were commenced with prayer by Rev. A. T. Hall, after which, J. B. Dawson, Chairman of the Association, delivered an address, of which the following is an abstract:

He congratulated the colored citizens of Chicago upon the repeal of the Black Laws. A sense of their forced degradation impelled them some months since to form a society called "The Repeal Association." They obtained several thousand signatures to their petitions, and delegated to Mr. John Jones the duty of laying them before the Legislature. Their confidence had not been misplaced. The Legislature were the instrument in the hands of God of wiping out the records of injustice. The status of the colored race had become materially changed.

John Jones announced himself as a representative of the African and European races. He asked his fellow-citizens if they were ready for the proper appreciation of the boon recently conferred. Should they use these rights without abusing them, others still greater were in store. Previous generations had conceded but little to the negro, and in return had asked but little. With augmented rights would come augmented duties. Education was the only safeguard. The right of suffrage was yet

Portrait of John Jones, ca. 1865, by Aaron E. Darling. *Courtesy Chicago History Museum*

to come. It would, however, be based upon an educational qualification, and they must prepare for the duty. They would wage eternal war upon all proscription of color. The war would have a radical effect upon the southern colored population.

Chicago Tribune, February 14, 1865.

JOHN WENTWORTH WAVES THE BLOODY SHIRT

John Wentworth was born and raised in New Hampshire and migrated to Chicago in the 1830s. Here he helped establish the city's first newspaper, the Chicago Democrat, entered the law, and became one of antebellum Chicago's more popular and colorful Democratic leaders. He served five terms in the U.S. Congress, but after the Kansas-Nebraska Act, Wentworth left the party of Jackson in favor of the Republican Party, serving two terms as mayor of the Windy City in the late 1850s. War's end saw Wentworth return to Congress as a Republican in favor of granting civil and political rights to African Americans. In this excerpt of a June 1865 speech he delivered to the returning Eighty-Second Illinois Infantry, Wentworth weaves together a number of themes that suggest some of the war's legacies. He contrasts the patriotism of the Eighty-Second, a regiment made up entirely of Chicago immigrants, with the "treason" of many American-born citizens, North and South; he endorses black voting rights, especially as a counterweight to the vote of "disloyal" Americans. Wentworth's larger frame of reference is the enormous toll exacted by the Civil War. In this way Wentworth offers an early version of a Republican staple in the postwar years: the venerable Bloody Shirt speech, reminding voters of their sacrifices and holding Democrats responsible for the nation's most terrible ordeal.

Fellow citizens of the 82nd Illinois volunteers—better known as the Hecker regiment: It is with pride I am called upon to address you. The path you have taken in this war is historical. You were one of the first regiments to go forth to fight for the flag of your adopted country, and you were the last to come out. . . .

A few years since there was a cry raised that foreigners could not be trusted, and an attempt was made to disfranchise you, but when at last the time came that tried men's souls—when native born *Americans* proved false to their allegiance and their flag, and tried their utmost to tear down and trample underfoot the noble structure their fathers fought and died to rear up, then you foreigners came forward and showed yourselves true men—you have done honor to your native and to *your adopted countries. I say it:* You have proved that this country owes its existence to foreign emigrants. . . .

Natives to the manor born conspired to burn up this city, while you fought to preserve it. Native-born *Americans assassinated* our beloved President. [John Wilkes] Booth committed the deed, but he was not more guilty of the murder than the pistol with which the act was done; it was the power behind it—the Americans who won't pay the laborer his hire—the *damnable slave power.* But, fellow citizens, that power is at an end, and the 82nd did its part toward rooting it out. [Applause]

When the enemy was in our front and in our rear, we called upon our colored brethren to help us. Then there was a class of individuals—American traitors—who cried out, "Damn the niggers," because they were fighting to save our country. These traitors and scoundrels attacked the colored people in New York, and burned and hanged them, because they were loyal. The villains hated everyone who loved his country.

You have proved with the musket that foreign born citizens are true to their adopted country, and now that you have returned home, you will prove your loyalty and devotion still further at the ballot box. Those persons who killed *our* boys at Baltimore, who starved so many thousands to death at Andersonville, who are guilty of the assassination of our President, want to vote and have things their own way again. They are all loyal now—ever since Lee surrendered his army they have been intensely loyal. What they now are after is to get some military man to place them in power again, and when once there they will treat us to more Buchanans. Those traitors who for four years have been fighting to subvert the Constitution, trample liberty under foot, and set up a government of their own with slavery as its corner stone, now that all hopes in that direction are gone, have set up a furious cry against the negro being allowed to vote. Of course—the negro is and always has been loyal—he would vote the loyal ticket. If he were allowed elective franchise, . . . all their hopes of future power would be at an end. I am in favor of letting the colored man vote, *for I believe a loyal nigger* is a better man than a white traitor. [Tremendous applause, long continued.] . . .

Chicago Tribune, June 20, 1865.

"THERE IS ALMOST NO SUCH THING AS LOYALTY HERE"

For some months after Lee's surrender Union troops waiting to be mustered out of the army remained in the South. From this vantage point they gained firsthand knowledge of the condition, attitude, and temperament of the now defeated Southern people. What they saw was alarming, prompting some to write to their elected public officials. One concerned soldier was Colonel Charles E. Lippincott, from Chandlerville, of the Thirty-Third Illinois Infantry. Here he writes Senator Lyman Trumbull to describe scenes in the Deep South.

Meridian, Miss. Aug 29th 1865

Mr. Trumbull

Dear Sir:

It has occurred to me that you might not think it an impertinence if, from my stand-point, I should drop you some of my candid thoughts on the condition of

things in this part of the country. You will at least believe that I have and can have
no object but the expression of the truth as it seems to me.

Since the surrender, I have been all the time in Miss. and Ala. and have had
pretty fair opportunities to know the people, and to become acquainted with the
real sentiments of what has been, and to a great extent will be, the governing
class of these States. I am familiarly acquainted with many who pride themselves
upon their "blue blood," and their extensive influence.

In the first place let me assure you that there is almost no such thing as
loyalty here, as that word is understood in the North. The armed force of the
rebellion is crushed,—and that is all. Its animus remains. To the great mass of the
southern people the Government of the U.S. means only the hated embodiment
of *Yankeeism*. In swearing allegiance to it,—in accepting the Amnesty,—they
mean simply to transfer the contest from the field of arms to that of politics.
The Convention in this State which has just adjourned, and which passed an
ordinance of emancipation, was as strongly pro-slavery in feeling as that which
passed the Ordinance of Secession. It is their hope, and intention, under the
guise of Vagrant laws, etc., to restore all of slavery but its name. And it is the
belief of by far the largest part of the intelligent classes of this State and Ala.
that having once regained admission to Congress, they will be able, with what
assistance may be procured from Northern Allies, to control the Government
in the interest of the South quite as much as they ever did before the war. They
are sorry the war was ever begun, but only because they were unsuccessful. The
same doctrines of State supremacy which led to the rebellion are as generally
held and avowed now as ever.

In my mind it is an exceedingly dangerous thing to readmit all these states
to their old power in the Gov't while this is the case. Magnanimity is very well:
but to surrender the government bodily to the keeping of those who have not
learned to be ashamed or sorry that they attempted its destruction, seems
something else than magnanimity to me. . . .

The freedmen are ignorant. They have a general sense of gratitude and
loyalty to the government. They would wish to vote as the people who have
insisted on their emancipation desire. But they will not know how to make their
strength felt at the polls. Nor will they be permitted to vote—whatever may be
the laws on the subject. Take away garrisons from this Southern Country, and
the negroes will be subjected to every outrage. The poor freedom they now have
is secured to them only by the presence of bayonets. The utter want of all sense
of justice, right, honor, toward the negro on the part of the people of the South
is amazing. And as astonishing, almost, is the want of what we call *pluck* on the
part of the negro. Under proper influences, with good leaders, they will fight to
the death. But of that sturdy, patient self-asserting spirit by which the people of

England and much of Europe have wrung freedom from feudalism, the negro seems to have none whatever. They may attain it—pray God they may—but meantime it will not do to rest the safety of this Government, nor its honor, only upon their votes.

I believe—whatever may be the effect on personal popularity—that statesman who shall delay the readmission of these rebel states to their old share of power, will deserve the gratitude of the Country, and receive the applause of the future.

Rapid changes will occur. There will soon be a re-distribution of property— and of influence. Those who now control opinion in the South will speedily lose their power. And it seems wisest, to me, to be patient,—to wait for the inevitable dawning of a better day. I sincerely hope our Statesmen may not be in too great hurry to *re-construct*. . . .

Very Respectfully
Yr Obt Serv't
C. E. Lippincott

Lyman Trumbull Papers, Library of Congress, Washington, DC.

SENATOR TRUMBULL DEFENDS CONGRESSIONAL RECONSTRUCTION

Born in Colchester, Connecticut, Lyman Trumbull studied and practiced law in Georgia before moving to Belleville in the late 1830s. By 1855, when he was selected by the Illinois General Assembly to serve as U.S. senator, Trumbull was already one of Illinois's most experienced statesmen, having served previously in the general assembly, as secretary of state, and as a justice on the Illinois Supreme Court. In the postwar years, from his position as chair of the Senate Judiciary Committee, Trumbull played a key role in formulating the congressional Republican response to President Johnson's policies. The two speeches by Trumbull excerpted here define and defend congressional Reconstruction. The first deals with the 1866 Civil Rights Act, a historic piece of legislation authored by Trumbull. The second, a response to critics of the 1867 Reconstruction Act, suggests the constitutional and political issues that Republican lawmakers confronted during Reconstruction.

I regard the [Civil Rights] bill to which the attention of the Senate is now called as the most important measure that has been under its consideration since the adoption of the constitutional amendment abolishing slavery. That amendment declared that all persons in the United States should be free. This measure is intended to give effect to that declaration and secure to all persons within the United States practical freedom. There is very little importance in the general declaration of abstract truths and principles unless they can be carried into effect, unless the persons who are to be affected by them have some means of availing themselves of their benefits. Of what avail was the immortal declaration "that all men are created equal; that they are endowed by their Creator with certain inalienable rights; that among these are life, liberty, and the pursuit of happiness," and "that to secure these rights Governments are instituted among men," to the millions of the African race in this country who were ground down and degraded and subjected to a slavery more intolerable and cruel than the world ever before knew? . . . And of what avail will it now be that the Constitution of the United States has declared that slavery shall not exist, if in the late slaveholding States laws are to be enacted and enforced depriving persons of African descent of privileges which are essential to freemen? . . .

Since the abolition of slavery, the Legislatures which have assembled in the insurrectionary States have passed laws relating to the freedmen, and in nearly all the States they have discriminated against them. They deny them certain rights, subject them to severe penalties, and still impose upon them the very restrictions which were imposed upon them in consequence of the existence of slavery, and before it was abolished. The purpose of [this bill] is to destroy all these discriminations, and to carry into effect the [Thirteenth] amendment. The first section of the bill, as it is now proposed to be amended, declares that all persons of African descent shall be citizens of the United States, and—

"That there shall be no discrimination in civil rights or immunities among the inhabitants of any State or Territory of the United States on account of race, color, or previous condition of slavery; but the inhabitants, of every race and color, without regard to any previous condition of slavery or involuntary servitude . . . shall have the same right to make and enforce contracts, to sue, be parties, and give evidence, to inherit, purchase, lease, sell, hold, and convey real and personal property, and to full and equal benefit of all laws and proceedings for the security of person and property, and shall be subject to like punishment, pains and penalties, and to none other. . . ."

This section is the basis of the whole bill. The other provisions of the bill contain the necessary machinery to give effect to what are declared to be the rights of all persons in the first section, and the question will arise, has Congress authority to pass such a bill? Has Congress authority to give practical effect to the great declaration that slavery shall not exist in the United States? If it has not, then nothing has been accomplished by the adoption of the constitutional amendment. In my judgment, Congress has this authority. . . .

The third section of the bill provides for giving to the courts of the United States jurisdiction over all persons committing offenses against the provisions of this act, and also over the cases of persons who are discriminated against by State laws or customs. It provides further that no person whose equal civil rights are denied him in the State courts shall be tried by those courts for any offense, but that he shall have a right to remove his cause into the courts of the United States, and be there tried if it be for an offense against the laws of the United States, according to those laws, and if it be for an offense which is not provided for by the laws of the United States, then according to the common law as modified by the statutes and constitution of the State where the offense is committed, so far as they are not inconsistent with the Constitution and laws of the United States.

The other provisions of this bill I shall not go over in detail. Most of them are copied from the late fugitive slave act, adopted in 1850 for the purpose of returning fugitives from slavery into slavery again. The act that was passed at that time for the purpose of punishing persons who should aid negroes to escape to freedom is now to be applied by the provisions of this bill to the punishment of those who shall undertake to keep them in slavery. Surely we have the authority to enact a law as efficient in the interests of freedom, now that freedom prevails throughout the country, as we had in the interest of slavery when it prevailed in a portion of the country.

Lyman Trumbull, *Congressional Globe*, 39th Congress, 1st sess., January 29, 1866: 474–75.

[TRUMBULL'S SPEECH ON THE RECONSTRUCTION ACT]

A great portion of [Wisconsin senator, Democrat James R. Doolittle's] argument is based upon the assumption that there is an intention on the part of Congress to place the governments of the South under negro control. The answer to that is, it is not true in point of fact; it is a false assumption; and of course the whole argument based upon it falls. . . . Now, sir, what becomes of this assertion that there is an attempt to place the governments in the rebel States in the hands of negroes? If you will look at the registration you will find more whites than blacks registered in most of the States; but if the whites have not registered, whose fault is it? The fault of the Senator from Wisconsin, and just such speeches as he has made to-day, to prevent the white population from taking part in this work of reconstruction. . . .

It is in the power of Congress in its discretion at any time to recognize as legitimate any government which may be set up in any of the rebel States which comes within the constitutional definition of a republican form of government, and doubtless, if the Legislatures organized under the auspices of President Johnson had ratified the constitutional amendment known as the fourteenth article, Congress would have taken that as an evidence of their loyalty and submission to the Constitution, and would have recognized them as valid governments. But they did not do it. They refused to accept the proffered terms, and thereupon Congress was at perfect liberty to refuse to recognize them as legal governments, which it has always done. Congress acted with great deliberation in that matter. It waited to see what would be the result of the attempt to organize State governments made under Mr. Johnson's auspices. When it was found that that effort was a failure, when it was found that the State governments, instead of going into the hands of loyal men, were placed in the hands of the very leaders of the rebellion, when it was found that they rejected the terms proffered on the part of the Government, Congress refused to recognize them, and took the necessary steps for the formation of State governments in accordance with the Constitution and such as should be necessary for the future safety and peace of the country. . . .

In my judgment, Mr. President, the constitutional authority of Congress over these States is complete. . . .

Congress in the exercise of its discretion has decided that except in Tennessee no loyal, legal governments have yet been organized in the rebel States. That is the end of that question. Nobody else can decide it. It does not belong to the President; he has nothing to do with it. It does not belong to the judiciary; that department has nothing to do with it. . . . Congress says to the military, "stay there for the protection of this nation;" it says to the commanding officer, "preserve the peace there for the safety of the people; make use as far as you can of any local organizations or tribunals to assist you; but the moment you see that they are interfering with the peace of the country or with your military authority suppress them and establish others." That is military control, and that control must continue till legitimate civil governments can be established, of which Congress is a judge.

Lyman Trumbull, *Speech of Hon. Lyman Trumbull, of Illinois, in the Senate of the United States, January 23, 1868* (Washington: Congressional Globe Office, 1868), 2–3, 5–6.

RESOLUTIONS OF THE GALESBURG STATE CONVENTION

Following the historic repeal of the Illinois black laws, African Americans set their sights on obtaining equal citizenship in Illinois. John Jones and Rev. Richard De Baptiste were the principal organizers of the 1866 Illinois State Convention of Colored Men, which met in October at Galesburg and drew up the resolutions excerpted here.

Whereas, Taxation without representation is contrary to the genius and spirit of our republican institutions, and

Whereas, The colored people of the State of Illinois are taxed for the support of the public schools, and denied, by the laws of the State, the right of sending their children to said schools, therefore,

Resolved, That we regard it as a gross usurpation, unjustly shown toward the colored citizens of Illinois, and that this Convention do hereby recommend to the colored people of the State to send their petitions to our legislature, asking for the repeal of said law.

Resolved, That our State legislature, having ratified the amendment to the Constitution of the United States, abolishing slavery, and repealing a part of her black code, giving to colored men the right to *testify in the court of justice,* must be regarded as still remiss in her duty, until she educates the children of three thousand colored men who helped fill the quota of the State. . . .

Resolved, That in view of the services rendered by the loyal and patriotic black men of the State of Illinois, during the war which has just ended, wiping from our national escutcheon the foul stain of slavery, that we ask the legislature to give us the free exercise of our inherent right, namely, the elective franchise.

Resolved, That the constitutional disability under which colored men labor in this State, calls loudly for redress; it insults our manhood, and disgraces the name of our great State.

Resolved, That, in spite of every opposition, we recommend to our people the propriety of getting an interest in the soil, believing that there is power in so doing: moreover, to cultivate and improve the same is one of the great means of elevating ourselves and every disfranchised American. . . .

Resolved, That, as the government called upon us to help defend it in the hour of danger, and thus recognized us as citizens of the republic, it should now give to us the right of the ballot box, for the protection of ourselves and families; and that we will not cease to agitate the question, until we shall have been recognized in law as the equals of every American citizen.

Resolved, That among the means to be adopted by the colored people of Illinois, for insuring confidence from their white fellow citizens, is to form themselves into stock associations, for raising cattle of all kinds, thereby proving that we have the same pride and taste in enhancing the farming interests of the State, as those who have, and are still laboring for her future aggrandizement.

Resolved, That our efforts for the achievement of the suffrage question, the admission of our children into public schools, the acquirement of lands, and the raising of stock shall be unceasing; that we feel our manhood, and must exercise it on every occasion, until we are satisfied that the prejudice which now exists against us is done away, and that we shall be treated as men and brethren throughout the State. . . .

Resolved, That we do not ask our white friends to elevate us, but only desire them to give us the same opportunities of elevating ourselves, by admitting us to the right of franchise, and an equal chance for educating ourselves, by opening the doors of their free schools and colleges.

Illinois State Convention of Colored Men, *Proceedings of the Illinois State Convention of Colored Men, Assembled at Galesburg, October 16th, 17th, and 18th* (Chicago: Church, Goodman and Donnelley, printers 1867), 6–7.

<u>SEVEN YEARS AMONG THE FREEDMEN</u>

In 1867, Maria Waterbury, from Polo, traveled to Mississippi to teach in a newly opened school for former slaves. It was the first of several tours for Waterbury in the Deep South during Reconstruction. Her work was sponsored by the American Missionary Association, just one of several organizations that sent thousands of Northern teachers to the South both during and after the Civil War. Northern women such as Waterbury imagined themselves doing God's work among the freedpeople. They soon discovered that many white Southerners violently opposed them. Her memoir, Seven Years among the Freedmen, *chronicles her time in Alabama, Louisiana, and Mississippi.*

ONE ELECTION DAY.

The Colored voters met at their church, and went to the polls preceded by a band of music. The colored women formed a line of one hundred or more, and ran up and down near the line of voters, saying,

"Now, Sandy, ef you don'vote de radical ticket I won't live wid ye."

"Now, Jack, ef you don'vote for Lincum's men I'll leave ye."

As the blacks came near the place for voting, the democrats came out with their tickets, and bought the votes of several. One man sold his vote for a suit of clothes; one sold his for a gallon of whisky. The democrats declared they would have gained the day, if it hadn't been for the women.

The noise and the unfairness in voting seemed more like an Indian pow-wow, than like intelligent American citizens making laws; and some one said, rather than have such a farce going on, it would be wiser for the government to keep a standing army, as they do on the continent.

At the election the republicans gained the victory, and in a few days the colored school was told that General Grant was elected president. The whole school rose and sang the doxology. . . .

A FREEDMEN SCHOOL—CALLING THE ROLL.

. . . Two hundred and fifty scholars, of all shades of complexion, and of all ages, from five to seventy-five, the roll-call goes on until representatives of the names of many of the presidents and eminent statesmen, are found to be studying in the *"nigger school,"* and with arms folded, and in order in their school desks, that have been sent from the North, for the school, they answer "present!" at the call of their names. A building one hundred and fifty feet long, built twenty years ago for a boy's school in Mississippi—this is a high school. Yonder is a flaxen-haired mulatto girl studying out of the same book with a middle aged woman, as black as midnight; here is a gray-haired man who has been the slave of an ex-general, trying to master the alphabet. We accost him with the usual salutation in the South, "How d'ye, Uncle? Is this your first chance at school, and how do you get on?"

"Mighty well, thankee, ma'am. Yes'm; dis yer's de bery fust 'pertunity I's had fur book l'arnin,' an' I's jammed nigh onter a hundred years." . . .

KU-KLUX OUTRAGES.

. . . Here [the home of a white school teacher from South Carolina], for want of a county poor-house, were boarded the poor, who were a county charge, and here the northern teachers found a boarding house.

The family is large, and Mr. Sandsby, the father, having returned from the town, twenty-five miles away, is standing with his back to the great fire-place, telling the home circle of the doings in the county.

"The Ku-Klux have whipped the colonel, mad'am," addressing the teacher, "and have sent me word they will call on you. Of course I will defend you and my family, with my guns and dogs, as well as I can," said the tall South Carolina gentleman; "but they'll burn the house immediately, and what now is our wisest course, that's the question! There are many colored people here, and very much attached to the school they are; but it isn't safe to trust them in an emergency. They are not well armed, and they haven't dogs at their command; and the Ku-Klux have both arms and dogs, and they know if they are half of them killed, there is no jury in this state that will give them justice. . . .

"There's an election close at hand, and this raid is to scare them to vote the ticket they give them. So much for freedom in old Mississippi, madam; and you'll find, too, they are bent on so scaring the blacks, that the children will be afraid to attend the school.

"They've killed the colored man who ferried them over the Tombig[b]ee [River], and now, what's best to do? We must act promptly; they'll be here by to-morrow night." . . .

Singing, prayer, and calling the roll. The teacher tells the scholars she is going to take a vacation, and will send them word when the school is to begin again; gives each pupil a beautiful Scotch Bible, donated by the Y.M.C.A. of Scotland, which she has been saving to give at the end of the term. . . .

The case [involving the colonel] was brought before the civil courts, but the lawyers adjourned it from time to time for *three years,* then a southern jury *acquitted the Ku-Klux,* and when they returned from trial, a company of ladies met them at the depot, with a flag, and a band of music.

Soon the colonel went to Washington, and returned with soldiers, who were quartered for three years on the country, and we taught other schools in large towns, but never returned to our plantation school. . . .

ANOTHER RAID.

Miss Ada was a devoted Christian girl, the daughter of a first-class lawyer in Illinois. The missionary spirit had fired her soul, and filled with desire to benefit the ex-slaves, she left a home of luxury to come South and be a despised teacher of the colored race. She lived in one room of an old house. Aunt Melinda, a colored woman occupied a part of the house, cooked the food of the teacher, and carried it to her room. The school taught by the lady was a short distance away, in an uncomfortable shed-like building. The scholars were learning fast, and greatly attached to the teacher. A night school for adults was taught, and good progress was being made by all pupils.

The school had gone on not yet two months, what at two o'clock in the morning, the sound of many horsemen was heard, and soon a rap at the door announced the presence of the Ku-Klux. They ordered the door opened immediately, speaking in a guttural tone, behind a mask, saying they were in haste, as they had a long ways to go.

"Open the door or we'll break it open," came from the hasty night riders, and with a prayer for help, the teacher opened the door, to be greeted by a dozen masked and armed men. Masks of white, trimmed with black, and their pistols at half cock, they entered the room. The lady invited them to sit down, and said she felt such a sense of the presence of God with her, that a thought of fear never entered her mind. With pistol in hand the captain of the band gave his orders for her to leave in three days saying, "This is a white man's government," also inquiring if she had a home, and why she should leave it to engage in so mean a calling.

"We will not have white people mixed up with niggers," said the Captain, and after inquiring the time with her, thinking to get sight of her watch, said they must go. As they went out, said one to another, "She wa'n't scared a bit." . . .

Maria Waterbury, *Seven Years among the Freedmen* (Chicago: T. B. Arnold, 1891), 90–91, 104–5, 129–37.

CONGRESSMAN MCNEELY OPPOSES THE FREEDMEN'S BUREAU

In this excerpt of a speech delivered on the floor of the U.S. House of Representatives, Democratic congressman Thompson W. McNeely, from Petersburg, explains his opposition to a bill to reauthorize the Freedmen's Bureau. In opposing the Freedmen's Bureau, McNeely voices themes that were common among the growing number of Illinoisans opposed to congressional Reconstruction policies.

Mr. Speaker, we have reached the time when the Freedmen's Bureau and all that belong to it should be abolished. The people expect it. Sir, it never had a constitutional foundation, and so apparent was this fact that those who originated it based it upon certain war powers which they claimed in a time of war were superior to and outside of the Constitution. It was accordingly attached to the War Department, and became a part of the war establishment where civil law was unknown, and where might and right were synonymous terms. Its Commissioner and his agents were selected from the officers of the Army. Even the clerks required in the bureau were assigned to it by the order of the Secretary of War. Its authority was enforced at the point of the bayonet, and much of the funds it received and squandered were the fruits of forced levies upon a prostrated and conquered people.

But, sir, I will not go into the discussion of the constitutionality of the establishment of the Freedmen's Bureau, nor will I criticise at length the motives and conduct of those whom it has prospered and now feeds. Its founders did not intend to make it a permanent part of the Government, but limited its operations both as to territory and duration. The day has at last come when even the pretended reasons for its establishment no longer exist, and the time for its continuance, as declared when it was organized, has expired. Let it be discontinued. Let it pass away as a part of the war that gave it birth[.] . . .

Sir, since the organization of the bureau you have furnished the freedmen, for whose protection it was designed, with the ballot. In all the States intended to be reached by this bill, the colored voters are either in the majority or hold the balance of power as between contending parties.

You have persistently contended that the right to use the ballot would enable the negro to protect himself. He has at last not only become a voter but a legislator, supreme judge, United States Senator, foreign minister, and you have thrust him into many of the State and county offices of the late slaveholding States. By his vote he is able to tax the property of the white man and force him to educate his children. This right is unobstructed. You have been saying to us, "Give the colored man a chance." So say I. You have carried him long enough; now give him a chance. Drop him into the road to his destiny, and start him on his way amid the struggles and competitions of life. Encourage yourselves to think that you believed what you said about his capacity for self-government, and induce other people to believe you were sincere in your professions by your actions. You have poured out millions of treasure and sacrificed hundreds of thousands of lives for his freedom. You have overthrown sovereign States and willfully violated the Constitution of your country to make him a voter, and now you propose to rob the people to educate him. . . . [W]hen you attempt to put your hands into the pockets of the people of my State in order to pay your colored allies for their past services and to engage them for the future I have a right to protest against the robbery. . . .

It is claimed that the Federal Government has the power to control the subject of education under that part of the Constitution which makes it the duty of

Congress to provide for the general welfare of the United States. Well, sir, my answer to that is this: that every citizen is interested in a greater or less degree, and so is the General Government in the welfare of every other citizen of the Republic in every social, political, and financial act he may perform; and if it is our constitutional duty to regulate all those matters appertaining to the welfare of each citizen or class of citizens in detail there would not remain a single limitation on the powers of Congress. On the contrary, Congress can exercise no power that is not expressly granted by the Constitution. . . . The right to interfere in the educational affairs of the people and to vote away the public money for that purpose, especially when its pretended benefit is confined to only a portion of the Union, is nowhere to be found among the delegated powers specified in that instrument, but belongs to the reserved rights of the States and their people.

Speech of Hon. Thompson W. McNeely of Illinois, in the House of Representatives, March 31, 1870 (Washington, DC: Congressional Globe Office, 1870), 2–4, 7.

THE ILLINOIS WOMAN SUFFRAGE ASSOCIATION

On February 8–9, 1870, the newly formed Illinois Woman Suffrage Association met in Springfield. The IWSA timed its convention to pressure delegates to the state constitutional convention, then also meeting in Springfield. Excerpted here are reports of the convention, including the organization's resolutions and summaries of key speeches.

Springfield, Feb. 8

WOMAN'S SUFFRAGE CONVENTION.

The annual meeting of the Woman's Suffrage Association, to advocate the rights of the ballot and perfect equality before the law, convened at the Opera House here to-day . . . Mrs. Lucy Stone then made a speech . . . giving a brief review of woman's work, glancing at the woman of the past, who turned the spinning-wheel or kept school at one dollar a week. She commended the women who had gone into machine shops, because they could earn men's wages. She alluded to women as successful artists, shopkeepers, and doctors. One of the last earned $1,500 a year. She called for the ballot, not as a privilege, but as a right.

The following permanent officers were elected: President, James B. Bradwell; Vice Presidents, Dr. Edward Beecher, D.D.; Rev. E. O. Haven, D.D; Rev. Robert Collyer, Mrs. P. Noyes, Rev. J. K. McMann; Recording Secretary, Myra Bradwell; Corresponding Secretary, Mrs. Jenny Willing; Treasurer, Mrs. E. J. Loomis. . . .

The Committee on Resolutions furnished, through Mr. Babbitt, the following:

Resolved, That the distinction of sex as a condition of voting and holding office is as wrong and impolitic as is that of race or color upon which the American people have pronounced an emphatic condemnation in the adoption of the Fifteenth Amendment.

Resolved, That Congress take immediate steps for the adoption of the Sixteenth Amendment to the United States Constitution, to secure suffrage for women on the same terms as men. . . .

Mrs. Livermore was next introduced. She made one of her best—one of her most impassioned—speeches. . . . Nearly five years ago ministers of the gospel urged from their pulpits, that slaves should be returned to their masters, bringing in the Bible to prove slavery a divine institution. Who would dare to-day to advocate it. The speaker took up the Labor Reform movement; the question of political economy; the efficiency of women for the work now denied them; the maternal instinct and the housekeeping faculty were needed at Washington, to perfect loyal measures. One man needed one woman, and the two make a perfect whole. The speaker paid a glowing tribute to temperance, and assured all that women would close the saloons with the ballot. She then reviewed the scenes of the late war, in which women were prominent and necessary actors. The women who gave up their married and wounded heroes had set their faces toward the shining steps of the New Jerusalem, and would never falter until they met them again free as they. She closed amid a storm of applause.

Chicago Tribune, February 9, 1870.

THE FEMALE SUFFRAGE CONVENTION.

[Springfield, February 9]

The second resolution was then called up, and discussed. It reads as follows:

"That the Constitutional Convention now in session in this city owes it to the spirit of the age, and to the petitions of many citizens, both men and women, to take such measures for the amendment of the constitution that the women of this State may vote as well as adult sane men now do."

Mrs. Lucy Stone made a speech in explanation. The speaker thought that any question [involving state government] which came up interested them as much as men, and when the time comes, as it will, when women vote it will be realized. . . .

Mrs. Livermore offered the following:

"*Resolved*, That the Illinois Constitutional Convention, now in session, be requested, in their revisions and amendments of the constitution, to deal as justly and fairly with the women of the State as they do by the negro of the State." . . .

The first speech was made by Mary A. Livermore, who took up the common argument of men that women do not need the ballot, and do not ask for it. The

Republican party, now dominant, had forced the ballot upon the negro, who did not ask for it, as they force a cart upon a balky horse. Women would bring the ballot into repute. Men to-day had sold it.

Chicago Tribune, February 10, 1870.

THE GREAT FIRE AND THE BOUNDARIES OF CHARITY

The Great Fire of 1871 was a pivotal moment in the history of Chicago. As the scope of the tragedy became known, communities across Illinois and the nation sent money to relieve the 100,000 people made homeless by the disaster. Within days the relief fund totaled nearly five million dollars. It was up to Chicagoans to determine how best to spend the money. Three days after the Great Fire, Mayor Roswell Mason, fearing corruption and incompetence on the city council, turned over the relief fund to the Chicago Relief and Aid Society. By the time of the Great Fire this private voluntary association had evolved into a professionalized charity organization, complete with paid staff and a board of directors composed of the city's wealthiest luminaries, including Marshall Field and George Pullman. The entire relief effort was now in the hands of the CRAS staff and its millionaire patrons; CRAS agents would now decide who was, and who was not, fit for relief. In this document, the CRAS booster Rev. E. J. Goodspeed reveals the assumptions those professional humanitarians held as they went about defining charity.

While the boundless charity of the great-hearted American public made it possible to feed, clothe, and comfort one hundred thousand persons in an incredibly short period, so that the very poor fared better than it was their wont to do, and all classes were blest in some measure, the necessity of an efficient association for permanent and deeper work was instantly apparent, and grew more urgent every hour. This was the crisis, too, for the machinery of our Aid Society to be applied to the greatest problem of the century; and nobly has it met the emergency. . . . The accompanying directions and information were furnished by printed circulars:—
To all Superintendents, Assistants and Visitors in the Service of the Chicago Relief and Aid Society: . . .
Superintendents of Districts and Sub-Districts will so keep an account of their disbursements as to give a correct report to me at the end of each week, the number of families aided during the week, and the amount, in gross, of supplies distributed. . . .
In the issue of supplies you will discriminate according to the health and conditions of the family, furnishing to the aged, infirm, and delicate, supplies not ordinarily furnished to those in robust health. . . .
The Chicago Relief and Aid Society will, for the coming winter, have to provide for all of the poor of the city, as there will be no distribution of the out-door

relief by the County Agent as heretofore. While your first care should be for those who have lost all by the fire, those that are not direct sufferers by it must be aided according to their necessities. The loudest complaints will come from those least deserving, who are always on hand for their share when any distribution is to be made or relief given.

You will have to refuse the application of many worthy people, who, having lost heavily by the fire, will think themselves entitled to a share of the relief fund, although still possessed of the means or ability to meet their present wants. You will explain to such as kindly as possible that the relief fund is not intended to make good losses by the fire; that it can be used only to prevent and relieve actual suffering. . . .

I am informed that large numbers of servant girls are unemployed in the city, who refuse to go to employment at good wages in the country or other cities. Be sure that none such are fed by the Chicago Relief and Aid Society. If there was ever a time when every person capable of earning his or her own support should be made to do it, it is now. Help must even be withheld from families who harbor persons able to work, but who are unemployed. In all cases where help is discontinued or refused to families, your books must show the reason for such discontinuance or refusal.

There are several thousand men and boys working this week whose families we are feeding, who will be paid for their work on Saturday night, sufficient to meet all the wants of the family for food or fuel next week. Be sure that every such family is known in your district, and reported at the office, so that no more supplies be given to it. Our supplies are going at a *fearful* rate. If any men, boys, or women are not working, apply St. Paul's rule: "If any man among you will not *work*, neither let him *eat*." . . .

In all your intercourse with applicants for relief, your manners to and treatment of them should be kind and considerate. You will have to render aid to many families whose condition is one of chronic pauperism, resulting from their vices or improvidence. This class you can never satisfy; like the daughters of the horse-leech, their constant cry is "give," but the great majority of your applicants will be people who have suddenly been reduced from a condition of self-support, and in many cases affluence, to one of partial or entire dependence. Their case is a sufficiently painful one without anything in your intercourse with them to remind them that they are now dependent upon charity. You will give such persons the preference over the class first named, so far as it is possible for you to do so, in receiving their application and supplying their wants, and let your intercourse with them be such that they will ever after look upon you as a friend in their time of need.

Rev. E. J. Goodspeed, *History of the Great Fires in Chicago and the West* (New York: H. S. Goodspeed, 1871), 422–23, 425–28.

FARMERS AND RAILROADS

In April 1873 the newly formed State Farmers' Association, made up of town and county Granges and antimonopoly leagues, held a mass convention in Springfield to pressure lawmakers to enact stiffer regulations of the state's railroads. Thousands of farmers, representing 72 of the state's 102 counties, attended. The convention's resolutions suggest some of the economic problems Illinois farmers faced in the years following the Civil War.

RESOLUTIONS.

Resolved, By the farmers of Illinois, in mass meeting assembled,

First—That the chartered monopolies not regulated and controlled by law have proved in that respect detrimental to the public prosperity, corrupting in their management, and dangerous to [r]epublican institutions.

Second—The railways of the world, except in those countries where they have been held under the strict regulation and supervision of the Government, have proved themselves as arbitrary[,] extortion[ate] and opposed to free institutions and free commerce between the States as the feudal Barons of the Middle Ages.

Third—That we hold, declare, and resolve, that this despotism which defies our laws, plunders our shippers, impoverishes our people, and corrupts our Government shall be subdued and made to subserve the public interest at whatever cost.

Resolved, That we believe the State did not and could not confer any of its sovereign power upon any corporation, and that now is the most favorable time to settle the question, so that it may never be hereafter misunderstood, that a State cannot create a corporation it cannot thereafter control.

Resolved, That in view of the present extortions, we look with alarm upon the future of one interest, which can combine in the hands of a few men a capital of nearly two hundred and fifty millions of dollars in our own State, and four thousand millions of dollars in our Union, and we believe it essential to the prosperity of all classes, that this contest continue until those corporations acknowledge the supremacy of the law.

Resolved, That we regard it as the undoubted power and the imperative duty of the Legislature to pass laws fixing reasonable rates for freight and passengers, without classification of roads, and that we urge upon our General Assembly the passage of such laws. . . .

Resolved, That the presentation and acceptance of railroad passes to our Legislators, whatever may be the spirit and intent with which they are accepted, are demoralizing in their influence, and we look to our Legislature, now in session, to rise above all personal considerations of pecuniary interest or convenience, and to pass a law making it a misdemeanor for any Senator or Representative, or other State or county officers, to accept any railroad pass, knowing, as we do, that the people look upon the acceptance of these passes with decided, and almost universal, disapprobation. . . .

Chicago Tribune, April 3, 1873.

CITIES OF THE DEAD

No sooner had the war ended than the work of remembering began. In the first document, African Americans meet in Tuscola in 1869 to commemorate Emancipation Day. The second document excerpts a speech delivered on Decoration Day—later to be called Memorial Day—by John Logan, commander in chief of the Grand Army of the Republic, at Arlington National Cemetery, May 30, 1870. Each suggests how the Civil War had left a complex landscape of meanings and legacies for Illinoisans.

EMANCIPATION DAY

Demonstration by the Colored People of Tuscola, Ill.

Tuscola, Ill., Sept. 23

Our city was yesterday the scene of one of the most interesting occasions of the season. Notice was given, a few weeks ago . . . that on the 22d of September there would be a grand celebration, by the colored folks of this and the adjoining districts, of the issuing of the Emancipation Proclamation. Several speakers had been invited, and great arrangements had been made by the colored folks of our city to make the occasion one of the grandest of the kind.

Wednesday morning was ushered in by the roar of artillery and like demonstrations. The morning was quite cloudy, but about 9 o'clock the clouds rolled away and the sun beamed down in his splendor on the enthusiastic crowds of Africo-Americans fast assembling from different directions, many of whom the same sun had once shined upon as slaves, but now as freemen in a free land.

At 11 o'clock a procession was formed, teams having been procured with the expectation of going to the grove. The horses were gaily decorated with flags, while here and there throughout the long procession (little less than a mile in length) floated the "good old flag" in all its holiday splendor. The procession was conducted through the streets with the greatest skill by Grand Marshal Shedd, assisted by Under Marshals. At the head was a banner with these words: "All we ask is Liberty and Equal Rights." . . .

After parading the principle streets, they repaired to the Court House where the following programme was carried out: First, music by the band: then prayer by Rev. Mr. Nicols of the [Methodist] circuit; then the singing of the whole congregation of the hymn, "The Year of Jubilee has Come." Then followed orations by Hon. C. S. Jacobs, of Decatur, W. H. Anderson, of Terre Haute [Indiana], and others, interspersed by music, more spirited than sweet, from the band. When the speaking was through they repaired to the old Court House, where a dinner was prepaired that did justice to the occasion. After dinner the crowd dispersed until evening, when the same programme was repeated with the exception of the dinner. . . .

The whole affair was a grand success. The crowd was very orderly. The demonstration was worthy of the occasion. Who will say that the occasion was not worthy of a grand demonstration. It was but one little portion of the great cloud of incense that daily arises to the memory of him who, as the crowning act of his life, issued the Emancipation Proclamation.

Chicago Tribune, September 25, 1869.

[GENERAL LOGAN'S DECORATION DAY SPEECH]

Throughout the broad compass of our land, to-day, vast concourses of true men and women are voluntarily assembled to pay deserved homage to the nation's heroic dead, and to garland their quiet tombs with nature's jewels, as an appropriate tribute of respect and gratitude.

But why is this, that the great masses on this day pass many graves, the occupants of which they have loved and honored in life, and with a singular unanimity seek our soldiers' graves alone? The answer of the heart rushes up to the lips in the simple but pathetic response: "They fell in defense of our common country, for the preservation of our free Government and the perpetuation of our national unity."

Will he who comprehends the meaning of the phrase "my country," he in whose breast a spark of patriotism burns, ask for a reason more ample than this? . . . When the first roar of cannon sounded over the waters of Charleston harbor, when the first flash of fire sent the blasphemous challenge to the Stars and Stripes on the ramparts of Fort Sumter, then the forbearing indignation of the loyal sons of the Union burst forth into a blaze of enthusiastic wrath. The core of the nation was touched, and her giant energy was aroused to deeds which astounded the world. The sound of alarm had not yet ceased its vibrations when, as if by magic, an army had sprung into being, which, in its patriotic manhood, had no equal in the past. . . . Yet onward, steadily onward, the noble column moved toward the center of rebellion and the cradle of treason. Undaunted by reverses, they carved a road through defeat to victory, and unchecked by misfortune they swept away every obstacle. Every vacant space caused by the carnage of battle was filled by another brave warrior, who bade defiance to death, until at last the beam of hope shone through the clouds of smoke, and the bright rays of victory cheered the loyal hearts amidst the scenes of agony and horror.

At last the bloody drama was ended, and the jubilant shout of a nation, redeemed by the brave, was re-echoed from the starry concave over the land of the free. At last the Union was saved, and the old ship of State that had entered the tempest in the most perilous moment, and under the discouraging scorn of foreign rivals, who wished to see her go down beneath breakers of rebellion, floats as proudly as ever, and waves her glorious colors to the breeze. . . .

The anticipations of the most sanguine friends of our cause have been more than realized; the framework of our Government has been restored in all its firmness and beauty; the cancer which had crept into our national health has been eradicated; the evils of the past have been cured, and ample measures have been taken for our future welfare and permanent safety. Herculean was the task, but the valor of our people was equal to the dignity and magnitude of the crisis. . . .

The dead who sleep in the bosom of the earth or beneath the ocean waves hear our vows. They have helped us to erect that glorious superstructure of universal freedom and equal rights upon the foundation of our republic, and have contented it with their heart's blood. Let us complete the grand design and make our country truly the world's "Temple of Liberty."

John Alexander Logan, *Oration of General John A. Logan, Commander-in-Chief, Grand Army of the Republic, Delivered upon the Occasion of the Decoration of Union Soldiers' Graves, at the National Cemetery, Arlington, Va., on Memorial Day, May 30, 1870* (Washington, DC: Office of the Grand Army Journal, 1870), 6–12.

Timeline

February   The Treaty of Guadalupe Hidalgo ends the Mexican-American War.

March   Illinois voters ratify a new state constitution and vote to authorize the state legislature to prevent the migration of free blacks into Illinois.

              Chicago Board of Trade is founded, creating the nation's oldest commodities and futures exchange.

April   The Illinois-Michigan Canal, linking Chicago to LaSalle on the Illinois River, is completed and opened for traffic.

July   The nation's first women's rights convention is held in Seneca Falls, New York.

August   Illinois Democrat Augustus C. French is reelected governor.

              The Free-Soil Party is organized at Buffalo, New York.

              Congress organizes the Oregon Territory on the basis of free soil.

              The first state convention of the Illinois Free-Soil Party is held in Ottawa.

November   Democrat Lewis Cass carries Illinois in the presidential election; Whig Zachary Taylor is elected president.

              Free-Soil Party presidential candidate Martin Van Buren receives 12.7 percent of the vote in Illinois.

1849

January   The Illinois General Assembly, controlled by Democrats, passes a nonbinding resolution in favor of the Wilmot Proviso.

October   The general assembly elects Democrat James Shields U.S. senator.

November   The Territory of California adopts a free-soil state constitution.

1850

January   President Taylor urges Congress to accept California's free-soil state constitution and admit it into the Union.

Kentucky Senator Henry Clay introduces the Compromise of 1850 into Congress.

September   The measures making up the Compromise of 1850 are passed by Congress.

Congress authorizes land grants to various states in order to facilitate the creation of a railroad from Chicago to Mobile, Alabama.

October   Indignation meetings opposed to the Fugitive Slave Law are held in numerous northern Illinois towns, including Aurora, Chicago, and Ottawa.

Chicago's common council passes resolutions condemning the Fugitive Slave Law.

1851

January   The general assembly, controlled by Democrats, endorses the Compromise of 1850 and rescinds the 1849 Wilmot Proviso resolution.

February   The general assembly grants charter incorporation to the Illinois Central Railroad, making it the largest landholder in the state.

The general assembly passes the Free Banking Law, subject to approval by voters.

November   The Free Banking Law is ratified by 54 percent of the voters, facilitating the rapid creation of banks across the state.

1852

March   *Uncle Tom's Cabin,* by Harriet Beecher Stowe, is first published in Boston, having appeared in serial form the previous year.

November   Democrat Joel Matteson is elected governor.

Democratic presidential candidate Franklin Pierce carries Illinois and is elected president.

Free-Soil presidential candidate John Hale receives 5.7 percent of the vote in Illinois.

1853

January   The Illinois State Agricultural Society is formed.

March	The general assembly enacts the Black Exclusion Law.
October	The State Convention of Colored Citizens of the State of Illinois meets in Chicago to protest passage of the Black Exclusion Law and other forms of discrimination.
December	Zebina Eastman commences publication of the *Chicago Free West*, devoted to free-soil principles.

1854

January	Illinois senator Stephen A. Douglas introduces the Kansas-Nebraska bill.
March	The general assembly passes resolutions endorsing Douglas's bill.
May	Congress passes the Kansas-Nebraska Act.
May–June	Anti-Nebraska agitation commences in many towns across northern and central Illinois.
October	Abraham Lincoln delivers his Peoria speech, against the Kansas-Nebraska Act.

1855

January	The general assembly elects anti-Nebraska "Free Democrat" Lyman Trumbull to the U.S. Senate, replacing James Shields.
March	The anti-immigrant, antiliquor Know Nothing movement carries the municipal elections in Chicago; nativist Levi Boone is elected mayor.
April	German residents in Chicago's North Division stage the Lager Beer Riot against police and state militia to protest the city's recent increase of liquor license fees.
June	Voters narrowly reject a statewide "Maine law" that would prohibit the manufacture and sale of liquor in Illinois.

1856

March	Heavy German and Irish turnout defeats the nativist Know Nothing movement in Chicago's municipal elections; lower liquor license fees are restored.

May	Massachusetts senator Charles Sumner is caned on the Senate floor by South Carolina congressman Preston Brooks; the free-soil settlement of Lawrence is "sacked" by proslavery settlers in Kansas.
	An anti-Nebraska state convention is held in Bloomington, successfully combining Illinois's antislavery forces into a single organization.
November	Republican presidential candidate John C. Frémont receives 40 percent of the vote in Illinois; Democrat James Buchanan carries Illinois and is elected president.
	Republican William Bissell is elected governor.
	A convention of the Colored Citizens of the State of Illinois is held at Alton; the State Repeal Association, dedicated to repeal of the state's black laws, is formed.

1857

March	The U.S. Supreme Court renders its *Dred Scott v. Sandford* decision, ruling that blacks are not citizens and that slavery cannot be excluded from U.S. territories.
September	Financial panic and economic recession spread across the United States, precipitating bank failures and financial losses for railroads and manufacturers.
November	Senator Stephen Douglas opposes the admission of Kansas to the Union under the proslavery Lecompton constitution.

1858

June	The Republican Party's state convention is held in Springfield; Lincoln delivers his House Divided speech.
July	Republican State Committee leaders meet with Lincoln to discuss the idea of debating Stephen Douglas; Lincoln proposes the idea to Douglas and he accepts.
Aug.–Oct.	Lincoln and Douglas debate at Ottawa, Freeport, Jonesboro, Charleston, Galesburg, Quincy and Alton.
November	Democrats retain a slim majority in the general assembly; Republicans carry the only statewide offices of state treasurer and state superintendent of public instruction by narrow margins.

1859

January	The general assembly, controlled by Democrats, reelects Stephen Douglas U.S. senator.
February	Governor Bissell vetoes a redistricting bill designed to ensure Democratic dominance in the general assembly.
September	Jim Gray, a fugitive slave from New Madrid, Missouri, is apprehended in Union County, Illinois. A county judge at Jonesboro files a habeas petition with state supreme court chief justice John Caton, then sitting at Ottawa.
October	John Hossack leads a vigilance committee into Caton's courtroom in Ottawa and frees Gray, who eventually reaches freedom in Canada.
	John Brown leads his raid on the federal arsenal at Harpers Ferry, Virginia.
December	John Brown is hanged for his actions at Harpers Ferry.

1860

May	Illinois Republicans meet at Decatur and endorse Richard Yates for governor and Abraham Lincoln for president.
	Republicans convene their national convention in Chicago and nominate Lincoln for president.
	The Democratic national convention meets in Charleston, South Carolina, but fails to nominate a candidate amid divisions between supporters of Stephen Douglas and his Southern opponents.
June	Northern Democrats in Baltimore nominate Stephen A. Douglas for president; Southern Democrats refuse to accept Douglas's nomination and turn to John C. Breckinridge.
August	Illinois supporters of Constitutional Union candidate John Bell meet at Decatur to endorse Bell's candidacy.
October	John Hossack is tried and convicted in federal district court in Chicago for his role in the Jim Gray fugitive case.
November	Lincoln carries Illinois with nearly 51 percent of the vote; Republican Richard Yates is elected governor, and Republicans gain control of the general assembly for the first time in the state's history.

Illinois voters authorize a state constitutional convention, to convene January 1862.

December   South Carolina secedes from the Union.

1861

January   The general assembly reelects Lyman Trumbull to the U.S. Senate.

Mississippi, Florida, Alabama, Georgia, and Louisiana secede from the Union and join the Confederacy.

Coal miners in Belleville strike and form the American Miners' Association.

February   The Confederate States of America is established at Montgomery, Alabama; Mississippi's Jefferson Davis is elected the Confederacy's first president.

Texas secedes from the Union.

March   Lincoln is inaugurated.

April   Fort Sumter is attacked; Lincoln orders the mobilization of 75,000 volunteers to put down the rebellion.

Illinois's first units are organized into the Seventh through Twelfth Illinois Volunteer Infantry Regiments at Camp Yates, in Springfield.

Governor Richard Yates calls the general assembly into a ten-day emergency session; the assembly enacts legislation expanding and updating the state's militia, appropriates $3.5 million for military purposes, and authorizes the organization of four additional infantry regiments, one cavalry regiment, and one artillery regiment.

Governor Yates orders several companies to Camp Defiance, Cairo. Brigadier General Benjamin Prentiss is sent to command these initial forces.

The Illinois State Arsenal, at Springfield, begins manufacture of munitions.

Captain James Stokes leads a raid on the federal arsenal at St. Louis, Missouri, capturing arms and supplies for use by Illinois soldiers.

Colonel Benjamin Prentiss orders the capture of the steamers *C. E. Hillman* and *John D. Perry;* a large supply of arms and munitions are taken.

Virginia secedes from the Union.

May   Training camps for new recruits are founded at Anna, Belleville,
            Dixon, Freeport, Jacksonville, Joliet, Mattoon, Peoria, and Quincy.

            Arkansas, North Carolina, and Virginia secede from the Union.

            Union General Benjamin Butler, in command of Fort Monroe, in
            Virginia, declares runaway slaves "contraband" and puts them to
            work for the Union military effort at the fort.

June   Stephen A. Douglas dies.

            Tennessee secedes from the Union.

            The United States Sanitary Commission is founded.

            Southern Illinois Democratic leader John Logan publicly backs the
            Union and its effort to crush the rebellion through force of arms.

July   The battle of First Bull Run is fought; Confederate general Joseph
            Johnston defeats Union general Irwin McDowell.

            President Lincoln calls for 500,000 additional volunteers on three-
            year terms of service.

August   Congress enacts the First Confiscation Act.

            Camp Butler, Illinois's largest army training facility, is established at
            Springfield.

            Union general John C. Frémont issues an order freeing the slaves in
            Missouri; President Lincoln revokes the order in September.

            Construction of three iron-clad river gunboats commences at
            Mound City.

September   Brigadier General Ulysses S. Grant is appointed commander of the
            District of Southeast Missouri; Grant establishes his base at Cairo.

            Camp Douglas is established at Chicago.

October   The Chicago Sanitary Commission is founded.

November   The elections for delegates to the upcoming state constitutional
            convention are held, resulting in a Democratic victory.

            The battle of Belmont, Missouri, is fought: Grant battles
            Confederate general Gideon Pillow to a draw. Hundreds of
            casualties are sent to hospitals at Cairo and Mound City.

The Illinois State Arsenal closes its munitions factory.

December | Mary Livermore and Jane Hoge begin their tour of hospitals at Cairo, Mound City, and St. Louis.

Senator Lyman Trumbull introduces a bill for a second confiscation act.

1862

January | The state constitutional convention, controlled by Democrats, begins deliberations at Springfield.

February | Grant captures Forts Henry and Donelson.

Congress enacts the Legal Tender Act.

March | General George McClellan begins his Peninsula campaign, seeking to capture Richmond.

April | The battle of Shiloh is fought: Grant defeats General Albert Sidney Johnston's forces. Twenty-eight Illinois regiments are engaged and suffer nearly 4,500 casualties, more than any other state.

Admiral David Farragut captures New Orleans.

Congress abolishes slavery in the District of Columbia.

May | Union general David Hunter issues an order freeing the slaves in South Carolina, Georgia, and Florida; Lincoln revokes Hunter's order.

Congress enacts the Homestead Act, granting 160 acres of public land to settlers who live on and improve the land for five years.

June | Illinois voters narrowly reject the new state constitution but approve the ban on black migration into Illinois and the denial of suffrage rights to black males by wide margins in separate ballot questions.

The Seven Days Battles are fought; Robert E. Lee defeats McClellan, preventing the Army of the Potomac from capturing Richmond. McClellan retreats and begins evacuating the York-James peninsula.

July | Congress enacts the Pacific Railway Act.

Congress enacts the Militia Act.

Lincoln calls for an additional 300,000 volunteers.

Congress enacts the Second Confiscation Act.

Congress enacts the Morrill Land-Grant Act, creating the nation's land-grant colleges and universities.

August The battle of Second Bull Run is fought; Lee defeats General John Pope.

The War Department approves the enlistment of black troops in the Southern Department.

September Lee commences the invasion of Maryland.

Evangelical leaders from Illinois convene a giant meeting at Chicago's Bryan Hall and draft the Emancipation Memorial. William Weston Patton and John Dempster travel to Washington to present the memorial to Lincoln.

The battle of Antietam is fought; McClellan fights Lee to a draw; Lee returns to Virginia.

Secretary of War Edwin Stanton orders the shipment of runaway slaves housed at Cairo into rural communities across Illinois; he revokes the order in early October.

Lincoln announces his preliminary Emancipation Proclamation.

Lincoln suspends the writ of habeas corpus across the North.

October The battle of Perryville is fought; Union general Don Carlos Buell defeats Confederate general Braxton Bragg; Confederate forces withdraw from Kentucky.

November Illinois Democrats rout Republicans in state and national elections, and regain a majority in the general assembly.

McClellan is relieved of his command.

December The battle of Fredericksburg is fought; Lee defeats General Ambrose Burnside.

Grundy County coal miners at the Morris Coal Company go on strike for higher wages and union recognition, precipitating a series of strikes across Illinois in 1863.

1863

January	Lincoln issues the Emancipation Proclamation.
	The general assembly elects Democrat William Richardson to the U.S. Senate.
	The U.S. army Quartermaster Department's facility at Quincy begins manufacturing army uniforms for troops in the western theater.
February	The Illinois house passes the Peace Resolutions.
	Congress enacts the National Banking Act, establishing a nationwide system of banks chartered by the federal government.
March	Congress passes the Enrollment Act.
	The general assembly passes the LaSalle Black Laws, making it illegal to encourage strikes and picketing.
April	Grant commences his Vicksburg campaign.
May	The battle of Chancellorsville is fought; Lee defeats General Joseph Hooker.
	Grant begins his siege of Vicksburg.
June	Governor Richard Yates issues an order proroguing the general assembly, which will not convene again until 1865.
	Antidraft violence commences in southern and central Illinois. Mobs clash with U.S. marshals and local law enforcement in Fulton and Richland Counties, among other sites.
	General Burnside issues General Order no. 84, shutting down the *Chicago Times* and the *Jonesboro Gazette*.
	Lee begins his invasion into Pennsylvania.
July	The battle of Gettysburg is fought; General George Meade defeats Lee; Lee retreats back into Virginia.
	Vicksburg falls to Grant.
	Massive antidraft riots break out in New York City, leaving over 100 dead.
September	Lincoln's Conkling letter is read at a huge Union League meeting at Springfield.

The U.S. Army informs Governor Yates that Illinois has exceeded its quota for volunteers; plans for instituting the draft in Illinois are suspended.

October   The Northwest Sanitary Fair is held in Chicago.

The War Department calls for an additional 300,000 troops on three-year terms.

November   Lincoln delivers his Gettysburg Address.

The U.S. Navy orders its ordnance stores for the Mississippi River Squadron moved to Mound City.

The battle of Missionary Ridge is fought; Grant defeats Bragg; Chattanooga falls to Union forces.

1864

February   Lincoln calls for an additional 200,000 volunteers.

March   Lincoln names Grant lieutenant general of all Union forces.

Antiwar Democrats clash with furloughed soldiers from the Fifty-Fourth Illinois on the Charleston courthouse square. The so-called Charleston copperhead riot leaves nine dead and twelve wounded.

April   The Twenty-Ninth U.S. Colored Volunteers, the only black regiment raised in Illinois, is mustered at Quincy.

The U.S. Senate passes the Thirteenth Amendment.

May   Grant begins an offensive against Lee in Virginia.

June   The Republican national convention is held at Baltimore; Lincoln is nominated for reelection.

Grant begins his siege of Petersburg.

Chicago workers found the Chicago Trades Assembly.

July   Bond, Fayette, and Montgomery Counties witness sporadic violence at the hands of antiwar men led by Missourian Thomas Clingman.

Lincoln calls for an additional 500,000 volunteers.

August   The battle of Mobile Bay is fought; Farragut captures the last major Confederate port on the Gulf of Mexico.

Peace Democrats organize a massive rally at Peoria.

The Democratic National Convention is held at Chicago; the party nominates George McClellan for president on a peace platform.

September   Atlanta falls to General William Tecumseh Sherman.

The Illinois State Sanitary Fair is held at Decatur.

October   Union general Phillip Sheridan marches through the Shenandoah Valley, mauling General Jubal Early's army.

November   Lincoln is reelected president with 54 percent of the vote in Illinois.

Republicans sweep back into the general assembly, winning 11 of 14 congressional seats; and Republican Richard Oglesby is elected governor.

Sherman begins his March to the Sea.

The draft begins in Illinois after the state fails to meet its quota of volunteers.

December   The battle of Nashville is fought; General George Thomas defeats General John Bell Hood, annihilating the Confederacy's western army.

Sherman captures Savannah, Georgia.

1865

January   The Thirteenth Amendment is passed by Congress and sent to the states for ratification.

The general assembly, controlled by Republicans, elects Richard Yates to the U.S. Senate.

February   The general assembly ratifies the Thirteenth Amendment.

The general assembly repeals the state's black laws.

Sherman marches through South Carolina and occupies Columbia.

March   Congress creates the Freedmen's Bureau.

April   Lee evacuates his lines at Petersburg, surrenders at Appomattox Court House.

Lincoln is assassinated.

Joseph Johnston surrenders to Sherman in North Carolina.

May	Lincoln's body returns to Illinois, lies in state at the Springfield capitol.
	Jefferson Davis is captured.
	General Edmund Kirby Smith surrenders the last Confederate army at New Orleans.
	President Johnson unveils his Reconstruction policy.
December	The Thirteenth Amendment is ratified.
	The Thirty-Ninth Congress convenes; Lyman Trumbull, chairman of the Senate Judiciary Committee, begins work on the Civil Rights bill.

1866

February	Congress reauthorizes the Freedmen's Bureau. President Andrew Johnson vetoes the bill; in July, Congress passes a modified bill reauthorizing the Freedmen's Bureau.
March	Congress passes the Civil Rights bill. President Johnson vetoes the bill; Congress overrides Johnson's veto in April.
April	The Grand Army of the Republic, a national veterans' organization for Union soldiers, is established at Decatur.
May	The first branch of the Ku Klux Klan is established in Pulaski, Tennessee.
June	The Fourteenth Amendment is passed by Congress and sent to the states for ratification.
October	The State Convention of Colored Men meets at Galesburg.

1867

January	The general assembly ratifies the Fourteenth Amendment.
February	The general assembly passes a bill creating the University of Illinois.
March	Congress enacts the Military Reconstruction Act.
	The general assembly enacts an eight-hour-day law but provides exceptions for employers who negotiate contracts stipulating longer hours.

1868

February	President Andrew Johnson replaces Secretary of War Edwin Stanton with Lorenzo Thomas; House of Representatives votes to impeach Johnson for violating the Tenure of Office Act.
March	The impeachment trial of President Johnson begins in the U.S. Senate.
May	The U.S. Senate fails to convict Johnson on the articles of impeachment.
	John A. Logan, commander in chief of the Grand Army of the Republic, issues a General Order establishing Decoration Day— later to be called Memorial Day—to commemorate fallen Civil War soldiers.
July	The Fourteenth Amendment is ratified.
November	Ulysses S. Grant is elected president with 56 percent of the vote in Illinois.
	Republican John M. Palmer is elected governor of Illinois; Illinois voters approve a new constitutional convention, to meet in December 1869.

1869

February	Congress passes the Fifteenth Amendment and sends it to the states for ratification.
	The Illinois Woman's Suffrage Association is formed in Chicago.
March	The general assembly ratifies the Fifteenth Amendment.
December	The state constitutional convention opens at Springfield.

1870

February	The Fifteenth Amendment is ratified.
	The Illinois Woman's Suffrage Association meets at Springfield.
April	Farmers from across the state meet at a "producers' convention" at Bloomington.
July	Illinois voters approve a new state constitution.

Discussion Questions

CHAPTER 1: ILLINOIS AND THE POLITICS OF SLAVERY

1. Why was the Fugitive Slave Law so controversial in Illinois? What factors influenced the various reactions of Illinoisans to the law?

2. What does the 1853 Black Exclusion Law reveal about racial attitudes in Illinois before the Civil War? What problems in the law did its critics identify? How do you reconcile support for black exclusion in Illinois, on the one hand, with widespread opposition to the Kansas-Nebraska Act, on the other? What problems did Democrat Burrel T. Jones see in the rise of political antislavery in Illinois?

3. What problems did Illinoisans associate with foreign immigration? What were some of the changes taking place in the 1850s that help us understand the appeal of nativism in places like Chicago? What effects did the nativist movement have on Illinois politics in the mid-1850s?

4. What were the main concerns of the early Illinois Republican Party? In what ways were Republicans like Lincoln similar to and different from abolitionists like Ichabod Codding or Mary Jones? Where in the state was support for the Republican Party relatively weak, and why?

CHAPTER 2: THE EMERGENCE OF LINCOLN AND THE SECESSION CRISIS

1. What were the key issues of contention between Lincoln and Douglas in their 1858 debates? How did each man attempt to connect his position regarding slavery in the western territories with America's democratic and constitutional traditions? How and why did the issue of race figure in the debates?

2. Richard Yates said, "The great idea and basis of the Republican party . . . is free labor." What did he mean? How did the economic character and development of Illinois—and by extension, the North—contribute to the election of Lincoln? How might an abolitionist like John Hossack or Mary Jones have responded to Yates?

3. How did Illinoisans respond to the secession of South Carolina and the rest of the slave South? Why did some Illinoisans seem to blame the Republican Party for Southern secession? Was secession a legitimate act? Why or why not? Did the writer "Egypt" make a convincing case for the secession of southern Illinois?

CHAPTER 3: IMPROVISING WAR

1. How did Illinois respond to the fall of Fort Sumter and the beginning of the Civil War? What measures did Illinois take to prepare for war? How did social identity—class, ethnicity, gender, or race—figure in the process of war mobilization? What role did community play?

2. Why did the battle of Bull Run affect Illinoisans so much? What were the consequences of the battle for the home front? Why did the 1862 state constitutional convention become so divisive?

3. Jane Hoge said that women's wartime work "turned a new leaf in woman's history and development." Do you agree? In what ways was women's wartime volunteerism a new development, and in what ways was it an extension of antebellum patterns and traditions?

CHAPTER 4: ILLINOIS AND EMANCIPATION

1. What arguments did various Illinoisans make in favor of emancipating the slaves? What factors did Lincoln himself weigh in his momentous decision to issue the Emancipation Proclamation? Why might the factors that influenced Lincoln be different from those that influenced ordinary Illinoisans? Was Lincoln a leader or a follower on the issue of emancipation? To what extent can we say that runaway slaves such as Andrew Smith freed themselves?

2. Why were the Cairo contrabands so controversial in Illinois? How did the issue affect the Illinois home front? Why did so many Illinoisans oppose emancipation?

3. How might H. Ford Douglas have answered the question about runaways freeing themselves? How might he have answered the question about Lincoln's role in freeing the slaves?

CHAPTER 5: DIVIDED HOUSES

1. What grievances motivated Illinois Democrats by 1863? What do those grievances reveal about the Democrats' views of government, the Constitution, and society during the war? What distinguished War Democrats—for instance, Stephen A. Douglas before he died—from Peace Democrats in Illinois? What did soldiers think of the Peace Resolutions and other examples of Democratic opposition?

2. Why did Governor Yates prorogue the Illinois state legislature, and how did his order contribute to the Democrats' critique of the war? By 1863 many Illinois Democrats believed that the Civil War was no longer about restoring the Union,

but rather a war to achieve Republican goals. Was this a fair characterization? How did Lincoln respond to this view?

3. How did various Illinoisans account for the violence—both threatened and real—on the Illinois home front? What role did deserters play in the reports of violence and intimidation? What role did organized groups such as the Knights of the Golden Circle play? Why might officials have exaggerated the violence or the extent to which opposition leaders orchestrated it? Do you believe the opponents of the Lincoln administration, whether armed or otherwise, were practicing disloyalty? Why or why not?

4. In his letter to James Conkling, Lincoln claims to have acted consistently with the Constitution. Do you agree? How much room did Lincoln leave for dissent during wartime? How and why did Lincoln connect emancipation and the use of black troops to the goal of saving the Union?

CHAPTER 6: THE SOLDIERS' WAR

1. In what ways did Illinois soldiers' perceptions of the war change over time? In what ways did their experiences as soldiers remain fairly constant throughout the war?

2. How did soldiers attempt to convey the experience of battle? Did that experience conform to their expectations? How did fighting battles affect the soldiers?

3. How did soldiers view the Southern people? How did their views differ from those back home? How did their attitudes toward the Southern people change over time?

4. How did the experience of black soldiers differ from that of white soldiers? How did black soldiers influence the home front?

CHAPTER 7: HEARTS AND MINDS IN THE DAYS OF TOTAL WAR

1. In what ways had Illinoisans' views of the sectional conflict changed by the second half of the war? How did events on the battlefield influence the home front?

2. How did the war alter women's roles and wartime activism? How did the war contribute to women's self-confidence and sense of citizenship? Why did a labor movement emerge during the war? What kind of society did the workers seem to envision? How was that vision similar to and different from the vision of Republicans and Democrats before the war? How did the *Chicago Tribune* respond to the issues raised by workers?

3. Why did bloody violence erupt in Charleston in March 1864? What accounts for the competing narratives of the Copperhead Riot's causes and meaning?

CHAPTER 8: IN THE SHADOWS OF WAR

1. In what ways had the war altered the expectations of black Illinoisans? How did the war figure in the resolutions of the Galesburg State Convention of Colored Men? How do you explain the repeal of Illinois's black laws? What evidence do you see of continued racism in Illinois after the war? How do you explain the persistence of racism on the one hand and the evidence of some progress on the other?

2. What were the problems that Lyman Trumbull hoped to address with his Civil Rights bill? What motives did Republicans like Trumbull and missionaries like Maria Waterbury share during Reconstruction, and what motives were distinctive to each? How did Illinoisans like Thompson McNeely respond to the program of congressional Reconstruction? How might Maria Waterbury have responded to McNeely? In the end, how do you explain the failure of Reconstruction?

3. Why did the antimonopoly and women's suffrage movements in Illinois emerge after the war? What vision of society did each movement seem to possess? Why was it hard to link these movements in postwar Illinois? Why, for that matter, was it hard to join together the women's suffrage movement and the movement for black civil rights?

4. In what ways does the term Reconstruction apply to Illinois as much as to the defeated South?

5. How did race influence the ways in which Illinoisans remembered and ascribed meaning to the Civil War?

Notes

PREFACE

1. Horace White to Lyman Trumbull, December 30, 1860, Lyman Trumbull Papers, Library of Congress, Washington, DC.

2. The contingency of events during the Civil War era is also emphasized in James M. McPherson, *Battle Cry of Freedom* (New York: Oxford University Press, 1988) and Michael F. Holt, "Change and Continuity in the Party Period: The Substance and Structure of American Politics, 1835–1885," in *Contesting Democracy: Substance and Structure in American Political History, 1775–2000,* ed. Byron E. Shafer and Anthony J. Badger (Lawrence: University Press of Kansas, 2001), 93–115. Of course, such a perspective is inherent in the very structure of historical narrative. But for an influential critique, students should consider Hayden White, *Metahistory: The Historical Imagination in Nineteenth-Century Europe* (Baltimore: Johns Hopkins University Press, 1973).

INTRODUCTION

1. Douglas, quoted in Robert W. Johannsen, *Stephen A. Douglas* (1973; Urbana: University of Illinois Press, 1997), 21.

2. Hay, quoted in John Mack Faragher, *Sugar Creek: Life on the Illinois Prairie* (New Haven: Yale University Press, 1986), 221.

3. Abraham Lincoln, "The Repeal of the Missouri Compromise and the Propriety of Its Restoration: Speech at Peoria, Illinois, in Reply to Senator Douglas, October 16, 1854," in *Abraham Lincoln: His Speeches and Writings,* ed. Roy P. Basler (Cleveland: World Publishing, 1946), 291–92, 321–22.

CHAPTER 1: ILLINOIS AND THE POLITICS OF SLAVERY

1. Douglas, quoted in Leon Litwack, *North of Slavery: The Negro in the Free States, 1790–1860* (Chicago: University of Chicago Press, 1961), 67.

2. Wilmot, quoted in Eugene H. Berwanger, *The Frontier against Slavery: Western Anti-Negro Prejudice and the Slavery Extension Controversy* (Urbana: University of Illinois Press, 1967), 125–26.

3. Michael F. Holt, *The Political Crisis of the 1850s* (New York: Wiley, 1978).

4. William E. Gienapp, *The Origins of the Republican Party, 1852–1856* (New York: Oxford University Press, 1987), 413.

CHAPTER 2: THE EMERGENCE OF LINCOLN AND THE SECESSION CRISIS

1. Stephen B. Oates, *With Malice toward None: The Life of Abraham Lincoln* (New York: Penguin, 1977), 211.

2. *Cairo City Gazette,* December 6, 1860, quoted in Arthur C. Cole, *The Era of the Civil War: 1848–1870* (Springfield: Illinois Centennial Commission, 1919), 253.

CHAPTER 3: IMPROVISING WAR

1. *Chicago Tribune,* quoted in Benson Lossing, *Pictorial History of the Civil War in the United States of America,* 3 vols. (Hartford: T. Belknap, 1868), 1:342.
2. Orville Hickman Browning, *The Diary of Orville Hickman Browning,* vol. 1, *1850–1864* (Springfield: Trustees of the Illinois State Historical Library, 1925), 462.
3. *Chicago Times,* November 7, 1861.
4. *Chicago Tribune,* June 17, 1862.
5. Yates to Lyman Trumbull, February 14, 1862, Lyman Trumbull Papers, Library of Congress.

CHAPTER 4: ILLINOIS AND EMANCIPATION

1. By this time, Lincoln had privately decided to emancipate the slaves, but he gave no indication of that in his meeting with Patton and Dempster, receiving the Chicago leaders politely but cautiously.
2. William Herndon to Lyman Trumbull, November 20, 1861, quoted in Arthur C. Cole, *The Era of the Civil War, 1848–1870* (Springfield: Illinois Centennial Commission, 1919), 292.
3. *Macomb Eagle,* October 11, 1862.

CHAPTER 5: DIVIDED HOUSES

1. Victor Hicken, *Illinois in the Civil War* (Urbana: University of Illinois Press, 1966), 139.
2. *Fulton Democrat,* quoted in Jason Miller, "A Neighbor's War: Provost Marshals, Desertion, the Draft, and Political Violence on the Central Illinois Home Front, 1861–1865," (MA thesis, 2012, Department of History, Eastern Illinois University), 119–20.
3. Lieutenant Colonel James Oakes to Colonel James B. Fry, July 16, 1863, reprinted in United States, War Department, *The War of the Rebellion: Official Records of the Union and Confederate Armies,* ser. 3, vol. 3 (Washington, DC: U.S. Government Printing Office, 1899), 503.

CHAPTER 6: THE SOLDIERS' WAR

1. James Austin Connolly, "Major Connolly's Letters to His Wife, 1862–1865," *Transactions of the Illinois State Historical Society* (Springfield) 35 (1928): 233.
2. Second Lieutenant Friedrich Martens to Family, August 24, 1861, in *Germans in the Civil War: The Letters They Wrote Home,* ed. Walter D. Kamphoefner and Wolfgang Helbich, trans. Susan Carter Vogel (Chapel Hill: University of North Carolina Press, 2006), 319.
3. *Canton Weekly Register,* August 12, 1862, quoted in William M. Anderson, "The Fulton County War at Home and in the Field," *Journal of the Illinois State Historical Society* 85, no. 1 (Spring 1992): 24–25.
4. *Chicago Tribune,* August 14, 1862.
5. Owen Stuart to Margaret Cameron Stuart, December 17, 1864, Owen Stuart Letters, Abraham Lincoln Presidential Library, Springfield.

CHAPTER 7: HEARTS AND MINDS IN THE DAYS OF TOTAL WAR

1. *Chicago Tribune,* quoted in Theodore J. Karamanski, *Rally 'Round the Flag: Chicago and the Civil War* (Chicago: Nelson-Hall, 1993), 164.

2. Sarah Gregg, "Civil War Diary of Mrs. Sarah Gregg," typescript, quotes from entries dated January 16 and August 20, 1863, Abraham Lincoln Presidential Library, Springfield; Mrs. S. P. Cooper to Eliza D. Phillips, October 23, 1863, Eliza D. Phillips Papers, Lincoln Presidential Library.

3. Rev. 21:25 (New American Bible): "During the day its gates will never shut, and there will be no more night there."

CHAPTER 8: IN THE SHADOWS OF WAR

1. Letter from Decatur, in *Philadelphia Christian Recorder,* May 20, 1865.

2. Browning, quoted in Roger D. Bridges, "Equality Deferred: Civil Rights for Illinois Blacks, 1865–1885," *Journal of the Illinois State Historical Society* 74, no. 2 (Summer 1981): 93; *Rushville Times,* July 2, 1868, cited in Arthur C. Cole, *The Era of the Civil War, 1848–1870* (Springfield: Illinois Centennial Commission, 1919), 412.

3. *Chicago Tribune,* February 4, 1870.

4. Allan Pinkerton, *Strikers, Communists, Tramps and Detectives* (New York: G. W. Carleton and Company, 1878), 387. After the war Pinkerton hired out his National Detective Agency to assist employers in their efforts to defeat labor unions.

5. H. W. Thomas, quoted in Karen Sawislak, *Smoldering City: Chicagoans and the Great Fire, 1871–1874* (Chicago: University of Chicago Press, 1995), 24.

Selected Bibliography

INTRODUCTION

Biles, Roger. *Illinois: A History of the Land and Its People*. DeKalb: Northern Illinois University Press, 2005.

Cayton, Andrew R. L., and Peter S. Onuf, eds. *The Midwest and the Nation: Rethinking the History of an American Region*. Bloomington: Indiana University Press, 1990.

Cole, Arthur C. *The Era of the Civil War, 1848–1870*. Springfield: Illinois Centennial Commission, 1919.

Cronon, William. *Nature's Metropolis: Chicago and the Great West*. New York: Norton, 1991.

Doyle, Don H. *The Social Order of a Frontier Community: Jacksonville, Illinois, 1825–1870*. Urbana: University of Illinois Press, 1978.

Einhorn, Robin L. *Property Rules: Political Economy in Chicago, 1833–1872*. Chicago: University of Chicago Press, 1991.

Etchison, Nicole. *The Emerging Midwest: Upland Southerners and the Political Culture of the Old Northwest, 1787–1861*. Bloomington: Indiana University Press, 1996.

Faragher, John Mack. *Sugar Creek: Life on the Illinois Prairie*. New Haven: Yale University Press, 1986.

Foner, Eric. *The Fiery Trial: Abraham Lincoln and American Slavery*. New York: Norton, 2010.

Haeger, John Denis. "Eastern Money and the Urban Frontier: Chicago, 1833–1842." *Journal of the Illinois State Historical Society* 64, no. 3 (Autumn 1971): 267–84.

Jensen, Richard J. *Illinois: A History*. New York: Norton, 1978.

Johannsen, Robert W. *Stephen A. Douglas*. 1973. Urbana: University of Illinois Press, 1997.

Leonard, Gerald. *The Invention of Party Politics: Federalism, Popular Sovereignty, and Constitutional Development in Jacksonian Illinois*. Chapel Hill: University of North Carolina Press, 2002.

Meyer, Douglas K. *Making the Heartland Quilt: A Geographical History of Settlement and Migration in Early-Nineteenth-Century Illinois*. Carbondale: Southern Illinois University Press, 2000.

Pease, Theodore Calvin. *The Frontier State: 1818–1848*. Springfield: Illinois Centennial Commission, 1918.

Simeone, James. *Democracy and Slavery in Frontier Illinois: The Bottomland Republic*. DeKalb: Northern Illinois University Press, 2000.

CHAPTER 1: ILLINOIS AND THE POLITICS OF SLAVERY

Anbinder, Tyler. *Nativism and Slavery: The Northern Know Nothings and the Politics of the 1850s*. New York: Oxford University Press, 1992.

Berwanger, Eugene H. *The Frontier against Slavery: Western Anti-Negro Prejudice and the Slavery Extension Controversy*. Urbana: University of Illinois Press, 1967.

Dillon, Merton. "Abolition Comes to Illinois." *Journal of the Illinois State Historical Society* 53 (1960): 389–403.

228

Selected Bibliography

Foner, Eric. *Free Soil, Free Labor, Free Men: The Ideology of the Republican Party before the Civil War.* New York: Oxford University Press, 1970.

Gara, Larry. "The Underground Railroad in Illinois." *Journal of the Illinois State Historical Society* 56, no. 3 (Autumn 1963): 502–28.

Gertz, Elmer. "The Black Laws of Illinois." *Journal of the Illinois State Historical Society* 56, no. 3 (Autumn 1963): 454–73.

Gienapp, William E. *The Origins of the Republican Party, 1852–1856.* New York: Oxford University Press, 1987.

Gliozzo, Charles A. "John Jones: A Study of a Black Chicagoan." *Illinois Historical Journal* 80, no. 3 (Autumn 1987): 177–88.

Goodman, Paul. *Of One Blood: Abolitionism and the Origins of Racial Equality.* Berkeley: University of California Press, 1998.

Guasco, Suzanne. "'The Deadly Influence of Negro Capitalists': Southern Yeomen and Resistance to the Expansion of Slavery in Illinois." *Civil War History* 47 (2001): 7–29.

Hansen, Stephen L. *The Making of the Third Party System: Voters and Parties in Illinois, 1850–1876.* Ann Arbor: UMI Research Press, 1978.

Harris, N. Dwight. *The History of Negro Servitude in Illinois and of the Slavery Agitation in That State, 1719–1864.* Chicago: A. C. McClurg, 1904.

Harrold, Stanley. *Border War: Fighting Over Slavery before the Civil War.* Chapel Hill: University of North Carolina Press, 2010.

Holt, Michael F. *The Political Crisis of the 1850s.* New York: Wiley, 1978.

Johnson, Reinhard O. *The Liberty Party, 1840–1848: Antislavery Third-Party Politics in the United States.* Baton Rouge: Louisiana State University Press, 2009.

Litwack, Leon. *North of Slavery: The Negro in the Free States, 1790–1860.* Chicago: University of Chicago Press, 1961.

Robertson, Stacey M. *Hearts Beating for Liberty: Women Abolitionists in the Old Northwest.* Chapel Hill: University of North Carolina Press, 2010.

Rozett, John. "Racism and the Republican Emergence in Illinois, 1848–1860: A Reevaluation of Republican Negrophobia." *Civil War History* 22, no. 2 (June 1976): 101–15.

Simon, Paul. *Freedom's Champion: Elijah Lovejoy.* Carbondale: Southern Illinois University Press, 1994.

Voss-Hubbard, Mark. *Beyond Party: Cultures of Antipartisanship in Northern Politics before the Civil War.* Baltimore: Johns Hopkins University Press, 2002.

CHAPTER 2: THE EMERGENCE OF LINCOLN AND THE SECESSION CRISIS

Barney, William L. *The Road to Secession: A New Perspective on the Old South.* New York: Praeger, 1972.

Bergquist, James. "People and Politics in Transition: The Illinois Germans, 1850–1860." In *Ethnic Voters and the Election of Lincoln,* edited by Frederick C. Luebke. Lincoln: University of Nebraska Press, 1971.

Collins, Bruce. "The Lincoln-Douglas Contest of 1858 and Illinois' Electorate." *Journal of American Studies* 20, no. 3 (1986): 391–420.

Donald, David Herbert. *Lincoln.* New York: Simon and Schuster, 1995.

Fehrenbacher, Don E. *Prelude to Greatness: Lincoln in the 1850s.* Stanford: Stanford University Press, 1962.

Gienapp, William E. *Abraham Lincoln and Civil War America: A Biography.* New York: Oxford University Press, 2002.

Guelzo, Allen C. *Lincoln and Douglas: The Debates that Defined America.* New York: Simon and Schuster, 2008.

Potter, David M. *The Impending Crisis, 1848–1861.* Completed and edited by Don E. Fehrenbacher. New York: Harper and Row, 1976.

Stampp, Kenneth. *And the War Came: The North and the Secession Crisis, 1860–1861.* Baton Rouge: Louisiana State University Press, 1950.

CHAPTER 3: IMPROVISING WAR

Attie, Jeanie. *Patriotic Toil: Northern Women and the American Civil War.* Ithaca: Cornell University Press, 1998.

Clinton, Catherine, and Nina Silber, eds., *Divided Houses: Gender and the Civil War.* New York: Oxford University Press, 1992.

Davis, Rodney O. "Private Albert Cashier as Regarded by His/Her Comrades." *Illinois Historical Journal* 82, no. 2 (Summer 1989): 108–12.

Fischer, LeRoy H. "Cairo's Civil War Angel, Mary Jane Safford." *Journal of the Illinois State Historical Society* 54, no. 3 (Autumn 1961): 229–45.

Fredrickson, George M. *The Inner Civil War: Northern Intellectuals and the Crisis of the Union.* New York: Harper and Row, 1965.

Gallman, J. Matthew. *Mastering Wartime: A Social History of Philadelphia during the Civil War.* Cambridge: Cambridge University Press, 1990.

Ginzberg, Lori. D. *Women and the Work of Benevolence: Morality, Politics, and Class in the Nineteenth-Century United States.* New Haven: Yale University Press, 1990.

Jones, James Pickett. *Black Jack: John A. Logan and Southern Illinois in the Civil War Era.* Carbondale: Southern Illinois University Press, 1995.

Karamanski, Theodore J. *Rally 'Round the Flag: Chicago and the Civil War.* Chicago: Nelson-Hall, 1993.

McAdams, Benton. *Rebels at Rock Island: The Story of a Civil War Prison.* DeKalb: Northern Illinois University Press, 2000.

McPherson, James M. *Battle Cry of Freedom: The Civil War Era.* New York: Oxford University Press, 1988.

Merrill, James M. "Cairo, Illinois: Strategic Civil War River Port." *Journal of the Illinois State Historical Society* 76, no. 4 (Winter 1983): 242–56.

Paludan, Phillip Shaw. *A People's Contest: The Union and the Civil War, 1861–1865.* Lawrence: University Press of Kansas, 1988.

Peterson, William S. "A History of Camp Butler, 1861–1866." *Illinois Historical Journal* 82, no. 2 (Summer 1989): 74–92.

Pitkin, William A. "When Cairo Was Saved for the Union." *Journal of the Illinois State Historical Society* 51, no 3 (Autumn 1958): 284–305.

Wilson, Mark R. *The Business of Civil War: Military Mobilization and the State, 1861–1865.* Baltimore: Johns Hopkins University Press, 2006.

CHAPTER 4: ILLINOIS AND EMANCIPATION

Adams, David Wallace. "Illinois Soldiers and the Emancipation Proclamation." *Journal of the Illinois State Historical Society* 67 (September 1974): 406–21.

Allardice, Bruce S. "'Illinois is Rotten with Traitors!' The Republican Defeat in the 1862 State Election." *Journal of the Illinois State Historical Society* 104, nos. 1–2 (Spring–Summer 2011): 97–114.

Berlin, Ira, Barbara J. Fields, Steven F. Miller, Joseph P. Reidy, and Leslie S. Rowland. *Slaves No More: Three Essays on Emancipation and the Civil War.* Cambridge: Cambridge University Press, 1992.

Blight, David W., and Brooks D. Simpson, eds. *Union and Emancipation: Essays on Politics and Race in the Civil War Era.* Kent, OH: Kent State University Press, 1997.

Foner, Eric. *The Fiery Trial: Abraham Lincoln and American Slavery.* New York: Norton, 2010.

Fredrickson, George M. "A Man but Not a Brother." *Journal of Southern History* 41, no. 1 (1975): 39–58.

Harris, Robert L., Jr. "H. Ford Douglas: Afro-American Antislavery Emigrationist." *Journal of Negro History* 62, no. 3 (July 1977): 217–34.

Paludan, Phillip Shaw. *The Presidency of Abraham Lincoln.* Lawrence: University Press of Kansas, 1994.

Tap, Bruce. "Race, Rhetoric, and Emancipation: The Election of 1862 in Illinois." *Civil War History* 39, no. 2 (June 1993): 101–25.

Voegeli, Jacque V. *Free but Not Equal: The Midwest and the Negro during the Civil War.* Chicago: University of Chicago Press, 1967.

CHAPTER 5: DIVIDED HOUSES

Anderson, William M. "The Fulton County War at Home and in the Field." *Illinois Historical Journal* 85, no. 1 (Spring 1992): 23–36.

Bernstein, Iver. *The New York City Draft Riots: Their Significance for American Society and Politics in the Age of the Civil War.* New York: Oxford University Press, 1990.

Blake, Kellee Greene. "Aiding and Abetting: Disloyalty Prosecutions in the Federal Civil Courts of Southern Illinois, 1861–1866." *Illinois Historical Journal* 87, no. 2 (Summer 1994): 95–108.

Neely, Mark E., Jr. *The Fate of Liberty: Abraham Lincoln and Civil Liberties.* New York: Oxford University Press, 1991.

———. *The Union Divided: Party Conflict in the Civil War North.* Cambridge, MA: Harvard University Press, 2002.

Nortrup, Jack. "Yates, the Prorogued Legislature, and the Constitutional Convention." *Journal of the Illinois State Historical Society* 62, no. 1 (Spring 1969): 5–34.

Sanger, Donald Bridgman. "The *Chicago Times* and the Civil War." *Mississippi Valley Historical Review* 17, no. 4 (March 1931): 557–80.

Silbey, Joel H. *A Respectable Minority: The Democratic Party in the Civil War Era, 1860–1868.* New York: Norton, 1977.

Sterling, Robert E. "Civil War Draft Resistance in Illinois." *Journal of the Illinois State Historical Society* 64, no. 3 (Autumn 1971): 244–66.

Tenney, Craig D. "To Suppress or Not to Suppress: Abraham Lincoln and the *Chicago Times*." *Civil War History* 27, no. 3 (September 1981): 248–59.

Towne, Stephen E. "'Such Conduct Must Be Put Down' The Military Arrest of Judge Charles H. Constable during the Civil War." *Journal of Illinois History* 9, no. 2 (Spring 2006): 43–62.

Weber, Jennifer L. *Copperheads: The Rise and Fall of Lincoln's Opponents in the North* (New York: Oxford University Press, 2006.

CHAPTER 6: THE SOLDIERS' WAR

Ambrose, D. Leib. *From Shiloh to Savannah: The Seventh Illinois Infantry in the Civil War.* DeKalb: Northern Illinois University Press, 2003.

Benjaminson, Eric. "A Regiment of Immigrants: The 82nd Illinois Volunteer Infantry and the Letters of Captain Rudolph Mueller." *Journal of the Illinois State Historical Society* 94, no. 2 (Summer 2001): 137–80.

Blackwell, Samuel M. *In the First Line of Battle: The 12th Illinois Cavalry in the Civil War.* DeKalb: Northern Illinois University Press, 2002.

Brown, Thaddeus C. *Behind the Guns: The History of Battery I, 2nd Regiment, Illinois Light Artillery.* Carbondale: Southern Illinois University Press, 1965.

Connolly, James A. *Three Years in the Army of the Cumberland: The Letters and Diary of Major James A. Connolly.* Edited by Paul M. Angle. Bloomington: Indiana University Press, 1959.

Glatthaar, Joseph. *Forged in Battle: The Civil War Alliance of Black Soldiers and White Officers.* New York: Free Press, 1990.

Grimsley, Mark. *The Hard Hand of War: Union Military Policy toward Southern Civilians, 1861–1865.* Cambridge: Cambridge University Press, 1995.

Hattaway, Herman, and Archer Jones. *How the North Won: A Military History of the Civil War.* Urbana: University of Illinois Press, 1983.

Hicken, Victor. *Illinois in the Civil War.* Urbana: University of Illinois Press, 1966.

McFeely, William S. *Grant: A Biography.* New York: Norton, 2002.

McPherson, James M. *For Cause and Comrades: Why Men Fought in the Civil War.* New York: Oxford University Press, 1997.

———. *What They Fought For, 1861–1865.* Baton Rouge: Louisiana State University Press, 1994.

Miller, Edward A., Jr. *The Black Civil War Soldiers of Illinois: The Story of the Twenty-Ninth U.S. Colored Infantry.* Columbia: University of South Carolina Press, 1998.

Mitchell, Reid. *The Vacant Chair: The Northern Soldier Leaves Home.* New York: Oxford University Press, 1993.

Moore, Francis T. *The Story of My Campaign: The Civil War Memoir of Captain Francis T. Moore, Second Illinois Cavalry.* Edited by Thomas Bahde. DeKalb: Northern Illinois University Press, 2011.

Morrison, Marion. *A History of the Ninth Regiment Illinois Volunteer Infantry.* Carbondale: Southern Illinois University Press, 1997.

Noe, Kenneth W. "'Coming to Us Dead': A Civil War Casualty and His Estate." *Journal of Illinois History* 2 (Fall 1999): 289–304.

Sterling, Bob. "Discouragement, Weariness, and War Politics: Desertions from Illinois Regiments during the Civil War." *Illinois Historical Journal* 82, no. 4 (Winter 1989): 239–62.

Wiley, William. *The Civil War Diary of a Common Soldier: William Wiley of the 77th Illinois Infantry.* Edited by Terrence Winschel. Baton Rouge: Louisiana State University Press, 2001.

CHAPTER 7: HEARTS AND MINDS IN THE DAYS OF TOTAL WAR

Cashin, Joan E., ed. *The War Was You and Me: Civilians in the American Civil War.* Princeton: Princeton University Press, 2002.

Gallman, J. Matthew. *The North Fights the Civil War: The Home Front.* Chicago: I. R. Dee, 1994.

Hanchett, William. "An Illinois Physician and the Civil War Draft, 1864–1865: Letters of Dr. Joshua Nichols Speed." *Journal of the Illinois State Historical Society* 59 (Summer 1966): 143–60.

Leonard, Elizabeth D. *Yankee Women: Gender Battles in the Civil War.* New York: Norton, 1994.

Palladino, Grace. *Another Civil War: Labor, Capital, and the State in the Anthracite Regions of Pennsylvania, 1840–1868.* Urbana: University of Illinois Press, 1990.

Royster, Charles. *The Destructive War: William Tecumseh Sherman, Stonewall Jackson, and the Americans.* New York: Knopf, 1991.

Sampson, Robert D. "'Pretty Damned Warm Times': The 1864 Charleston Riot and 'The Inalienable Right of Revolution.'" *Illinois Historical Journal* 89 (Summer 1996): 99–116.

Venet, Wendy Hamand. *A Strong-Minded Woman: The Life of Mary Livermore.* Amherst: University of Massachusetts Press, 2005.

Wieck, Edward A. *The American Miners' Association: A Record of the Origin of Coal Miners' Unions in the United States.* New York: Russell Sage Foundation, 1940.

Williams, T. Harry. *Lincoln and His Generals.* New York: Vintage Books, 1952.

CHAPTER 8: IN THE SHADOWS OF WAR

Benedict, Michael Les. *A Compromise of Principle: Congressional Republicans and Reconstruction.* New York: Norton, 1974.

Blight, David. *Race and Reunion: The Civil War in American Memory.* Cambridge, MA: Belknap Press, 2000.

Bridges, Roger D. "Equality Deferred: Civil Rights for Illinois Blacks, 1865–1885." *Journal of the Illinois State Historical Society* 74, no. 2 (Summer 1981): 82–108.

Buck, Solon Justus. *The Granger Movement: A Study of Agricultural Organization and Its Political, Economic, and Social Manifestations, 1870–1880.* Lincoln: University of Nebraska Press, 1913.

DuBois, Ellen Carol. *Feminism and Suffrage: The Emergence of an Independent Women's Movement in America, 1848-1869.* Ithaca: Cornell University Press, 1978.

Edwards, Laura F. *Gendered Strife and Confusion: The Political Culture of Reconstruction.* Urbana: University of Illinois Press, 1997.

Foner, Eric. *Reconstruction: America's Unfinished Revolution, 1863–1877.* New York: Harper and Row, 1988.

Garb, Margaret. "The Political Education of John Jones: Black Politics in a Northern City, 1845–1879." *Journal of the Historical Society* 8, no. 1 (March 2008): 29–60.

Grant, Susan-Mary, and Peter J. Parish, eds. *Legacy of Disunion: The Enduring Significance of the American Civil War.* Baton Rouge: Louisiana State University Press, 2003.

Montgomery, David. *Beyond Equality: Labor and the Radical Republicans, 1862–1872.* Urbana: University of Illinois Press, 1967.

Perman, Michael. *The Road to Redemption: Southern Politics, 1869–1879.* Chapel Hill: University of North Carolina Press, 1984.

Plummer, Mark A. *Lincoln's Rail Splitter: Governor Richard J. Oglesby.* Urbana: University of Illinois Press, 2001.

Richardson, Heather Cox. *The Death of Reconstruction: Race, Labor, and Politics in the Post–Civil War North, 1865-1901.* Cambridge, MA: Harvard University Press, 2001.

Sawislak, Karen. *Smoldering City: Chicagoans and the Great Fire, 1871–1874.* Chicago: University of Chicago Press, 1995.

Schneirov, Richard. *Labor and Urban Politics: Class Conflict and the Origins of Modern Liberalism in Chicago, 1864–1897.* Urbana: University of Illinois Press, 1998.

Schwalm, Leslie A. *Emancipation's Diaspora: Race and Reconstruction in the Upper Midwest.* Chapel Hill: University of North Carolina Press, 2009.

Silber, Nina. *The Romance of Reunion: Northerners and the South, 1865–1900.* Chapel Hill: University of North Carolina Press, 1993.

Swenson, Phillip D. "Illinois: Disillusionment with State Activism." In *Radical Republicans in the North: State Politics During Reconstruction,* edited by James C. Mohr. Baltimore: Johns Hopkins University Press, 1976.

Vorenberg, Michael. *Final Freedom: The Civil War, the Abolition of Slavery, and the Thirteenth Amendment.* Cambridge: Cambridge University Press, 2001.

Index

Bross, John A., 146
Brown, John: attitudes toward, 35, 46–47; in
    Chicago, 16–17; in Kansas Territory, 12; at
    Harpers Ferry, 35, 46–47
Browning, Orville H., 12, 36, 83, 101, 177; views of
    home front during war, 57, 61–62
Bruinsburg, MS, 142
Buchanan, James, 14, 34, 208
Buell, Don Carlos, 130
Buffalo, NY, 9, 205
Bull Run, battle of, 57, 72, 211; effects of, 69–71, 81
Bull Run, second battle of, 133, 213
Burnside, Ambrose, and order no. 84, 104
Bush, Eliot N., 100
Butler, Benjamin, 211

C. E. Hillman (steamer), 57, 210
Cairo, IL, 1, 59, 74, 77, 88, 126, 128, 155, 159, 178;
    contraband camp at, 81, 83, 93–96; strategic
    significance of, 56–57
Cairo City Gazette, 38
California, 10, 14, 126, 205
Camp Butler, 58, 114, 116, 211
Camp Defiance, 56, 93, 210
Camp Douglas, 1, 155, 211
Camp Manchester, 115
Camp Yates, 56, 210
Canada, 15, 22, 32
Canton, IL, 171–73
Carbondale, IL, 118
Carrington, George, at Vicksburg, 142–45
Carrington, Henry B., 103
Caseyville, IL, 56
Cashier, Albert, 59
Cass, Lewis, 205
Cass County, IL, 115
Caton, John D., 107, 209
Causeway, battle of the, 87
Centralia (IL) Soldiers' Home, 154
Champaign County, IL, wartime politics in, 72–73
Champaign County Democrat, 71
Champion's Hill, battle of, 142
Chancellorsville, battle of, 101
Chandlerville, IL, 185
Charleston, IL, 40, 43, 148; 1864 copperhead riot
    in, 155, 167–69
Charleston, SC, 56, 87, 145, 170, 209
Chase, Salmon P., 36, 156
Chattanooga, 127, 171, 172
Chester Picket Guard, 155
Chicago, IL, 1, 2, 6, 18, 57, 80, 111, 154; *Agitator*,
    178; Board of Trade, 180, 205; city council
    condemns Fugitive Slave Law, 10;
    copperheads in, 115, 155, 178; Douglas's last
    speech in, 62–64; economic growth of, 3,

32–33, 153, 164–65; 1860 National Republican
    Party Convention at, 36, 49–50; 1864
    National Democratic Party Convention
    at, 155; elections in, 11–12, 184, 207; First
    Congregational Church of, 91; and Great
    Fire of 1871, 179–80, 198–99; immigrants
    in, 11, 23–26, 64–67, 125, 179, 184–85; Know
    Nothing movement in, 11–12, 23; Lager Beer
    Riot, 12, 23–36; meeting of evangelicals at
    Bryan Hall in, 81, 91–93; Northwest Sanitary
    Fair in, 165–66; trial of John Hossack in, 35,
    47–48; Twenty-Ninth U.S. Colored Infantry
    in, 146–47; and Underground Railroad, 15–17;
    Western Citizen, 9. *See also* Chicago Repeal
    Association; Chicago Sanitary Commission;
    Chicago Times; Chicago Trades Assembly;
    Chicago Tribune; Wentworth, John
Chicago Daily Evening Journal, 38
Chicago Democrat, 184
Chicago Free West, 207
Chicago Relief and Aid Society, 198–99
Chicago Repeal Association, and black codes,
    182–83
Chicago River, 179
Chicago Sanitary Commission: activities
    described, 59, 73–76; established, 59, 211;
    renamed the Northwest Branch of the U.S.
    Sanitary Commission, 154. *See also* Northwest
    Branch of the United States Sanitary
    Commission
Chicago Times, 60, 69, 110; on battle of Bull Run,
    70–71; shut down by General Burnside, 104
Chicago Trades Assembly: established, 154;
    platform of, 173–74
Chicago Tribune, 72, 74, 108, 110; on African
    American soldiers, 146–47; on Cairo
    contrabands, 94–95; on Chicago's wartime
    economy, 164; on Lager Beer Riot, 23–26;
    predicts quick Union victory, 56; on war
    mobilization in Chicago, 64–67
Chickahominy River, 147
Chickamauga, battle of, 148
Chipman, Albert, 157
Chipman, Sophronia, and farm work during war,
    157, 159–60
Cincinnati, 153
Civil Rights Act (1866), 176, 187–89
Clark County, IL, 103
Clarke, George R., 116
Clay, Henry, 6, 51, 206
Cleveland, OH, 111
Clingman, Thomas, raid of, 155, 215
Clinton, IL, 85–87, 90
Codding, Ichabod, views of, 70–71
Colchester, CT, 187